EMPOWERING PARENTS

Meeting children's learning needs in the kindergarten/primary

years

Dale Shipley

Empowering Parents: Meeting children's learning needs in the kindergarten/primary years

Pandamonium Publishing House

www.pandamoniumpublishing.com
ISBN: 978-1-989506-28-8

Dedication

Dedicated to the parents who struggle to support their children's learning and success in school

Empowering Parents: Meeting children's learning needs in the kindergarten/primary years

TABLE OF CONTENTS

Empowering Parents: Meeting children's learning needs in the
primary years K to 3

ACKNOWLEDGMENTS

Writing a book is a journey; this book represents for me a
'culminating outcome' of a long and diverse career in education
during which I never stopped learning. I might have aspired to
create and invent, but I am much more a student who gathers the
bright ideas of others and works to reconcile them with my
experience and perspectives acquired in most education sectors and
at all levels. Writing this book during a pandemic added to my
challenge but I have been encouraged and supported along the way
by family, friends, other educators, and parents who shared their
concerns about how we educate and prepare our children for the
challenges that this century has already visited upon us. School
principals described their issues and experience; teachers described
daily frustrations but nearly always spoke eloquently about the
rewards of teaching children that keep them in the profession.
Maya Shipley encouraged me throughout, read the manuscript in
its early stages and always offered constructive, balanced feedback
and mature suggestions well beyond her years.

A special thank you to Diane Kay, a coach and consultant
for parents of school-age children, who provided insights on
parents' attempts to guide their children's education and keep them
interested in school. Diane reinforced the need for a book for
parents seeking to know how to help their children be and feel
successful at school, prepare them to sustain the rigours of
uncertainty and change, and find ways they might express their
concerns as parents and be 'heard'. Gary Chivers shared
perspectives he gained over several years as a school-based tutor
while helping children overcome their fear of math, win their
struggles to understand math and regain their confidence as

effective learners. Leaders and authors have for several years warned about the consequences of tired school systems that no longer serve today's urgent needs and the dangers our nation faces if education continues to resist transformational change.

Throughout my career in education, I worked with leaders in education and colleagues whose faith in the capacity of children to develop and grow way beyond expectations, when they are in the right learning environments, inspired and motivated my work. I also met those who go to great lengths to protect the status quo. I appreciate the opportunity and support provided to me by Pandamonium Publishing House who have encouraged this writing project on the understanding that it may offer guidance to parents of school-age children and keep hope alive for equitable and motivating school-based learning opportunities and experiences for all children in our public schools.

I am most indebted to Pierre Giroux, a leader among educators who is also my valued critic and meaningful support system. He sustained me through the writing of five editions of a textbook – and now this. My hope is that this book will provide insights to parents about how to navigate the schools with their children and enable and encourage them to love learning.

Dale Shipley, Ed.D.

Introduction

"The significant problems we face cannot be solved at the same level we were at when we created them." (Albert Einstein)

When parents ask their children what they did in kindergarten today, the typical response is "we played". If they push a little harder and ask what they played, they might hear, "we sang", "we went outside", and "we heard a story". Most parents know that these answers do not provide the whole story and are often at a loss to know what really did happen at school. When parents ask teachers questions about the "play-based" kindergarten approach, they typically hear, "the children learn while they play", as if something magical happens when children pass through the kindergarten doors and begin to play. This explanation is partly right; something magical does happen when children play, but that is not the whole picture either.

Parents' have a right to know what and how their children are learning at school starting with the kindergarten years and throughout their schooling. The anxious days of the pandemic and the extended school closures exposed the need for parents to be better informed about their children's learning needs and expectations for their grade level. There were gaps in communication between schools and their communities and an absence of clarity about the developmental and learning priorities for children at each learning level. Parents had little understanding of how they might provide learning experiences at home for their children to practise and maintain what they had already achieved during the school year. The impact of the gap was uneven across the population and its effects perhaps most detrimental among the kindergarten/primary children whose developmental trajectories are rapid and time-sensitive. The impact was even harsher for the children with disabilities and their parents.

My intention in writing this book was to empower parents by providing information about what they should expect of the schools and explain the learning expectations for children during the early school years (i.e., the primary division). The book should let parents know how they might support their child's early learning, communicate with teachers, and engage with the curriculum, the school and the education system. It appears imperative now, that parents have more information about how schools work, what they should expect from them, what and how their children should be learning, and how they are performing. This information should enable parents to reinforce at home the skills, knowledge, concepts, and dispositions for learning that are emphasized at school. My goal is that parents will become better able to express their expectations regarding the accountability of schools, their children's right to effective education services, and their right as parents to be properly heard and informed.

This book focuses on the junior and senior kindergarten years and the primary grades one to three – that is, from about ages four to

eight years. The developmental continuum of this four-or-five-year
period (depending on whether kindergarten is one or two years) includes
an important cognitive transition from preoperational (sensory-based)
thought from about age four to about six to the concrete-operational
period that begins about age six or seven. This is a sensitive period
during which children make an important cognitive transition as well as
growing rapidly in size, developing communication skills, expanding
their social networks and interactions, sharpening perceptual skills, and
learning to manage their behaviours and emotions. Children's thought
processes become less reliant on their senses and they experience the
contradictions between what they see and what they know. Gradually,
they learn to trust what they have learned conceptually even though they
continue to depend on the physical presence of objects that allow them to
verify what they are beginning to know and understand. The timeframe
for this cognitive transition is not fixed, as individual development
during this sensitive period depends a lot on the quality of children's
preschool play experiences in the environments they inhabit and the time
they need to make the transition at their own pace. Navigating this
transition successfully is crucial to later learning as it is during this
period that children exercise and develop their dispositions for learning,
readily acquire habits of mind, grapple with learning challenges (e.g.,
reading and understanding number), and experience rapid and dramatic
physical growth and brain development. As their introduction to
schooling, this early period from age four to about age eight lays a
crucial foundation for the educational journey ahead.

Schools are exceedingly powerful and frequently closed
institutions that purport to follow and represent the values, norms and

conventions of the societies in which they are embedded, but they tend to erect boundaries, protect the status quo and discourage activism. Education systems do not change voluntarily. Empowered parents are entitled to ask questions, expect answers and require accountability. They should expect that gains and progress begun in the kindergarten/primary years are carried into the junior and intermediate division grades and beyond. Parental expectations do not yet have the momentum of a full-scale movement, but pressures for change at all levels are gathering on several fronts and parents have become more aware of the serious gaps in our education systems and more engaged. For example, we recently witnessed parents organizing successfully to force a newly-elected Ontario government to abandon its intention to replace a new sex education curriculum launched by the previous government with the old, outdated curriculum. Meanwhile, the business community renewed earlier calls for aggressive education reform that would be more closely attuned to global challenges including the technological advances that continue to have a dramatic impact on the world of work and employment. Corporations and governments have, for years, clamoured for graduates with the creative thinking and problem-solving skills that seed invention and innovation that would improve life for all and contribute to Canada's influence and prosperity.

I was writing this book at a time when the Ontario government had the teachers in all major school boards involved in work-to-rule and rotating strike campaigns during fall 2019 and winter 2020. The priorities for negotiations in this latest round were much like they had been for decades: government wanting to reduce or contain costs by implementing cuts to educational services and resources, increase class sizes for some grades, and keep annual wage increments for teachers as low as possible. About the same time, the government announced that it expected improved provincial standardized test results for elementary school students in grades three and six, especially in math, notwithstanding the increased class sizes they proposed and their reluctance to add meaningful resources to the education system. It was a classic case of knowing that educational outcomes should be improved while maintaining the same policies, funding levels and parsimony and still expecting different results. Making the essential investments in education that are relevant to today's changing social, demographic, economic and environmental contexts on local, provincial and national levels is a no-brainer. On the other side of the bargaining table, teacher unions have held out for annual wage increments, smaller class sizes and more resources without linking these 'asks' to improved teacher training and other broad systemic reforms that teachers know are badly needed. Negotiations between teacher unions and governments have not changed significantly in decades, yet the social and economic environments in which today's education systems strive to meet their obligations to children and society have altered remarkably.

Teachers have for decades borne the burdens of children with mental health issues, child poverty and nutritional deficits and the mild to serious disabilities experienced by larger numbers of children, along with limited and often diminishing resources needed to alleviate the pressure on children and the system. Teachers have been in the front lines of bullying incidents between children and required to assume greater responsibility for children's health, sex education and character-building that used to fall mostly to parents and extended families. The potential

for additional demands on teachers related to disruptive climate change
and economic events, relocation of families and more school
interruptions caused by societal upheavals all remain. Yet, there is little
evidence that governments and unions are thinking ahead, let alone
addressing the increasingly disabling deficits in educational investment
and the urgent need for a transformed vision and plan for education that
would solve or alleviate problems on both sides of this persistent divide.

Business and government think tanks have reminded us since the
turn of the century that nations which thrive in spite of monumental
challenges need novel thinkers, problem solvers and creative people who
compete successfully, remain relevant, and anticipate demands and
needs. The quality and relevance of their education systems are usually a
bellwether of successful nations. Yet, in much of Canada, public
elementary education remains stalled in Industrial Age school design and
outdated delivery systems, pedagogies, curriculum, and evaluation
approaches that are unsuited to the education needs of the Information
Age. Schools that were built in the post-war period (in some instances,
that's post-World War I!) have been renovated many times, but the ways
in which schools are used and how education is delivered have remained
much the same for a century.

Over about five decades, the value attached to education in
Canada has been linked increasingly with economic issues and
workplace demands and has become less connected to the development
of children's individual potential. Unparalleled inequality in the
economic and social security between the privileged and lower and
middle-income groups is warning us of the economic and social
disruption ahead. Education for its own sake used to be a hallmark of

civilized societies and nations began for a time in the mid-20th century to
invest more in education. When governments later started to view
education mainly as an engine for economic growth and business
success, and as an instrument for social control using streaming
strategies, equality of opportunity, a fair and balanced economy and the
development of human potential took second place. Education systems
that are tied to national economic goals tend to perpetuate inequality
among the socioeconomic classes and favour those with wealth and
power. While in some nations, that is the covert goal, most Canadians
never intended this to be so in Canada. The steady erosion of Canada's
investment on a per capita basis in the public education system, the
absence of a clear vision for its future, and the apparent incapacity of
past and present governments to bring about effective change are key
factors related to this startling wakeup call for education that has been
exposed by the pandemic.

The significant change that education systems have been forced
to contemplate in order to address persistent threats to health and
survival should be factored into new demands for transforming our
education systems that no longer meet the needs of individuals or the
nation. Although transformative change is required to adequately prepare
children for this 21st century world, the education institution seldom
leads change; it usually follows society at a snail's pace and often veers
off-course. Kindergarten and the primary division may be the vanguard
of growing public demand to restructure elementary education, apply
state-of-the-art strategies for teaching and learning, and establish
education outcomes relevant to the times we live in and the challenges
we face. The kindergarten/primary division in education is where the

foundation for learning is laid and where the impact of education is greatest. Perhaps the best hope we have for mitigating the power that education systems wield over children, families and communities is to empower and equip parent stakeholders as reliable partners in primary education and advocates and leaders for essential change.

Parents and teachers are natural partners in children's education, and parents are the senior partners. The disruption that education has experienced makes information, parental support and involvement with teachers and the schools a compelling challenge. Parents are better positioned now than ever to influence change and help solve persistent problems in public schooling that have been exposed by the pandemic. They need to raise questions, offer potential solutions, and expect their perspectives to be heard. They have questions about their own obligations and what their child faces as they start school. How does play enable a child's transition in kindergarten to becoming ready and eager for grade one? How do I assess my child's progress and learning? What essential learning should my child achieve in kindergarten? This book answers questions and describes what children are developmentally ready to learn and do and ways parents can navigate schooling with their children during the primary years from kindergarten to grade three.

Parents who understand the mandates of the kindergarten/primary years, the special nature of early learning and the developmental tasks of early childhood are better equipped to support children's learning progress at home. They discovered during the pandemic how unexpectedly they can be thrust into the role of teacher and how helpful it would be to know the essential learning their child should acquire to continue the learning process at home. Parents usually approach schools with reference points they remember from their own elementary schooling and although they see some differences, much appears the same to them - the roles of the teacher, principal and office staff, the intervals and mechanisms for reporting to parents, and the usual configuration of classrooms. Despite superficial changes, so much about the schools remains sufficiently recognizable that parents sometimes revert to behaviours they acquired while students themselves – that is, deference to real and perceived authority and a desire to "fit in" and help their children do the same. Parents often believe they should neither stand out nor rock the boat and the school system regularly perpetuates this learned helplessness. Education systems do not change unless they are compelled to do so but this generation of parents is under no illusion that they should accept being kept largely in the dark about their child's schooling. They have a right to expect direct answers to questions and to have a voice and be heard in the context of education reform. Active partnerships between parents and teachers may be a fundamental missing ingredient in releasing children's learning potential. Parents who accept this challenge may find that many more teachers and principals than they had imagined are as convinced as they are of the need for education reform.

The structure of this book

Chapter 1 addresses the nature of learning and development during the kindergarten/ primary years from age four to about age eight (grade three). During the first eight years of life, children's minds and bodies develop more rapidly than at any other period in the lifespan and the nature of their learning differs markedly from that of older children and

adults. The kindergarten experience sets the stage for how children
perceive school and how parents understand the school's influence on
their child's development in all domains – physical, cognitive
(intellectual), social, and emotional – that together lay the foundation for
ongoing learning success. When parents undertake their role in
supporting the teacher's efforts, they interact positively with them and
become connected with other parents and the school, a factor that also
pleases their children.

Chapter 2 describes the learning-to-learn skills; some are referred
to as "executive functions" and others include attitudes and dispositions
for learning, attending skills and habits of mind that influence lifelong
learning. These skills and habits form early in life - for example, an
ability to block out distractions, attend to the task at hand, choose, start
and finish an activity – and are all skills that should be practised in
kindergarten. Habits of avoidance and inattention develop early in
children if learning-to-learn skills and constructive habits of mind are not
practised when they encounter obstacles and challenges. Chapter 2
should resonate with parents who learned early the importance of good
learning habits or regretted that they did not do so. These skills are much
harder to achieve the older one gets, as the adverse habits children can
fall into early have to be unlearned so that better habits can replace them.
When constructive learning habits and skills are acquired early, they set
the scene for lifelong dispositions for learning, motivation to succeed and
a concept of self as an effective learner.

Chapter 3 describes the power of play and its unique role in
early learning from birth to age seven or eight and beyond. Ability to
play evolves from infancy when play is largely sensory and becomes

increasingly elaborate as children develop. A developmental task of
kindergarten is for the child to become a sophisticated 'player', a
learning outcome that is practised in the context of sociodramatic play.
When environments are rich in play and learning potential indoors and
outdoors, children become astute 'players' which, in turn, promotes
learning. This chapter discusses the characteristics, styles, and social
contexts of play that becomes more elaborate as play experiences
challenge their bodies and minds, guide their choices, and promote
participation, risk-taking, and a balance of individual learning and
collaboration. Children need play-based learning experiences that let
them realize their plans, overcome obstacles, test ideas, use resources,
finish what they start, and feel successful.

Chapter 4 discusses the social, administrative and political
environment of schools and the economic and cultural needs they should
serve. School locations matter but current trends in housing development
have led to widespread closures of established neighbourhood schools in
favour of large new schools on the fringe of communities where denser
populations of families often live. This means that most children have to
be bused and parents are distanced from the school physically and
socially. School personnel and the roles they hold influence a school's
tone and social climate. The most important figures are the child's
teachers, including ECEs and education assistants and other resource
persons who work directly with the children. The climate of welcome
and security they all project to families are important to the young child
who must navigate five days a week with many new people. Chapter 4
introduces the school and the classroom and helps parents 'read' the
learning potential and emotional climate and understand the social,

physical, and cognitive challenges their children may encounter there.

Chapters 5 - 9 describe the kindergarten program, curriculum and how play influences development and learning in the major domains: social and emotional competence; physical literacy; language and literacy; numeracy and concept learning; and creative literacy. These chapters discuss developmental tasks, play-based teaching and other strategies that support and promote children's progress. When parents know how play influences children's learning, they make the connection between classroom design and organization, learning centres, activities and play materials, and the learning outcomes that children are likely to achieve. When they also appreciate the role of the outdoors in learning and the impact of both group and independent learning, parents are better equipped to ask questions and provide play experiences at home that complement their school-based learning.

Chapter 10 addresses the central issue in education that has the capacity to keep everything the same or turn everything on its head – that is, the assessment and evaluation of learning. Teachers need updated skills and intensive pre-service training related to the nature of learning, learning-to-learn skills, a range of teaching methods, and the observation and assessment skills that enable them to assess children's progress, detect gaps in learning, and identify the resources and support systems that help them develop and learn. This is especially important during early childhood when physical and brain development are rapid and the body and mind are at their most flexible and 'plastic'. Children who function in ways that reflect their potential at every stage not only feel more fulfilled; they are also prepared to contribute to a better functioning collective in which more people find a niche and fully participate. The

instruction-centred methods inherited from the past and widespread use
of standardized tests to determine rank and standing - instead of
promoting and assessing individual development and learning potential -
are among many factors still present in education that are out-of-sync
with today's pressing educational challenges.

Empowering Parents: Meeting children's learning needs in the
primary years K to 3

1

THE NATURE OF LEARNING

"Realize that the way we do school is entirely unnatural".
Susan Wise Bauer, 2018.

Re-thinking School: How to take charge of your child's education.

Learning involves being able to do, know or understand something for the first time and to integrate that learning in ways that influence one's beliefs, knowledge, skills, and competence. Learning brings about meaningful change in the learner; it inhabits the mind and body, senses and emotion, builds intelligence and wisdom and adds to one's repertoire of behaviour. It reconfigures who we are, what we are capable of, and how we understand our world and our place in it. It may represent small or large change, but it is usually something that one can feel and that others might

observe. When we have learned, our behaviours change, we are able to defend newly acquired attitudes, demonstrate strengthened abilities and performance, and enhance our self-concept. Learning has staying power, but if the new learning is not exercised it may falter and eventually disappear. For a time, however, new learning lends confidence and has an impact on self-esteem. We become able to detect new patterns, make new connections, behave differently, and feel more capable. Learning is the essence of living and being human; the best outcome is that the more of it we acquire the richer our lives become.

We learn in many ways that are influenced by a pattern and sequence of human development that is universal. Young children learn differently from older children and adults; this is an important distinction to understand and fully accommodate in our schools and homes. Individuals also differ at any age and stage in terms of how much and what they learn and in the way they approach and manage learning challenges. Each person brings unique abilities, knowledge, and interests to a learning context. Learning is gained through experience in the sensory, physical world as we interact with the environment, in the social-emotional realm as we encounter new people and life experiences, develop relationships and perspectives, and in the intellectual world of the mind as the brain *assimilates* and *accommodates* new information, concepts, patterns, and ideas. [1]

Learning should be valued first and foremost according to the progress each child makes toward achieving his or her human potential; some say this is the significant purpose of education. [2] This purpose presumes that the education system treats children as individuals. Some education goals are to prepare them for a niche in society that enables them to be productive, participate successfully as citizens, broaden their intellectual and physical horizons, and feel that they belong to something larger than themselves. When parents understand the long-term goals for their children's education and understand the nature of learning and how it evolves as they mature, parents should feel empowered to guide and advocate for them during the school years and raise questions when they meet roadblocks in learning.

Parents should not assume that the difficulties they see their child grappling with at school are due to the child's ineptness. They should not accept, for example, that their child's difficulty with math means that "my child is not good at math" nor believe that "my child has trouble with learning" as if their child is unable to learn. It is the right of all children to receive an education that is relevant to the times in which they live and to develop their potential. They also need home support that helps them over the inevitable hurdles most children encounter at some point in their schooling. All children are capable of learning but their aptitudes, learning preferences and the pace at which they learn vary widely. The challenge of parents and teachers is to determine in what contexts the child learns most readily, what interests her most, and what motivates her to persist and succeed. This calls for patience, a positive outlook, observation and assessment skills, and confidence in the child.

Children with learning disabilities

Children who bear the burden of disabilities are capable of learning and achieving but they require specialized support, the right learning environment and time to reach their potential. Many renowned persons with disabilities have overcome obstacles to learning and excelled beyond their own expectations despite extraordinary challenges. The human mind moves through the stages in cognitive development and learning at its own pace but usually follows a typical developmental sequence irrespective of disabilities. Since the 1980s, increased investment has been made in the provision of resource teachers and other professionals trained to enable children with disabilities to learn by modifying the learning environments and adapting curriculum and assessment strategies according to their special needs. Allowing children to learn at their own speed and using a range of teaching approaches usually yields positive results. But our governments have not yet

fully understood that failure to develop the potential of all children
is one of the most wasteful and encumbering costs many nations
bear. When the education system does not capitalize on the interest
and willingness of individuals to prepare themselves for
constructive participation in society, the toll of waste and the cost
of mitigation for those who cannot sustain themselves weigh
heavily on the performance, productivity and progress of a nation.

Individualized education for kindergarten and the primary grades

Education that focuses on the needs of each child
individually is sometimes referred to as *personalized education*
that customizes learning for each child's particular interests, the
pace at which the child usually learns, and culminates in a *learning
plan* that is based on observations and assessment of the child's
progress. Personalized education is not as regulated as
individualized learning is for children with disabilities nor as
applicable to children in the kindergarten/primary years.
Individualized education for children with disabilities leads to an
individual education plan (IEP) that is intended mainly for
children with disabilities who usually work closely with resource
teachers. As this book emphasizes the importance of a building a
strong foundation for learning, I am using the term 'individualized
learning' here to reflect the importance of closer monitoring of the
progress of all kindergarten/primary children in all domains –
physical, social, emotional, and cognitive. In the past,
kindergartens and the primary grades were driven largely by group
expectations and averages and the learning pace of the group
although some positive changes have been made in recent years
with the introduction of play-based learning in many
kindergartens.

These first five years of schooling lay the foundation for
development and learning and the pattern of habits and

dispositions for their later lives. The IEP for K to grade three should reflect needs to adapt the learning environment and personalize activities according to the progress of each child. The plan for each child's individualized learning should be guided by a *Kindergarten Individual Education Plan* (KIEP) that resembles many features of the IEP for children with disabilities. The KIEP should follow the child from junior kindergarten through to grade three, monitoring and assessing the pace at which the child learns, his achievement, or otherwise, of developmental tasks and learning outcomes for each level, hurdles he may encounter and supports needed to address them, learning preferences, and physical and emotional factors that may be present. The KIEP becomes the assessment record that provides the basis for reporting to parents at regular intervals. Each child's KIEP is intended to prevent or minimize gaps in their foundation for learning that might otherwise inhibit progress; it also documents children's special interests and apparent strengths. Education that strives to enable all children to achieve their human potential should treat the first five years of kindergarten/primary schooling as one continuum of development and learning through which children proceed as they demonstrate their readiness for the next steps. This approach documents the paths they take to achieving a sound foundation for the junior division grades four to six.

How does learning occur?

One answer lies in knowing a few facts about the structure of the brain, what happens when the brain is stimulated and exercised, and how it may be modified by interventions and learning experiences that stretch minds. Some experts recommend "brain-based assessments" [3] to determine the strengths and weaknesses in an individual's brain that would suggest a way to intervene early in the brain's development. An approach like this might not become mainstream for some time, if ever. When

parents know, however, that the number of synaptic connections
among neurons in the brains of young children is fifty percent
greater than in the adult brain, and greater also than in the
adolescent brain, they begin to understand that early childhood is
an exceedingly 'sensitive period' for appropriate educational
intervention, accurate assessment, expert teaching and generous
investment. The significant "pruning back" of the neural
connections in the child's brain which have not been used or
exercised that occurs during adolescence presents a stark example
of "use it or lose it". [4] This evidence suggests that all areas of the
brain should be exercised and challenged throughout the early
childhood period while the number of neural connections is
increasing rapidly and the brain is at its most amenable and plastic.
The primary school years are therefore prime time for employing
and strengthening the "muscle" of the brain and for exercising and
fortifying the child's experiences physically, cognitively and
affectively using a wide range of strategies, providing interesting
experiences and activities and using diverse resources indoors and
outdoors. To achieve this goal requires creative educational
delivery approaches, an individualized education model, more
intense and improved teacher training, and collaboration between
teachers and parents during these first five years of schooling.

Constructivist learning theory

Much of the theoretical base for early learning as it is
practised today originated in the Constructivist child development
and learning theories that gained prominence from the 1970s and
were based largely on the work of Jean Piaget and the neo-
Piagetians. [5] Constructivist approaches evolved from the study of
brain and body development that have contributed immensely to an
understanding of how learning occurs. It took nearly three decades
before this theoretical foundation was expressed in teacher training
for kindergartens. Prior to that period much of teacher training was

grounded in intuition, culture and conventions that were based on
instruction-based practice (6) for all grade levels. Jean
Piaget,1920s to 1980s, was a Swiss genetic epistemologist and
pioneer in the study of how young children come to know and
understand. His seminal work proposed that learning involves the
joint processes of *assimilation* (changing what is out there to be
learned), *accommodation* (change that happens within the person
to accommodate the new learning), and *equilibration,* (an internal
balance that is achieved when one has firmed up new learning and
understanding). Piaget believed that learning in early childhood is
an uneven, repetitive process that relies on sensory stimulation and
exploration and includes active interaction with concrete objects in
the environment during play.[7] The child requires time and
diverse play experiences before new learning is fully integrated
and becomes a permanent part of the child's repertoire.

Consider the example of a two-year-old who is trying to
build a tower with blocks. She explores and manipulates the blocks
as she tries to put one on top of another, eventually finds the flat
surfaces and juxtaposes them, may also experiment with larger
blocks, and finally builds a tall tower. At this stage, the learner is
engaged in *assimilation* or altering what is out there which, in this
case, means finding the flat surfaces and sizes that balance one on
top of another. During this learning process, the child adjusts her
behaviour by making a "fit" between what she has already learned
– that is, to make a tower that stands, blocks need a flat, usually
larger surface to stand on. Piaget called this internal process
accommodation, a process that involves integrating the new
learning in order to make the new learning a part of the child's
larger repertoire. Once a fit has been achieved between what the
child understands and can do and the new learning challenge, she
is able to return to a state of balance (equilibrium). Regaining
equilibrium is a process that Piaget called *equilibration* that

happens when the new learning has been integrated through these joint processes of *assimilation* and *accommodation.*

Learning at any age begins when one encounters something new and unfamiliar and is challenged to master it. The process that Piaget described applies for most ages and stages and to acquiring knowledge (days of the week), learning skills (balancing on skates, forming letters) and understanding concepts (eight pennies and eight elephants are equal in number so size does not influence number). What is to be learned might be imposed externally by the school system (e.g., learn to read), later by one's job (e.g., become a good team member) or voluntarily chosen by the individual (e.g., learn to play tennis or bridge). Taking on the challenge to learn is usually accompanied by an imbalance or feeling of discomfort by the learner (*disequilibrium*) as he tries to master the new learning. Disequilibrium can last for as long as it takes an individual to acquire the new knowledge, perform a new skill consistently or explain and apply a new concept.

Think back to when you first learned to ride a bicycle and retrace the steps and what you felt as you grappled with this new learning. You had to do something different with parts of your body above the mid-line (hold the handlebars) and those below the mid-line of the body (pump the pedals) while simultaneously doing something different between the left and right sides of the body (steer the handlebars with one hand and make hand traffic signals or apply the handbrake with the other hand). In addition, you had to maintain your posture and distribute your weight while gliding and balancing. All these physical skills had to be coordinated and executed smoothly to remain on the bike and move forward while also obeying the rules of the road and avoiding collisions. Riding a bicycle is, nonetheless, a complex learning task that most children can begin to learn with support and practice from about age four.

Learning to drive a car with manual transmission later in life in heavy traffic and exiting and entering freeways involves a similar process. When we master the smooth execution of the physical, cognitive, and emotional skills involved in high-stakes tasks like these, we feel that equilibrium has been restored. A similar learning process applies to intellectual tasks like learning geometry, writing a viable essay, or planning a research project. The pace at which an individual is able to balance the physical, perceptual, cognitive and emotional skills involved in learning complex tasks differs from person to person and depends on the skills, knowledge and understanding one brings to the new learning.

The learning process is facilitated by choosing an approach that fits one's style, native abilities such as perceptual skills, motivation to learn something more complicated than usual, and ability to attend to the task at hand and persevere. Some people give up quickly while others persist and try different ways to achieve their goal. In most cases, interest, motivation, and persistence count more than native ability when learning. [8] Some people find it easier to master the winning moves in playing chess than trying to drive a golf ball or draw a portrait.

Many current educational theories may be traced back to the observations of Jean-Jacques Rousseau, an 18th century philosopher who wrote about the "malleability of the natural child" and its "perfectibility". [9] The early kindergartens of Friedrich Froebel, Maria Montessori's understanding of "sensitive period" and "method", and Lawrence Kohlberg's (1972) "cognitive-developmental model" all emphasized "early education of the senses" and the importance of reaching one's natural potential. [10] These philosophers agreed that play is the young child's natural context for learning.

In early childhood, learning occurs as children explore and
interact with concrete objects while they play and during the
process, they build the mental structures and neural connections in
the brain that become increasingly more elaborate with time and
play experiences. They discover the physical characteristics of
things such as size, shape, and texture as they manipulate objects
and learn physically through touching, seeing, and hearing. A rich
variety of play experiences with concrete objects in the
environment facilitates the "formation of mental structures" [11]
and promotes the brain's increasing flexibility, plasticity, memory,
and readiness for more complex learning.

Preoperational period (from sensorimotor thought to preoperational
thought)

The preoperational period of cognitive development
features two distinct phases in learning and the development of
thought: *symbolic thinking* (about age two to four) when their
thought processes are linked to using concrete symbols, and
representational thinking (about age four to six) when they learn to
represent in a number of ways what they are capable of thinking.
During the symbolic phase, children use play materials and words
as symbols to stand for what they are thinking or imagining – e.g. a
toddler (age two) using a realistic toy telephone when he imitates a
phone conversation; a preschooler (age three) may use a block as a
stand-in for a telephone. These actions mark children's evolving
cognitive abilities to use first, a realistic toy, then an abstract object
(a block) as a symbol in their pretend play. Four-year-olds
typically identify numbers and letters by name and recognize them
as symbols that have meaning. Children's books for this stage
encourage them to link number, letter, and word symbols with
pictures of things.

Representational thinking

The kindergarten years are prime time for the development
and practice of intuitive thought that is characterized by children's
representation through role play what they are thinking, by
negotiating roles, inventing a script, and using props as symbols to
support their play episode. From about age four to six, children
also represent what they are thinking using a variety of media such
as art, music and movement, and storytelling. Sociodramatic role
play is the capstone of play during this *representational* stage
when kindergarten children use dialogue that they invent as they
play and actions to represent what they imagine or remember and
have agreed to dramatize. The ability to act out an event that all
children in a small group can relate to, or to imagine a scenario and
invent a script for their dramatization, is a sophisticated stage of
play that all children should be encouraged to achieve because it is
so rich in learning. Chapter 3 addresses in greater detail the
learning achieved through sociodramatic play.

The concrete operational period – thinking and learning

An implicit aim of the kindergarten years is to move
children from preoperational thought to *concrete operational
thought* often beginning by grade one and progressing throughout
the primary years, that represents another cognitive stage. The
developmental tasks [12] of grade one increasingly rely on an
ability to know and understand in the absence of concrete objects
to manipulate even though children typically continue to use
fingers to count on or beads to verify their sums and subtractions.
The ability to know and understand cognitively, instead of
depending on the senses and manipulation of concrete objects, is
apparent, for example, when children can sort and classify sets of
objects with ease and define their own categories (*classification*),
put things in order by size and sequence following specified rules
(*seriation*), and understand the constancy of number (groups of
things can be equal in number despite differences in their size,

27

shape or configuration). Acquiring these fundamental logical concepts, along with other concepts, makes it easier for children to understand arithmetic operations and solve word problems. Chapter 8 addresses logical concepts and early math learning.

Children who are concrete operational in their thinking relate to spatial and directional concepts – up/down, in front of/behind, above, and below. They understand causality (cause and effect) and can separate their own perspective from that of others. They see themselves as separate from other things and people in the world and become more objective about experiences and events around them. The child who has not yet achieved concrete operational thought attributes human characteristics to non-human and inanimate things like the sun, moon and stars, trees, wind, and cars (animism). This child also exhibits egocentric thinking whereby she believes that everything in the world happens because of her; for example, "I lost my mittens because I behaved badly yesterday"; or, "the car got stuck in the snow because daddy said a bad word". These changes in the thought processes evolve gradually from about age five or six. The transition has been made from preoperational to concrete operational thought when the child demonstrates consistently that she has understood concepts that defy perception – for example, those which confirm relationships between things and people that go beyond direct or observable connections and appearances. Consider examples such as: my mommy and my aunt are sisters just like my sister and I are sisters; the small rubber ball will travel faster and farther than the large beach ball when thrown.

From concrete operational thought to formal operational thought

The cognitive transition of preoperational children to concrete operational thought is different in content and substance from the transition that occurs later on, from about twelve years (or puberty) to adolescence. This later cognitive transition occurs as children move from concrete operations to *formal operational thought*. At the formal operational stage, children achieve the ability to think in ideas and at higher levels of abstraction that depend on their cognitive maturity. Their learning evolves as children meet experiences which confront them with learning challenges that their minds are either ready to tackle, or not. For example, the child in grade one or two who struggles with subtraction questions may need to review with her teacher the concept of *"reversibility"* (i.e., understand that actions can be done and undone or reversed) and needs more play time with materials that may help her understand the subtraction operation. The child who is moving from concrete operational thought to formal operational thought (approximately age twelve or puberty) needs to juggle several ideas, rules, and frameworks in his mind.

As children move toward secondary school, they have to compose an essay on a topic that requires an introduction, a clear explanation, perhaps an opinion or argument, and a conclusion that together requires them to hold a number of ideas in their minds while framing a coherent explanation or argument. Many children need plenty of practice to be ready for this challenge and waiting until high school to achieve the underlying skills and level of mental organization can pose a setback to the child's concept of self as a learner. The complexity of this assignment requires a multitude of literacy skills but also the ability to organize one's thinking and explain a rationale, a complex task that cannot be accomplished without the essential foundational skills. Some of these skills include an ability to use and apply symbols, use clear language, and put oneself in the position of the listener, all skills that are introduced and practised in elementary school, even as early as kindergarten.

Facilitating the transitions in thinking and learning

Understanding the transitions in the development of thought and learning facilitates understanding of how children's learning progress at any stage is buttressed by skills they learned effectively at an earlier stage. As thought patterns and learning strategies change significantly over time, teaching and coaching should start where the child is developmentally and move him to the next step when he is ready, not when the curriculum says it's time to move on. This is another rationale for individualized primary education while children are learning the foundational (generic) skills for later learning. Some children learn to read in kindergarten while others learn to read in grade two or three. How quickly they learn often depends on children's opportunities to practise the foundational skills and concepts. For example, the immaturity of the child's cognitive-perceptual or physical-perceptual skills might slow down the child's learning to read. [13] This implies going back to provide more practice activities to develop the child's perceptual skills. A child who has not yet developed eye-hand coordination and depth perception finds it hard to connect the bat he is holding with the ball that is thrown to him, a shaming in front of his friends that might turn him off baseball forever. Instead of keeping the child in the outfield or using a pinch-hitter, it is better to find games and play activities for the child to practise the underlying perceptual skills. As the child matures, the role of play in all aspects of learning diminishes but play can and should remain a useful vehicle for practice and learning throughout life. Yet, play is employed in remediation and in later stages of learning and life far less than it should be.

Types of knowledge children acquire

Piaget proposed three types of knowledge: *physical, social conventional* and *logical-mathematical.*

Physical knowledge

This type refers to information children acquire by exploring and manipulating the physical characteristics and composition of concrete objects around them. They test the strength, feel textures, and find out if they bounce or roll. The environment should be restaged regularly with new materials for children to explore as their hands-on manipulation of objects helps them know their environment. Children also need opportunities to become aware of what their bodies can do and to acquire a *concept of self*. This discovery occurs through physical activity indoors and outdoors that include games with rules and fitness exercises. Five-year-olds are proud when they are able to tie shoelaces, gallop and skip, and ride their bikes. The acquisition of physical learning depends on regular active play, practice and repetition, often in a variety of contexts in order to achieve full mastery. The importance of planned, physical programming for kindergarten and primary grades, in school and outside, cannot be over-stated and is the subject of Chapter 6.

Social-conventional knowledge

Kindergarten children learn facts and labels related to things in their world that are usually taught directly. This learning is referred to as *social-conventional knowledge* that is influenced by culture, history, and precedents such as good manners, respect for cultural traditions, and protecting the natural environment. Knowledge of rules related to personal safety and how to behave in a group is essential knowledge for health, good citizenship and getting along with others that are usually taught at home and reinforced in school. Children absorb social-conventional knowledge quickly and are proud to tell what they have learned. This type of knowledge often originates from direct experience – learning the rules of games, bicycle safety, how to navigate the neighbourhood and find one's way home. Learning to observe conventions, respect others' rights and appreciate cultural customs

depends on children's environments so the school has a large role
to play.

Learning one's home address and names of local landmarks
like churches and fire stations represent factual knowledge about
everyday things that is acquired through lived experience, field
trips and listening to others. Social conventions reflect knowledge
that society deems to be important for children to learn such as
saying please and thank you and standing for the national anthem.
It is mostly straightforward to acquire factual knowledge that relies
on listening, repetition, and the motivation to remember, and
children eagerly soak up facts that interest them. Remembering
jokes, reciting rhymes, and counting numbers all involve facts that
are typically easy to learn and fun to know.

Logical-mathematical knowledge i.e., concept learning

Children begin to form concepts in preschool and in
kindergarten they should be ready to practise logical-mathematical
concepts that depend more on knowing and understanding than
sensory input. Thinking logically and reasoning involve
understanding relationships among things, patterns and ideas that
are not readily perceived through the senses nor necessarily
understood through direct instruction. When children engage with
play activities that exploit the difference that exists between what
they see and what exists, they are exposed to concepts that depend
on reasoning and logical thinking about the invisible action of
forces or factors on each other. This cognitive transformation is
eased by first introducing children to phenomena that they can see
occur before introducing concepts that cannot be seen and must be
understood such as magnetism. Concept formation continues
throughout life, but the most rapid period of growth is from about
age three or four to eight especially for the logical-mathematical
concepts that are addressed in Chapter 8.

Some people claim that logical-mathematical thinking is the hardest learning to acquire; others dispute that claim based on their early learning experiences and what comes easiest to them. The differences among individuals may be attributed to factors including early play experiences, the coaching support they received when discrepancies occurred between what they perceived and what was alleged to be 'true', and children's emotional ability to confront and overcome obstacles. Howard Gardner [14] proposed that people possess multiple intelligences in unequal amounts that are based on genetic inheritance, individual experiences, and exposure at the right time to clear explanations, examples, and practice. Children's aptitudes toward some intelligences more than others influence how easily they learn some skills and concepts and struggle with others. *Teachable moments* when children's learning is stalled can occur at home and in school at any time, but they are 'moments' that pass by quickly.

Informal and formal learning

Learning occurs in informal and formal contexts throughout life. Informal learning is a byproduct of the play activities and experiences in which young children engage; it occurs at home, in recreational pursuits and by observing and listening to others. The kindergarten child's understanding continues to be impacted by messages received through the senses. During this 'sensitive period' when learning by doing is most effective, informal play continues to be the learning strategy of choice. Informal learning seldom involves rules that children have to follow and little expectation that children will achieve learning outcomes within a specified timeframe. Children learn informally through activities and games that are mostly elective and self-directed and free play that is engaged in for its own sake. For example, children love to play tag for fun, but in doing so, they also practise physical abilities that include agility, flexibility,

stamina, and balance. Playing with puzzles develops fine motor
coordination, ocular-motor and other perceptual skills, as well as
cognitive skills - just as adults learn to curl for its own sake but in
the process also maintain balance and depth perception and
exercise cognitive skills such as estimation and probability.
Informal learning settings should offer progressively complex
challenges that capitalize on children's curiosity and eagerness to
know that motivate them to practise and understand concepts.

Sociodramatic play is a particularly dynamic type of
informal learning that requires kindergarten/primary children to
represent an episode they imagine, dream or understand using
symbols, imitation and drama. As they play out their scenarios,
children may read or write, navigate twists and turns in the script
they evolve, sort out disagreements, submit their own ideas to the
rule of the majority, imagine unexplored places like space stations
or pioneer homes, and practise communicating with new words
and language structures. The learning gained from this play style is
exceedingly rich; it is also *informal* because it is embedded in play
that is governed by the children and only limited by their
imaginations and ability to express themselves.

Sociodramatic play that may include fantasy play requires
imagination, risk-taking, planning and setting goals,
communication, and negotiation skills. These skills are also
possessed by successful leaders, craftsmen, artists, and innovators,
yet remarkably, the acquisition of these habits and skills can begin
informally in kindergartens during sociodramatic play. Teachers
provide props, may ask questions, or suggest themes for episodes,
and they prompt children if or when the play stalls; they might also
review the episode with the children at the end. This type of
informal learning helps children become 'sophisticated players'
whereby they practise skills that many adults never acquire such as
the ability to hold a script in their heads, think on their feet and

compromise.

Informal learning also occurs in the context of projects in which children strive together to achieve a concrete outcome and in the process they practise and learn skills that contribute both individually and collectively to the result. This is another interactive approach that is rich in learning especially when the project has multiple stages and takes place over several days or weeks. Projects that are well-planned enhance communication (develop fluency in speaking and negotiation), improve social skills (active listening, providing feedback), and support creative thinking (representing, visioning, and adapting). [15]

Contrast these informal learning opportunities with sitting at a table doing prescribed paper and pencil tasks that have a format and pattern to follow and an explicit endpoint like tracing numbers, connecting dots, cutting out and matching shapes. Prescriptive activities provide essential practice with fine motor and perceptual skills, eye-hand coordination, and starting and finishing tasks, all of which have a clear purpose in kindergarten. They should not, however, replace the time and energy needed to facilitate the learning inherent in creative activities such as sociodramatic play that simultaneously challenge children's social, emotional, physical, and cognitive abilities and introduce complexity. Prescriptive (convergent) activities and child-initiated creative (divergent) activities are both viable. Education practice should not move from one end of the pedagogical spectrum of teacher-directed learning to the other end that leaves children totally in charge of what they try and learn. Nor should education let children fend for themselves when learning does not readily occur. Education does not have to reject past practices that work in their appropriate contexts in order to embrace progressive practices that are evidence-based. The irrational swings of the pendulum from one teaching approach to something new and shiny at the other end happen way too often in education and should be rejected by parents.

Formal learning in middle childhood (about age eight to puberty)

Formal learning relies on academic skills that include reading, writing, inquiry, work-study skills, problem solving, and technological literacy that enable study, research and production. An important mandate of elementary school education is to prepare children gradually for formal learning that occurs mainly in secondary schools but may also be acquired and practised in informal and community settings and workplace practicum assignments. In addition to reading, writing, mathematics and science, children learn academic skills such as finding resources for projects (e.g., books, articles), writing essays and reports and using devices to improve the accuracy and quality of their productions. All children need proficient formal learning skills in order to solve problems, communicate clear explanations, devise questions and research answers. Most of these skills can also be practised and learned in informal settings. This acknowledgement supports the case for expecting high performance standards in academic skills from children who learn best in the context of hands-on, experiential learning and occupational programs. Most children can become quite capable of competent performance in the generic skills including reading and communicating effectively, mathematical problem solving, analysis, and critical thinking when this is the expectation we have for them. They should not be assumed to be weak learners just because they learn best by doing and they should never be satisfied with 'watered-down' courses and expectations in the generic skills. Low expectations produce low levels of performance.

The importance of achieving formal operational thought

Formal operational thought usually occurs at the end of a
continuum of cognitive development from sensorimotor,
preoperational, and concrete operational thought and should
culminate in formal operations which rely on reason and logical
thinking. These higher levels of intellectual activity range from
remembering and understanding at one end of the cognitive
spectrum to analysis, synthesis, evaluation, and possibly invention
at the higher end. [16] Children usually achieve elements of formal
operational thought as they reach puberty (about age 12 to 14) after
they have let go of their earlier dependence on sensory,
knowledge-based learning and are able to balance ideas and
perspectives in their heads. Although their achievement of a
measure of abstract thought as they begin high school is an
important goal, not all children achieve the same levels of abstract
thinking in all learning contexts. The extent to which children
achieve formal operational thinking depends to a great extent on
the quality and nature of their learning experiences in the primary
school years.

A major challenge for 21st century education is to ensure
that many more children attain higher levels of intellectual activity
that are essential to creativity, invention, and innovation. Not only
do occupational, entrepreneurial, professional roles, and most
economically secure jobs increasingly depend on more complex
performances. The future of democracy also rests in part on a
voting population that has the capacity to analyze, evaluate and
make viable choices based on evidence and is able to contribute to
the health and wellbeing of the nation and all its citizens.

Industrial Age education (19th and 20th centuries) was
predicated on the understanding that a minority of students needed
to be educated to attain levels of abstract thinking and higher
intellectual performance for professional roles and the sciences, as
the majority of the population would find work in industrial

production, in-person services and manual labour. The thinking
then was that most children would not, therefore, receive the same
level of educational investment. The revised economic base of the
nation from the dawn of the Information Age (about the late
1990s) altered the ratio of *routine production* jobs to *systems
analysts*. This re-ordering, at the turn of this century recommended
education reform to accommodate a massive shift in the
performance levels of the largest segment of the workforce. Some
of this shift was accommodated at the postsecondary level with the
broad expansion of university and college education for many
more students that began in the 1970s and 80s.

Change should occur now in the elementary school system
to broaden education delivery systems and diversify learning
venues, update curriculum, and improve teacher training, teacher
recruitment and the resources and support systems for teaching.
Significant shifts made at the postsecondary level and tried to some
extent at the secondary school level happen too late in the lives of
children to make a significant difference in their performance.
Education reform is essential at the elementary school level
because that is where the foundation is laid, or not, for complex
thinking and attainment of higher levels of performance. The
platform for extensive reform that began with the introduction in
some jurisdictions of full-day, play-based kindergartens was a
good start. Now, the kindergarten/ primary sector should lead the
essential paradigm shift that would put public elementary school
systems on a constructive new trajectory.

Alternate schooling opportunities

Differences in learning styles among children should be
respected as legitimate by elementary schools and offer options to
children who do not thrive in conventional classrooms. If the first
five-years in school were individualized to the end of grade three,

children's projected learning needs would be well-documented and supported by evidence in their KIEP. Education reform should include the provision of a wider array and high-quality alternative delivery choices for the remaining elementary school years. Some progressive jurisdictions already provide alternative schools that emphasize experiential learning for children in the intermediate division, but they are not yet mainstream choices. Children who favour academic studies tend to do well in the security and predictability of formal learning classrooms and appreciate drill and practice routines they can practise by themselves. Learners who choose experiential settings are more likely to achieve their potential in non-conventional, less didactic ways. All children are entitled to educational experiences that enable them to become literate, numerate and independent thinkers - competencies that influence the quality of their adult lives - and these learning experiences and challenges should be tailored to their interests, talents and aptitudes for learning.

The elephant in the room is a stigma that has diminished the value of experiential learning in apprenticeships, vocational and technical education next to misguided perceptions that 'academic' schooling is somehow superior and should be reserved for those who exhibit talent in conventional, academic ways. Children's preferences for experiential learning environments do not imply that they do not have to perform at the same levels of proficiency and 'literacy' in the generic skills as those who prefer academic pathways. All children require proficiency in the generic skills known today as "essential employability skills", such as numeracy, literacy, technological literacy and analytic skills, although some children will choose experiential pathways in order to practise and acquire these skills instead of the conventional academic ways. Who decided that children who prefer non-academic learning pathways and destinations should not also

require proficient communication skills (i.e., spoken language,
writing skills), numeracy and analytic skills just because they
choose to be a plumber, a cabinet maker, or a cook? They are
unlikely to require the writing proficiency of a print journalist, but
competent use of the language in print and spoken form, and an
ability to apply numeracy skills effectively in business and work
transactions as well as for the management of personal finances are
now essential life skills for all.

The stigma linked to mental illness is being exposed and
challenged and progress is occurring, but an education stigma
persists, although it is seldom acknowledged in education contexts.
Backlash against the educated elites of our time seems to have
been powered by widespread but subtle depreciation of people
'without university degrees' who are increasingly protesting
political correctness and the disdain they feel from the educated
who typically do the clean, regular, well-compensated work. Our
democracy is in danger of being undermined by attributions of
superiority and entitlement to the 'educated' that casts those
'without university or college degrees or diplomas' and even those
who lack the right credentials from the 'right' universities as
inferior and therefore unworthy of power and wealth. This
perversion of human rights and social standing taints society and
contributes to the current populist backlash against the educated
elites. Michael Sandel (2020. *The Tyranny of Merit: What's
Become of the Common Good?* New York: Farrar, Strauss and
Giroux. p. 26) states: "Elites have so valorized a college degree –
both as an avenue for advancement and as the basis for social
esteem – that they have difficulty understanding the hubris a
meritocracy can generate, and the harsh judgement it imposes on
those who have not gone to college".

Learning in multi-age groupings in primary classrooms

Parents have learned to fear that their child might be placed in a multi-age classroom which often happens when enrollments dip in a school and it is deemed necessary to merge two or three grade levels. There are several reasons why multi-age classrooms, especially in the primary years, may benefit children, especially when older children are able to mentor younger ones and, in doing so, re-learn for themselves. "Teaching is to learn twice" is an adage that fits this context. It is also easier for children to experience diverse perspectives in a multi-age environment. There is little evidence that same-age classrooms contribute to uniformity in the pace at which children learn. The popularity of the Montessori model that exploits the benefits of multi-age learning is a testament to children's versatility as they move seamlessly from teaching to learning; older children may help the younger ones solve puzzles while younger children feel proud to observe and contribute to the project of an older child.

A climate of cooperation infuses a multi-age classroom more readily than a same-age class where children cannot resist competing with one another. Children develop empathy as they offer help to younger children and while doing so are able to discern how much they have learned themselves. The cooperative atmosphere and self-confidence of children who discover they can 'teach' another child, as well as the pride a younger child feels in having the attention of an older child, adds energy to the interpersonal dynamics in the classroom. Younger children observe the abilities of older children and anticipate their own learning of skills that will allow them to produce or do something similar.

Enhanced learning in schools

In middle childhood (about age eight to twelve), children are attracted by issues and situations they meet in books and films and by stimuli that challenge their imaginations and creativity.

They are eager for new experiences and have a thirst for invention. Finding learning pursuits in which they can shine augments their self-concept and self-esteem. The school-age child is energetic and wants to attempt everything he sees; if his interest is captured and he believes he will be successful, he will pursue it vigorously. Primary school children also benefit from exposure to music, art, martial arts, dance, fitness, and sports - any activities that challenge their bodies and minds, and these programs should be accessible throughout elementary school. Yet, even at a time that calls for creativity and invention, school systems continue to threaten access to subjects like physical education, intramural sports, and the arts when budgets are tight. This is a frequent response to financial pressures by ministries and school boards that parents should vigorously oppose. Physical, music and arts education should be a fixture in elementary school curriculum, not only for their own worth, but also because they provide a balance that improves children's readiness and motivation for learning of all kinds. Attempts by school systems to reduce children's access to physical education and the creative arts is unhealthy for children and an assault on the intrinsic value of education.

The 'discovery learning' debate

The adoption of discovery learning in early childhood education was influenced by research results from the 1970s on that produced evidence of the success of informal, play-oriented preschool programs on children's later school performance and as young adults. This pioneering research demonstrated that play-based programs which contain large elements of exploration and discovery had a significant impact on children's lower incidence of school dropout later on, lower crime rates, fewer teen pregnancies, and better outcomes overall. Later research confirmed the early evidence based on children who were preoperational in their thinking. [17]

These success stories and Constructivist cognitive-developmental theory that began to predominate in early childhood education in the 1980s eventually influenced thinking related to kindergarten education. This led to long-overdue pressure early in the new century for full-day, play-based kindergartens that relied on the proven effectiveness of discovery learning for young children. Ministries of education began to take notice and they assumed that if discovery learning enhances young children's education outcomes, its principles should be imported into the junior and intermediate grades especially for math education. This debate is addressed again in Chapter 8.

The decision to adopt discovery learning and inquiry methods in elementary schools led to the widespread abandonment of conventional instruction for some subjects. Didactic teaching, memorization, and rules to follow were deemed to be ineffective, even for subjects like math for which understanding is cumulative and depends on understanding one concept and building another on that conceptual foundation. Math teaching was changed without much warning or consultation to 'discovery' and 'inquiry-based' learning. [18] Former requirements for children to memorize multiplication tables and learn protocols for long division, for example, were discarded in favour of teachers who, "engage with the children in inquiries that enable the children to explore their questions and wonderings as *co-learners* with the educators…(who) offer provocations that build on the children's thinking or invite the children to engage in new ways of learning"! [19]

Discovery learning has been interpreted in many ways, but its meaning for the decision-makers in education seemed to originate with their belief that elementary school children should discover and work out basic math principles and the steps to follow for themselves and that thinking through a problem would lead

them to discover the solution. The curriculum designers connected
their convictions to the Constructivist view of learning that
'children construct their own understanding of concepts and build
their mental structures' but forgot the piece related to 'in the
context of their active manipulation of concrete objects while their
immature cognitive processes are largely tied to direct experience
and reliance on the senses'. This misapplication of discovery
learning methods to junior and intermediate schooling, when it was
intended primarily for children in preschool, kindergarten and
those in grade one whose 'knowing' is largely sensory-bound, led
to years of declining performance in math for many children in the
junior and intermediate grades and beyond. In the backlash that
followed this misadventure, the discovery learning approach to
math teaching and learning was blamed on Constructivist theory,
another misinterpretation which ensured that this viable cognitive-
developmental theory also suffered an undeserved attack on its
credibility. For a generation or more of children in the elementary
schools, the indiscriminate abandonment of some 'best practices'
in direct instruction for math and the pendulum swing toward
'thinking through', estimating and discovering, failed to account
for the fact that mathematics understanding is cumulative, based on
understanding concepts and applying the tools and concepts in
appropriate contexts.

Discovery learning has been widely criticized in recent
years by claims it is responsible for the decline in students'
performance on standardized tests, especially mathematics. The
implementation of discovery learning in the absence of a firm
foundation in logical concepts, reasoning skills and in the practical
application of tools and strategies for mathematical problem-
solving was problematic. The gaps in children's understanding of
math concepts made math unnecessarily difficult for children who
need clear instruction, some rules to follow, tools they can

memorize, and enlightened coaching and explanations at the right time. Another challenge was the inadequate preparation of teachers to implement discovery learning which also depends on a teacher's command of the subject, in this case math, their understanding of when and how to use hands-on manipulation of objects, and their ability to explain the underlying concepts clearly when children encounter obstacles.

Mathematics has always been a subject in which most children require competent instruction and explanations that target the precise area where and when they experience a gap in their logical understanding of the problem. Teacher training in most universities has usually assumed, but not verified, that certified teachers understand the subjects they teach and are able to identify where a child is having trouble. Teachers should be able to explain the underlying concepts and provide examples and alternate pathways to understanding and applying principles. They should also verify that children have understood foundational concepts and principles before they are required to proceed to the next step in learning. Many parents lacked these skills and became frustrated by their inability to address their child's math problems. Children's performance deteriorated and discovery learning was identified as the culprit while the other factors, such as its misapplication to junior and intermediate math learning, were ignored.

The swing of the pendulum into discovery learning and away from instruction and equipping children with the essential tools for success in elementary school math, has been problematic for school systems, teachers, children and their parents, and the public has also raised concerns. Decades ago, primary and middle school teachers believed in brain fitness through rote learning, memory challenges, and the brain-eye-hand fine motor activities involved in printing and handwriting. When these structured tasks and others such as memorizing multiplication tables, public speaking without notes, and committing long passages of poetry to memory were removed from elementary school curriculum on grounds that they were too "structured and boring", education lost significant ways to strengthen the fitness of the brain, stabilize neural connections and take advantage of the brain's 'plasticity' in childhood. [21]

There are several instances in education of embracing new theory and abandoning the old without due regard for the wisdom of several past practices that were identified as "best practices". Many of the pendulum swings in education occur because people with power and influence in education either misunderstand or disregard the hazards of change in the absence of sufficient knowledge and evidence to support when and for whom an application is appropriate and advised. The decision to jump full-throttle into discovery learning contributed to almost two decades of disruption in public schools. In just a few years, some valued direct-teaching methods were replaced by discovery-based practices. Meanwhile, children continued to be subjected to standardized testing that revealed declining performance on tests of the generic skills, especially numeracy and literacy. High schools, colleges, and universities complained that students were arriving with poor math, literacy, and work-study skills. Colleges developed remedial courses to help incoming students succeed in programs that required functional performance in literacy, numeracy and analytic skills. The casualties of the pendulum swing were those young people who wanted postsecondary training and education, or good jobs right out of high school, but could not meet the entrance or employment requirements.

Today, many educators and the public are calling for "back to the basics" approaches of the past to solve this problem and demanding that discovery learning be abandoned altogether. Fortunately, other educators are warning against teaching "the

basics" in the same conventional ways they were taught years ago
while ignoring that the application of structured learning and direct
teaching approaches of the last century do not work on their own,
nor for all children. There are benefits to be had from discovery
learning and inquiry methods for junior and intermediate grades
that encourage children to think through solutions to problems.
Direct instruction and discovery approaches may be combined to
assist the learning process when teachers know how to do so, have
sufficient training, and are able to explain underlying concepts,
especially in math. Some educators are recommending "balanced
approaches" that combine the best of formal learning and
instruction with discovery learning. [22] A balanced approach has
a better chance of addressing much that we now understand about
the nature of learning and how it changes as children develop, gain
experience and mature.

2

LEARNING TO LEARN

**"Persistence is the difference between mediocrity and
enormous success."** David Shenk 2009. [1]

What does it mean to "learn to learn"?

Learning to learn is an important mandate of kindergarten
that includes skills children can practise while they play.
Kindergarten is the right environment and time to introduce skills
such as positive dispositions for learning, the right habits of mind,
ability to attend and task orientation, and the "executive
functions". [2] This chapter includes psychological and
environmental influences on learning to learn such as theory of
mind, metacognition and motivation. Social, temperamental,
emotional, and many cognitive factors also support early learning
and influence lifelong learning. Ability to learn is not something
that one either has or does not have; becoming an effective learner
has to be learned. Children are born with various abilities and
aptitudes for certain types of learning, but effective learning
involves the acquisition of skills, dispositions and character traits
that should be actively nurtured by parents and teachers in the
early years. When this happens, the skills and aptitudes usually last
for a lifetime.

Theory of mind

Theory of mind is a way to understand how children learn
to mentally take the perspective of someone else and consider it
alongside their own. It asks them to think about thought,
understand their own thoughts and the thoughts and feelings of
others, and is an awareness that individuals have different beliefs,
intentions, and perspectives. Theory of mind grows in relationship
with others. As they play, children learn that perspectives vary
widely, especially when they try to hang onto a toy that another
child wants or negotiate who plays what role in a scenario.
Children who understand the perspectives of others do better in
school from kindergarten on because they are able to anticipate
what their teachers want and expect, and they appreciate why their
peers feel and respond the way they do. [3] Perspective-taking is as
important for children to learn as independent thinking [4].

Theory of mind is relevant to effective learning as it
cultivates and sustains *cognitive flexibility* such as the ability to
change one's mind and alter how one thinks, or, at a mature level,
the capacity for analysis that requires objective assessment of facts,
opinions and judgements. Children begin to develop a theory of
mind from age three; it develops as their play becomes more social
and group-based and as they are confronted by the ideas and needs
of others that conflict with their own. The challenge is to
encourage children to watch how other children approach an
activity and contrast what their peers do with their own approach.
As they observe others, children may amend their strategies and
attempt the activity again, especially if they did not reach their goal
the first time. Trying out a range of ways to tackle an activity
encourages flexible thinking, willingness to risk taking on
unfamiliar challenges and may influence a child to change a plan
to achieve a goal. Theory of mind supports the ability to persevere
– to start an activity, deal with obstacles, adjust one's approach,
pick up new skills, recognize that the goal might take longer to
reach than originally planned, and stick with it anyway. When
parents and teachers observe this process closely, they can help a
child adjust his approach, find resources to support his efforts and

persist, even when he must face up to his own mistakes or wrong assumptions. When we allow children to simply walk away from a challenge and find something easier and less threatening to tackle, children lose the benefits of an important teachable moment that may not reappear. Theory of mind gives children confidence to engage with unfamiliar activities, think their own thoughts and explore new pathways that might lead to originality and invention.

Metacognition

Theory of mind is related to metacognition which includes the mental processes of reasoning, strategizing, problem-solving, and evaluating or judging. Metacognition originates in experience; it involves ability to reflect on one's mental processing and to discover how false thoughts or inaccurate perceptions can become habits of mind that we adhere to because of inexperience, personality traits and personal needs. When children learn early to consider how they arrived at a certain plan or perspective and realize there may be other ways to plan or find a solution, they exercise the mental flexibility they need to persist with a task or solve a problem by trying a different approach instead of giving up and walking away.

Habits of mind

Habits of mind are mental skills people practise actively or maybe drift into unwittingly and eventually establish as a modus operandi for tackling learning challenges and dealing with life in general. There are positive and constructive habits of mind, like regularly completing projects before their due dates and following through with what one has committed to, or they can be habits of avoidance, procrastination and denial that inhibit learning. Positive habits of mind encourage children to focus on the task at hand (task orientation), or return to an activity after an interruption, or to block out distractions so that they meet their learning commitments (ability to attend); they also play a supporting role in learning to delay gratification. Acquiring positive habits of mind and the right dispositions for learning influence school success and lifelong learning at least as much as native intelligence does.[5]

High levels of performance in school, work and life in
general are nearly always related to qualities that enable self-
direction, positive habits of mind and intrinsic (inner) motivation.
We all know people who, despite their apparent talents, were
thwarted by character traits and habits such as inability to persist,
absence of self-control and a tendency to avoid risk,
disappointment or failure when confronted by a challenge. These
are sometimes the same people who excel at playing cards, are the
first to solve puzzles, can readily see abstract relationships, use
analogies with ease, and are the first to draw insightful or funny
connections between unrelated subjects or ideas. Too often these
talented people neither excel in school, nor distinguish themselves
in their work. When asked, they might say they disliked school
because of limits they perceived as constraints, pressures to
conform and compete, endless rules, and bland, uninteresting
environments. Many wish they had been steered actively toward
learning to learn, positive habits and authentic, interesting
opportunities to practise them. While they may live happy, fulfilled
lives, they sometimes feel remorse later in life about opportunities
they failed to pursue. Given 21st century needs for talent, higher-
level thinking skills, creative thinking and invention, society also
loses the benefit of their talents and potential contributions.

Dispositions for learning

Children possess dispositions and characteristics of
temperament that make it easier or harder for them to develop
good learning habits; however, children are nearly always curious
explorers by nature. Dispositions for learning include personality
traits such as mental energy and motivation and are supported by
positive environmental conditions such as freedom from anxiety
and stress, nutritious food, loving caregivers, shelter, security, and
a reasonable level of routine and dependability. Dispositions for
learning are also influenced by life-sustaining attributes that
contribute to children's inner confidence that the world around
them is stable. When children are hungry, anxious, lonely, or
subjected to stressful living conditions and poverty that fails to
meet their basic needs, it is much more difficult for them to acquire

positive dispositions for learning.

Finding the right balance between optimism and pessimism plays a role in acquiring the right dispositions for learning. When pessimism sets in, children are tempted to believe there is nothing they can achieve and too many factors that prevent them from achieving their goals. Too much pessimism provides tempting excuses not to invest the time, sacrifice, and energy to pursue goals. [6]

The role of environment versus genetic inheritance

Parents want their children to succeed in school and they usually understand that success depends on good learning habits. Jerome Kagan, a noted 20th century child development researcher, believed that nurture (environmental factors such as love, care, security) is more important than inherited intellectual or temperamental traits. The 20th century "nature-nurture" debate about the impact of '*nature versus nurture*' on human development and education systems, i.e. genetic inheritance versus environmental factors, preoccupied psychology from about the 1920s to the 1970s. The nature side emphasized the role of the environment and conditioning children to behave and learn in conventional ways by using positive (or negative) reinforcement. [7] The commonly-held belief was that inappropriate behaviours could be erased and replaced by conditioned responses that helped manage behaviour and temperament. The later contribution of Arnold Gesell [8] and the child development (maturationist) movement from the 1950s on made convincing arguments which favoured nature (genetic inheritance) that persisted to the end of the century. The science of learning today promotes the dual influences of nature and nurture, (along with neuroscience that has revealed so much about brain development) on whether children are able to achieve their potential for learning and achievement. [9]

When play environments are motivating and interesting, children more readily engage with the environment, choose and start playing and try new play styles. In a repetitive environment they become fidgety and may self-stimulate to satisfy their need to be active and fight boredom. At home, they may be tempted to turn to easy pastimes such as mindlessly leafing through books or watching television or other devices. Over time, these 'line-of-least resistance' behaviours become the norm for children and a pattern sets in that is difficult to break. When they have regular opportunities to play indoors and outdoors and explore and interact, they develop habits of mind and dispositions for learning that can last a lifetime. The right amount of engaging play choices encourages children to choose, follow through and finish, move on to something else, perhaps return to an activity not mastered earlier, finally master its challenges, and feel satisfaction when he succeeds. Becoming able to represent a vision they have in their minds, using building or other creative materials, encourages children to plan, take risks, elaborate, and maybe reframe the activity. Children are not born with these skills - they learn them. The kindergarten/primary years are prime time to begin this learning journey through play before they are required to learn by relying heavily on their academic skills.

Most parents know that it is usually too late and much harder to change the behaviours, motivations and working styles of the adolescent or adult whose slack learning habits have become ingrained. The kindergarten years are the time to introduce, facilitate and reinforce effective learning skills and work habits by providing uninterrupted time, positive role models, indirect teaching methods, and expectations that children will practise the skills and make progress. When children acquire these habits and dispositions early, all future learning is easier for them and positive behaviours and attitudes toward learning are more likely to endure throughout life.

How many instances can you recall of peers who were full of bright ideas, and learned easily when young, who later learned to regret that they had lacked the self-discipline to persevere, accept challenges and master tasks that require time and effort. These children often "sampled" activities rather than persisting with those that posed elements of challenge. Children who flit from one activity to another, resist tidying up, and are easily

discouraged when their plans do not turn out, often become
adolescents who fall short of completing projects that require
diligence, patience, and perseverance.

The role of temperament, emotional factors and interest

Temperament

Temperament is a combination of characteristics related to
emotions, mood, dispositions, and physical and mental responses
to one's environment. Temperamental characteristics can help
parents and teachers predict how a child will respond to school and
whether she is likely to join in readily, feel she belongs, and adjust
easily to the presence of many new people in her life.
Temperamental preferences also affect the readiness with which a
child adopts the right habits of mind, attending skills, and the
executive functions that influence learning. Each temperamental
distinction has both advantages and disadvantages in learning to
learn that should influence what teachers expect of each child
socially and emotionally and how they are likely to respond to the
social demands of groups and activities.

Introverted and extroverted personality styles

It is worth teachers' time to consider toward which end of
the introversion-extroversion spectrum a child trends, although
stereotyping children as introverted or extroverted should be
avoided. Children who trend toward the extroversion end of the
scale are usually social, like to be active and may find it more
difficult to settle to quiet, sedentary activities. They often wriggle
and speak out when asked to listen and have to be redirected to
something more active. Teachers usually find ways to subdue
boisterous children by encouraging them to take leadership within
the group, but these are sometimes the children who tune out and
neither hear the story, learn the song nor pick up on the
conversation. Extroverted children may find it harder to attend to
the task at hand (task orientation) for sedentary, independent
activities with paper and pencil while sitting at tables, but they still
need to develop the perceptual and literacy skills that these

activities often target. Experienced teachers usually discover during games, fitness activities and while practising skilled movements in the gymnasium or outdoor play that there are more effective ways to promote the child's ability to focus, block out distractions, finish what they start and exercise self-control. They choose teaching methods to fit the child, instead of trying to fit the child to the methods - a choice that usually fails to the child's detriment. Outdoor play usually offers relevant opportunities to engage boisterous children in activities that address attending skills and task orientation.

A tendency toward introversion influences the ease with which children adapt to expectations such as having to attend school each day, fall in with routines and sit still. These children more often approach independent activities with enthusiasm, focus and lose themselves in the process. Attention to detail and self-reliance also makes it easier to overcome obstacles and seek help and persist until the task is finished according to standards she has set for herself. Introverted children are often more interested in pleasing themselves than with earning praise or recognition from others and their motivations originate from within (intrinsic motivation) rather than from the approval or praise provided by an adult.[10] This child's attention is captured by solitary tasks even in a room of boisterous children and sometimes becomes most productive when confronted by detail she has to unravel and many materials to sort, test and use.

Children who tend toward introversion may get lost in the mix of extroverted children who significantly outnumber the introverts, are the first to raise their hands, speak out and be heard, like to be first in line, have the loudest voice in the playground, and enjoy being the self-appointed leader of the group. I will never forget visiting a kindergarten where I met Massimo who greeted me at the door with a big smile: "Hi, I'm Massimo. I'm the leader here. Who are you? I can show you around!" And Massimo did just that while the teacher worked individually across the room with a child at a table. Massimo knew everyone's name, took me to every table and then told me where I could sit, which I did. Every

teacher likes to have at least one Massimo in her class. But, as
charmed as a child like this makes us feel, many extroverted
personalities in one classroom can overwhelm the quiet, timid
child who prefers not to be singled out. In fact, introverted children
are often overlooked for just that reason – they simply prefer not to
be noticed.

There is a widely-held belief that children who do not
respond eagerly to group contexts, prefer to play quietly and alone,
and do not crave teacher approval should become more group
oriented. They are deemed to be aberrations from the norm. As
more extroverted children tend to occupy the foreground of the
environment, teachers are usually happy to have a few quiet, non-
demanding children they can count on to be self-sufficient much of
the time. There is, however, a tendency for teachers (and parents)
to express concern about the child who prefers to play alone or
with one other person rather than join the group. These children are
often channeled by teachers into group activities, teamwork, and
collaboration on the understanding that they should learn to enjoy
groups. Sociability, willingness to interact and play in groups are
often believed to be "normal" behaviours, whereas children who
shun groups, however quietly and without a fuss, are sometimes
deemed to need subtle but persistent redirection. Even their report
cards may state, "does not relate well with peers" or "needs to
spend more time on group activities" or "prefers to play alone and
avoids group play". Experts who have studied the matter, tell us
that one-third of the population exhibits introverted personalities
but much of their potential contribution to the wider population is
lost because their strengths go unnoticed and unrewarded. [11]

Human traits such as spontaneity, a need for stimulation,
the drive to be active and crave immediate gratification can
complicate the acquisition of learning to learn skills. The
extroverted personality may shun boundaries, respond eagerly to
external stimulation and distraction, prefers action – any action –
rather than quiet, focused effort and concentration. One can usually
trace the work behaviour of an extroverted adult back to the child
who was easily distracted, found it hard to sit still for stretches of

time and preferred the stimulation of the group. They are the adults
who need frequent social breaks throughout the workday and
prefer occupations like sales, performing arts and group animation
that involve people skills and dynamic work environments.

The retiring, independent child who quietly pursues his
own goals can go just as far, just as fast, but is often lost amid the
din created by extroverts. It takes more effort by teachers to draw
out the quiet strengths of the introvert without remaking them into
a style that does not match their strengths. The introvert does his
best work alone, perhaps with a partner, usually purposefully and
with little need for fanfare. The 21st century world needs more
introverts to come out of hiding and more recognition for their
learning style.

Some children require restorative niches where they can
retreat to connect with their own drives and personalities in order
to function optimally. What is restorative for the introvert is very
different than for the extrovert. One requires a place set apart from
others; the other demands boisterous outlets that usually involve
people, noise and lots of action. Brian Little found that everyone
needs to have time, space and permission to reconnect with their
original natures.[12] The education system that was created for the
industrialized society of the 20th century under-estimated
individual potential and achievement and, instead, reinforced a
system and values that sorted individuals into classes and skill sets
that would meet the needs of industry and organizations. Today's
challenge is to ensure that education systems motivate and educate
individuals for independent work, creativity and invention and a
broad range of skills, dispositions and habits that support the
realization of individual talents and learning potential. So how do
teachers tackle this challenge?

The role of interest and talents in learning to learn

Learning occurs when children practise skills in the context
of interesting activities that also suit their temperament. In literacy
learning this may mean engaging an active child in learning to read
by following printed instructions for an obstacle course at each

station or reading signs and words for a treasure hunt. He might
learn constancy of number by forming teams of equal number for a
game. Instead of sitting him down to cut, paste and produce a
collage while practising eye-hand coordination and fine motor
skills, he would likely prefer to build a low brick wall in the
playground or assemble the small parts of a model car.

Children vary as widely as adults do in the strengths they
possess. Some children are gifted communicators from an early
age; some seem destined for athletic achievement from
toddlerhood; others are extraordinarily sensitive to people. There
are children who exhibit early musical talent; others can take apart
and reassemble a complex tool or appliance in a flash. Howard
Gardner's research on "multiple intelligences" demonstrated that
children (and adults) usually possess one or more types of
intelligence that surpass their less remarkable skills and interests.
He proposed nine "intelligences" - linguistic, logical-
mathematical, visual-spatial, musical, bodily-kinesthetic,
interpersonal, intrapersonal, naturalistic, and existential.[13] Some
secondary school systems offer a diversity of choice in programs
and courses that specifically accommodate children's special
aptitudes and talents. Their choices usually indicate their preferred
pathways toward trades, occupational or professional vocations.
Elementary schools have much more they should do to
accommodate children's temperaments, talents and learning styles
by reconfiguring learning environments, curriculum, delivery
methods, and evaluation.

The child who is uniquely well-coordinated, skilled in
fundamental movements and physical abilities, who is usually the
first out the door to the playground, sends clear signals to teachers
about how best to engage him in learning. It is the teacher's
challenge to have a repertoire of active games, activities, tasks, and
resources that are needed to teach a full range of developmental
and learning skills during the daily physical program. Active social
play and group games are a hook that interests most children in the
development of physical abilities in the gymnasium or outdoors
but also provide practice in communication, reasoning and logical-

mathematical thinking, emotional control, and social intelligence.

Emotional factors

A disposition to balance dreams with a commitment to making dreams come true contributes to lifelong learning. The ability to inject some reality into fantasizing a desired future, such as accounting for obstacles and proposing concrete ways to overcome them, is called "mental contrasting".[14] Developing this disposition requires rules – both self-imposed and externally driven – as well as practice balancing dreams and hard work. Setting one's own rules can also remove the temptation to resist external authority and a commitment to do the right thing. When rules are reasonable, children generally defend the rules and readily adopt them. When they learn to accept rules such as tidying up after playing with the blocks, their attention is drawn to the importance of an organized environment. Two years in kindergarten allows time for habits such as these to become second nature to the child. A kindergarten mandate is to encourage children to adopt learning habits and behaviours that become an integral element of character that remains with them lifelong.[15]

The relationship between self-esteem and learning to learn

Success in learning builds confidence and feeds self-worth especially when the child has set his own goals, persists in the face of obstacles, and experiences the thrill of achieving what he set out to accomplish. Experiencing success with activities that are matched to his developmental level buttress a child from disappointment and the temptation to drop an activity he finds more difficult, in which he may be less interested or that require him to stretch his skills and persist. We want children to believe that they are effective learners and successful experiences motivate them to try again, choose and persevere toward a different, perhaps more distant goal. Failure to achieve calls for a significant adjustment to one's self-concept but this can also be turned into a positive learning experience for a child. The child who faces keen competition and the threat of failure, who does not know how pick up and persist, and has not been encouraged to set realistic goals will sooner or later reach a fork in the road. Either she has to climb down from her former perception of self and pursue more manageable options or she denies the validity and importance of the goals that she had set.

The attitudes of parents and teachers are crucial at these junctures. When they guide the child to set a more feasible goal and take a different approach – perhaps to take smaller steps and allow for more time and practice - they teach the child to make necessary adjustments and start again along a slightly different path. If they praise the child's achievement even though he has missed the goal by a mile, the child develops a false sense of his own capabilities or dismisses the adult's assessment altogether. What matters ultimately to the child is the authenticity of the adult who is passing judgement. The child who is accustomed to praise without regard for the standard he has achieved and the level of effort he has expended, even when he knows he could have done better, is unlikely to strive toward challenging goals that risk damaging his self-esteem. At a juncture like this that occurs when some children begin, for example, to have difficulty with math, it is important that parents not assume a 'can't do math' fixed mindset or believe that the child is "unintelligent". This is a time when referencing Gardner's "multiple intelligences" can remind parent and child of his strengths in other areas.

Mindset matters

The ways in which we think about our cognitive processes and our capacity to influence the mindset we bring to learning have a significant bearing on the outcomes we achieve. A *growth mindset* allows us to believe that we will become smarter if we work at it and our competence may increase over time if we persist. A *fixed mindset* believes that abilities are static and predetermined at birth and there is little we can do to alter our cognitive capacity.[16] Mindset influences how motivated we are to choose goals, expend the necessary effort to meet them and how likely we are to seek new challenges.

The learning mindsets of parents and teachers (and others

close to the child) influence how they present learning challenges
to a child and address them when the child wants to walk away.
Those who believe in a fixed mindset emphasize external
conditioning, control and reward systems that train the child and
help her achieve right answers. When the child still does not
succeed, they try to guide the child in a different direction, perhaps
toward something easier but also less fulfilling. Those with a
growth mindset believe that as children learn about themselves and
understand their capabilities, they will continue to strive,
emphasize their strengths, overcome obstacles, and deal with
failure if it occurs.

An abundance of self-confidence and self-esteem that is not
based on authentic success can misguide and thwart ambition and
initiative. There are children who seldom win prizes or accolades,
never place first, plod through school largely unnoticed by peers
and teachers, and then go on to accomplish great things. These are
often children who learn the value of hard work, accept challenge
and risk-taking to achieve goals and understand the significance of
tenacity and effort. There are almost as many external influences
on becoming an effective learner as there are internal influences.

The 1970s 'me generation' era emphasized self-
actualization and open education practices in education that put
children's self-esteem at the forefront of schooling ahead of the
achievement of learning outcomes, apparently seeing them as
separate pursuits. This was an era of praising the child's product or
performance even if it was mediocre by the child's own standards.
This mindset reinforced a sense that children's standards of
performance are less important than how others respond to them.
The practice increased children's dependence on the approval and
praise by others (extrinsic rewards) instead of guiding children to
assess their own performance realistically and set goals based on a
desire to succeed and feel justifiably proud of their achievements.
The gradual decline in educational standards and student
performance lasted at least to the end of the 20th century. Literacy
and numeracy levels declined, and students began to show up in
colleges and universities unable to read, write, or function in math

at levels of scholarship that postsecondary institutions used to require. The preservation of self-esteem out-ranked scholarship and academic excellence for about two decades.

Today, it is generally understood that self-esteem is intrinsically driven, not doled out by adults with agendas. As children's self-esteem depends on recognition of their authentic successes, the development of learning to learn skills from an early age becomes even more crucial. Very little injures a child's self-esteem more than feeling they are unsuccessful. Education in the early years should emphasize positive dispositions for learning and habits of mind, learning to learn skills, and the executive functions that enable children to assess their own performances, overcome setbacks, and make choices and adjustments as needed in their approach to meeting goals.

The role of motivation

Motivation is triggered by sets of factors that invite a response of some kind – either extrinsic factors such as running fast to escape a predator or working late to please a demanding boss – or intrinsic factors such as an inner drive to excel at something one enjoys doing or has decided to do, such as getting up early to practise hockey or eating healthier foods to lose weight. In infancy, motivation to walk comes from a determination to be mobile, to explore and be more independent. The preschool child flips her jacket over her head, arms into arms to put on her own coat so she can go outside sooner. Learning skills at a young age involves intrinsic motivation, i.e., an internal decision to get what one wants, an ability to imitate others, and a feeling of power and being in charge of something.

Motivation in early childhood is a mix of curiosity and a desire for independence. The task of the kindergarten is to capitalize on both factors while guiding the child to curb impulsive actions, persist with challenges, accept some limitations both externally and internally imposed, know one's own capabilities, and use time wisely. Learning to gauge the time an activity will take and how to tackle increasingly complex activities in a sequence of stages are important factors that influence self-motivation. Kindergarten should nurture children's self-motivation, help them visualize and believe in their own potential success, and introduce a sense of time passing and time-limited activity, like getting dressed in the morning to leave in time for school.

Kindergarten is a transition time

The kindergarten years form an important bridge between the preoperational thinking of the preschooler who depends on the senses and hands-on play to learn, and the concrete operational stage when children move away from "seeing is believing" and begin to reason logically with the support of physical objects to verify they are on the right track. Senior kindergarten and the next three years of school are transitional as there is no set pace or age by which children move from preoperational to concrete operational thought in all domains. The transition depends on the child's experiences, environment, the support and guidance he receives, and his maturational timetable. Although the transition occurs gradually between ages four and seven, it is the irregularity and unpredictability of children's progress in all domains that make individualized education in the kindergarten/primary years so important. This is also why all primary school children (K to 3) should have an Individual Education Plan (KIEP) that records their maturation and learning for all domains and moves with them throughout all five years. The KIEPs provide benchmarks for teachers to know where to begin with each child each year and to move them further along the learning continuum so as to finish the primary division successfully.

The learning to learn skills

Learning to learn skills may be grouped according to three categories: attending; task orientation; executive functions.

Attending

Attending skills include the ability to focus, block out

distractions while involved in an activity that requires attention, return to an activity after an interruption, and being able to delay gratification in order to complete something started. Ability to attend involves becoming able to concentrate on what one is doing and leave other things aside until finished. Attending skills are fostered by responsive activities that have a start and end point, that engage them for a meaningful length of time and motivate them to finish the activity before moving on to something else. The process of learning to attend to a task or activity and finishing it also requires children to seek help when they need it, use the materials for the purpose intended and overcome obstacles they encounter. To promote ability to attend, children do best with one- or two- step activities for which the finishing point is clear, the activities may be completed in a relatively short timeframe, and the number of steps involved and the time it usually takes to complete them increase gradually. When children master these skills, they are ready to engage in open-ended, creative activities in which the children decide for themselves when they have finished what they set out to do.

Attention span

In the course of tackling more complex activities, children are often challenged to block out distractions, return to an activity after an interruption and increase their ability to attend for longer periods of time. Attending skills do not only refer to time spent on an activity (i.e., attention span), as the amount of time children spend on activities always depends on how familiar they are with the materials, their readiness for and the complexity of the activity, and the level of challenge it presents to them. The duration of time they spend on an activity is usually age- and stage-related and also depends on the maturation of the nervous system and individual needs to be physically active. Attention span is less important than learning to start, follow through and finish an activity no matter how long or short it is. As children mature and engage in increasingly complex multi-stage activities, their attention spans increase accordingly assuming that the activities are interesting to them and are designed to take some time and effort to complete.

This is another reason why the climate for learning and
organization of the classroom have to be compatible with the
learning goals that children are expected to achieve. Children do
not learn to attend when the time allocation for learning activities
is too short, routines keep interrupting the children's play and
learning time, or when all the activities can be finished in short
order.

Delay gratification

The challenge involved in learning to delay gratification is
why this skill is usually addressed together with the other learning
to learn skills – attending, task orientation and the executive
functions. Being able to resist the temptation to leave what one is
doing to tackle something easier or more interesting, or delaying a
snack, usually involves a struggle no matter how disciplined we
may become or how old we are. An inability to delay gratification
can be an obstacle to becoming a productive and effective learner
and is so often the main reason why people fail at what they set out
to do.

Play experiences of longer duration enable children to
practise delaying gratification. Becoming a "sophisticated player"
includes the ability to stay with an activity or a project instead of
leaving it unfinished if the intention is to finish in one sitting.
Mastery of this skill is a lot to ask of children in kindergarten but
making the attempt to wait a little while instead of getting what
one wants immediately is a good way to begin and to practise. As
the ability is not inborn but has profound influence on schooling
and lifelong learning, ability to delay gratification should be
introduced in kindergarten and practised often in the primary
grades or it becomes much harder to acquire later on after
contradictory habits have become ingrained. When a child enters
grade four unable to delay gratification, she is more likely to
continue the habits that compete with effective learning and work-
study behaviours. Mindless activity, distractibility, procrastination,
or insufficient motivation to complete a task that is unfamiliar and
more difficult are the usual stumbling blocks. When these contrary
habits are observed in children, the challenges for parents and

teachers are doubled and long-lasting as the child has to unlearn
bad habits in order to replace them with positive ones.

Task orientation

Task orientation skills are learned abilities that children
acquire through observing positive role models, learning to choose
an activity, begin and follow through, overcome obstacles, seek
help and resources as needed, finish what they started, and report
on what they achieved. Children notice the habits of others close to
them, including teachers and parents who should try to model the
habits and behaviours we want children to learn. The achievement
of task orientation skills also depends on how organized the
environment appears to them. It is futile to expect a child to
become task-oriented if the environment is disorganized and
discrete activities are difficult to find amid general disarray. When
the activities provide clear messages about how to begin, figure out
what the activity requires, follow through and finish, they invite
children's participation. If the activity is complex and unfolds in
several stages, the presence of an adult as a guide is essential at
least at the beginning. If the child encounters obstacles, the teacher
or parent should intervene to ask helpful questions that guide the
child over the hump, support morale and demonstrate or suggest
what the child might try instead.

Activities should offer opportunities for children to adapt
an activity to fit with their own skills and know-how or to make it
more interesting. In kindergarten they should be encouraged to risk
not being able to do right away what some activities require and to
begin regardless. Teaching children to decide and state when they
have finished with an activity and describe what they have
accomplished reinforces the importance of finishing what they start
or indicating that they will return to the activity later to try again.
Activities with a clear starting and end point make it easier for the
child to know she has finished; others are open-ended for the child
to decide. It is also important that children be encouraged to finish
whatever plan they had in mind for their project or to announce
changes to the plan. Parental input matters a lot to children in this
context. Task orientation skills are not as straightforward to learn

as they sometimes appear, and children usually need plenty of leeway and numerous opportunities to apply these skills. Children need the time it takes to practise and make progress in learning to learn which is another benefit that individualized primary schooling can and should provide.

The roles of the teacher and parent are to monitor the child's task orientation abilities, try a different path or strategy to encourage her to stick with a challenge, take time to reflect on what they might do to finish the task, and to recognize her persistence. When teachers are too busy managing children's behaviours, or if the activities do not keep the other children in the group engaged, or if a positive learning climate has not been established, children are easily distracted. The teacher is forced to manage classroom behaviour and does not have time to work with individual children or small groups. Engaging ECEs and education assistants throughout the primary years as team members, to maintain a positive learning climate and facilitate children's individual practice of task orientation and other learning to learn skills, would be a significant bonus.

Executive functions

Executive functions manage the way the brain works when children tackle challenges and control emotions as they confront obstacles. The executive functions weave together social, emotional, and intellectual capacities. If they are practised throughout childhood they contribute to success in postsecondary education, the workplace and lifelong learning. Galinsky identifies executive functions that should be introduced in kindergarten: focus (concentration); self-control; memory and remembering what is required; commitment to a goal; ability to consider perspectives of others alongside our own, and the mental flexibility to see a problem or situation in different ways. [17] Children's attention should be drawn toward making connections that are not obvious among ideas and things that require imagination and creative thinking to discern the connection. The rudiments of these skills may be practised during children's sociodramatic play episodes and projects that occur over time and in stages; they are also

present in the more advanced classification activities (Chapter 8).
Adele Diamond [18] believes that being introduced to executive
functions and ongoing experiences that challenge them may predict
children's achievements and school success better than tests of
native intelligence. Recognizing children who succeed today at
something they could not do yesterday or when they achieve a
"personal best" fosters enthusiasm for the learning journey.

Reflection and cognitive flexibility

Self-regulation or self-control are linked to emotional and
social development and to motivational drives to overcome
hurdles. Activities that involve self-regulation have an impact on
deliberate, intentional learning that requires effort, planning,
choosing a strategy, and ability to evaluate what one has learned.
[19] Cognitive flexibility is seeing a situation in different ways,
inhibiting our thoughts and feelings to consider the perspectives of
another and reflecting on someone else's thinking alongside our
own. Children learn from storybook characters who get themselves
into or out of a situation by considering what someone else might
do in a similar predicament and the choices they faced. Teachers
and parents promote executive functions with questions about what
a child might do in a similar situation, the alternatives they have
and how they might choose a path forward. The answers children
provide often reveal some understanding that most problems have
several possible solutions and that children have different
perspectives on the best path to follow. Stories that require
reflection and perspective-taking also encourage the mental
flexibility to hold multiple ideas in one's mind at any given time.
Kindergarten is time to begin probing these depths with children
and to emphasize conversation skills, self-control, and ability to
inhibit one's impulses and point of view in order to understand
what others might be thinking.

Learning while playing

Children are astute observers when they are not distracted,
and, if left to their own devices for a while, they often figure out
what they want to do or learn and may ask for the resources they

need. Learning through play in kindergarten does not mean allowing children to play when the "real work" of learning is finished; it means planning and setting up an environment with learning-rich materials they are developmentally ready to use and letting them play. For the environment to hold children's attention, it should change as they achieve the outcomes embedded in the activities and as they want to play with new sets of materials and activities. The observant teacher who possesses a wide repertoire of activities that teach skills and concepts and knows each child's learning and practice needs, also knows which activities and resources offer alternative pathways to learning the child is ready to tackle.

The role of kindergarten curriculum in fostering lifelong learning

Above all, children should acquire positive feelings about school, excitement about learning, and the ability to cope with groups and the competing interests of other children. Effective kindergartens prepare children for a world that is still organized in groups socially, culturally, politically, and economically. During early childhood, a one-size-fits-all curriculum with everyone doing the same thing at the same time to reach the same goal is neither appropriate nor viable. Although there are times when that may happen, such as during planned physical programs, kindergartens should be hives of activity with children engaged in various activities, alone or in small, fluid groupings.

An individualized kindergarten/primary curriculum allows latitude for the child to connect in his or her own way with the learning experience and encourages teachers to set realistic expectations, goals, and outcomes for each child. Just as children begin kindergarten at diverse developmental physical, cognitive, and social-emotional levels, they do not all achieve the same learning outcomes at the end of their two kindergarten years. When the kindergarten experience accommodates the needs, interests and developmental readiness of each child and the curriculum is individualized, all children make progress, but they end their two years of kindergarten at various stages and levels of competence in a whole range of skills, knowledge and concepts. The KIEP lets teachers know where each child is set to begin with activities and learning tasks that tackle the next level in the primary school curriculum.

Two years of kindergarten expose children to a wide range of opportunities that encourage them to explore, take risks, and persist. Kindergarten curriculum should provide a developmental framework of values and learning expectations that function like a roadmap toward a destination that has been negotiated by the education system and the society in which the system resides, but not all children will reach this destination at the same time and in the same ways. Children need three more years (i.e. primary grades one to three) to continue their early learning journey in the individualized program format that allows them to progress at their own pace, documents their progress and builds a sound foundation for formal learning and a more standardized curriculum that begins in grade four and continues for many more years.

3

TEACHING THE WAY CHILDREN LEARN

"The intelligent person is not someone who merely does well on a test or in the classroom but one who can use his or her mind to fullest advantage in all the various transactions of everyday life." Robert Sternberg, 1987 [1]

Young children have always discovered their world through play. From Greek and Roman times to the present, play has been recorded in drawings, music, and stories. The history of childhood describes play activities and games of children through the centuries as well as the clothes they wore and how they were treated by adults. Adult attitudes toward play and the value attributed to childhood have always influenced how children are dressed, the behaviours they learned, their status in families, and the freedom they were allowed, or otherwise, to "just play". Play provides a crucial vehicle for learning, from the reflexive sensory play of infancy and the repetitive practice play of toddlerhood to the interactive, representational play of kindergarten that fosters children's acquisition of knowledge, skills and concepts. This chapter explains how play motivates children's learning in kindergarten and influences later schooling and lifelong learning. It

may also help parents and teachers support or intervene in
children's play to extend their learning or help them overcome
setbacks in an otherwise successful experience.

Brief history of the evolution of play theory in teaching young children

Pioneers in child development, play and education,
including Friedrich Froebel in the 19th century and Maria
Montessori in the early 20th century, thought of play as either the
business of childhood or "children's work". Play-based pedagogy
built on the foundation of Froebel's kindergartens appeared in
North America as early as the 1920s. [2] The translation during the
1970s of Jean Piaget's five decades of research and writing (1920s
to 1970s) added seminal insights on children's cognitive thought
processes that eventually transformed early education and play
theory throughout the Western world. The neo-Piagetians (1970s
onward) crystallized Piaget's research into a theory of cognitive
development that became a foundation of the Constructivist
movement in early childhood education. The work of Lev
Vygotsky, a Russian researcher who promoted the influence of
social interaction on cognitive development was later integrated
into theConstructivist tradition. [3]

The Constructivists emphasize the integral role of play in
children's cognitive development during the first seven or eight
years of life when children's brains are developing most rapidly.
Constructivist approaches assert that children build their mental
structures (schema) through their active interaction with concrete
objects in the environment that provide a context for and add
meaning to their experience. [4] Therefore, play and learning
environments should be designed and equipped to optimize and
respond to children's actions so they build their mental structures
and revise their earlier understanding of their immediate world.

In a Constructivist learning context, it is important to "scaffold" learning challenges by presenting them in "bite-sized chunks" and in engaging contexts that exercise the mind, body and perceptual abilities.[5] Responsive environments add a crucial dynamic to the process of mental structure building and facilitate the formation of neural connections in the brain that contribute to intelligence. For example, Constructivist pedagogy facilitates children's acquisition of logical-mathematical concepts, reasoning abilities and later math education. The pedagogy also guides the organization of learning environments, encourages active participation, coaches children who need support and guidance, and documents children's participation, development and learning progress. Constructivist theory continues to contribute to and learn from neuroscience that influences the ongoing evolution of early childhood learning theory and educational practice in this century. A question parents may ask relates to what they can do at home to facilitate their child's building of mental structures during the early years. Most parents struggle with space and time issues and offering guidance in setting up the home environment for play and finding resources that can be acquired at low cost may alleviate some pressures.

Play is serious for children

The active market in educational play materials and books for young children is evidence that parents are aware of the impact of play on children's development and their role in their child's learning. When parents know the developmental progressions in play and the diversity of play styles, they understand how play influences early learning and their physical and mental health when children are doing something they are naturally inclined to do. Parents of earlier generations saw kindergarten as an introduction to the routines of schooling, socialization with peers and appropriate school behaviours, and not necessarily as an extended time for playing in order to learn.

The organization of classroom space, the resources to enhance play and the social-emotional climate in the kindergarten all contribute to the influence of play on development, concept formation and positive dispositions toward learning. When parents understand the power of play, they begin to understand their own roles in extending play and learning begun at school to their child's experience at home, indoors and outdoors. Developing a partnership with their child's teachers assumes added importance when they also learn what their child is working on at school. During the pandemic, parents who had already partnered with teachers found their relationship useful, reassuring and one that worked both ways. Play has always been a serious enterprise for children, one into which they can escape, relax and become fully invested in what they are doing. Play motivates children to explore, test, risk, and confirm, especially when the social-emotional climate also supports their efforts. A gradually changing play environment encourages them to try something new, persist, finish and move forward.

Play enhances children's learning potential

Children begin their lives as active, curious explorers. They are intrepid scientists almost from the moment they are born. By the time they enter kindergarten, some are already able to engage and communicate with others in their play and eager to learn new skills, strengthen their bodies, express their feelings appropriately, and exercise their imaginations and natural creativity. Those who have had limited opportunities for play have a steeper hill to climb and need support and guidance. All children benefit from well-timed interventions in their dispositions for learning and their motivation to tackle new challenges and take risks. Kindergartens should meet these needs and exploit the attractions of interesting, meaningful play.

Children's development thrives on positive experiences in the concrete world and trust in the people with whom they interact. By definition, authentic play is freely chosen by children from an accessible array of materials, supplies and equipment that pique curiosity and present a learning challenge for the child. At other times, children find their own instruments for play, often outdoors in nature with its infinite attractions and resources, and also with things they find casually at home such as throws on chairs or drawers they can sort. What matters is that the things in their environment change when they finish or tire of these explorations and are replaced by other safe household items that can serve many play purposes.

Families with limited space indoors and outdoors might find that their most economical and durable investment for their child's play is two or more sets of blocks – one set table-sized, the other one or two sets that are floor-size wooden blocks with a shelf they can be stacked on and a partially-enclosed carpeted area for one or two children to play. As they should be encouraged to continue playing for as long as it holds their interest and achieves their goals, responsive materials like blocks are usually a good investment as they capture children's attention over several years, keep growing and changing as they build and adapt to children's developing skills and maturity. The enclosure of a space on three sides for block play allows the blocks to remain protected on the floor, lets children preserve or modify their block structures over time and offers the comfort of knowing that this is their space.

Effective kindergarten environments introduce children to schooling by providing many kinds of play activities in diverse settings. Their play with well-chosen and various types of concrete materials usually moves them during kindergarten from sensory-bound actors into children who reflect, think and understand in the context of concrete objects but without depending as much on the senses as they did earlier. Play that encourages them to figure out, test and try again promotes problem solving as materials become more challenging and interactive. An important mandate of kindergarten is to facilitate play that moves from dependence on "seeing is believing" toward thinking through and understanding more complex play challenges that lead to mature and sophisticated forms of play. In kindergarten, children should become "sophisticated players".

The features of real-play

Play is "a deeply intellectual and meaningful activity for children" [6] that provides its own reward. It is also "a sublimely human activity that fills a need to explore and release oneself into a world of pleasure and surrender to momentary fascination" [7]. Play is absorbing and fulfilling when it offers opportunities for uninterrupted, freely chosen, meaningful activity. One of life's great pleasures is to watch a child wholly immersed in play with things that command his scrutiny and attention for what seems like an endless period. Play might be described as a psychological state during which the young child's inner life, intentions and curiosity drive his actions more than directions and actions prescribed by teachers or parents.

When children play, they escape from daily demands and enter a world that is often known only to them, and they re-enter the real world only when distracted by someone or something else that commands their attention. The more interesting the play is to the child, the more likely it is that she will stay with the play, pursue her own goal and complete a process she has in mind. Play is a renewable resource that can be resumed at any moment, follow any path the child desires and end when the child chooses.[8]

A responsive play environment works best when children are preoperational, one that lets them manipulate, take apart and put together and interact in diverse ways with the environment and the people in it. Often their play seems random but is not as random as it may appear to adults. The play of kindergarten children becomes more purposeful as they begin to anticipate certain results like taking apart and putting back together, combining various materials and implements to see what happens or building or drawing to represent a plan they have in mind. The more relevant the environment is to the child's interests and physical, social and cognitive abilities, the more likely it is that their learning will progress rapidly. This implies that teachers observe and assess children's participation and progress with the activities presented and make adjustments as needed. This is why kindergarten teachers and ECEs should be well-trained in child development, observation, assessment of children's progress, and know the learning potential of all play materials.

Play versus not-play

An activity in which a child is asked to participate and follow a prescribed pattern is "not-play" even though it can be a valid and meaningful kindergarten activity. For example, an activity that guides children to produce someone else's idea of what the outcome should be, such as pasting pre-cut hats on pre-cut bunnies is also not-play. These activities might be just busywork but they are effective when they provide practice in eye-hand coordination, visual perception and hand control and this practice-time is valuable and necessary. Real-play follows the child's intention and finishes when the child decides. However, activity is not-play if it involves flitting aimlessly from one thing to another or mindless exploration that is devoid of attention and interest. [9] The urge to play arises from within the child (intrinsic motivation) and is not motivated by social demands, competition or adult requirements.

Play focuses on means, not ends, and the process is more important than the product. It is usually free of the externally imposed rules that characterize games. Play occurs easily when the objects for play are familiar; when objects are unfamiliar or not understood, children engage in exploration of the objects rather than play but exploration is also useful. Convergent activities (those for which the results are prescribed), such as crafts, help children acquire fine motor skills and practise manipulating tools like scissors or brushes and have value but they are also not-play. Connecting dots and colouring inside the lines may teach children how to start and finish a task and develop perceptual and coordination skills but they are also not-play.

Play at its best

The key feature of play is its freedom from expectations or constraints beyond the potential limitations of the materials being played with or the conditions necessary to continue playing. Play depends on the child's freedom to choose an activity, figure out its purpose and potential, formulate and pursue his plan, and decide when the play has ended – activities like deciding to build a pathway in a woods with rocks and stones, paint a portrait, or carve out a hut in a snowbank.

Play at its best involves pretending and includes 'as if' representation that is especially important when children are at the peak of their natural creativity or what Gardner calls their "creative orientation".[10] Kindergarten children should be encouraged to become something other than they are and to pretend and act out what they imagine. Pretend (and imitative) play and drama encourage children to form a substitute in their minds for something they cannot perceive – i.e. touch or see – that frees them from the presence of concrete objects so they can imagine them for themselves. Ages four to seven are prime time for fantasy, and dramatic play in social groups. Developing children's ability to think symbolically and represent what they are thinking and imagining is a key mandate of the kindergarten. Watching videos for children is not-play although limited exposure to them can furnish children's minds with ideas for sociodramatic play episodes. Selective screen-time can also acculturate children and expose them to super-heroes that become temporary idols who feed their imaginations and whom they imitate in their role play.

Why do children need to play?

Children who do not play risk being exposed too soon to immediate demands, anxiety over things they cannot control, and experiences they are unable to understand. When children abandon themselves to the moment they are in, they explore, try out things, and imagine. Play can become a child's escape hatch from the present into a time and place that exists somewhere between the here and now, the past or the future, between the familiar and the unknown, with others or by themselves. Play offers release from the concrete world into a remembered time and place, or plants them in a moment of anticipation, for example as they wait for a special holiday or the arrival of grandparents.

The uniquely human ability to move oneself mentally into a different head space is fundamental to novel thinking, projecting, and inventing and should be nourished and cultivated. Opportunities for expansive play foster habits of mind and flexibility of purpose and thought that have the power to transform the child's existence from one of daily rituals and routines to the excitement of wonder, anticipation and inspiration. When children's play is always restricted to a time or place, the same materials and activities day in and day out, an unchanging environment, and 'busyness' that ends up in the same place each time, children's minds become fenced in, their spirit muted, and their imaginations and aspirations frustrated.

Play allows children to focus on tiny details they choose to pursue while also practising skills and dispositions for learning. Play that is always closely linked to specific types of learning changes the nature of play. That is another reason why the boundaries of play in kindergarten should expand to the outdoors, so that what they explore becomes more spontaneous and abstract for part of every day. It is also why inventing their own play scenarios with classmates (i.e. sociodramatic play) is so important. Later on, the purpose that children attach to play may become more instrumental as they understand that play can also help them improve their skipping, throwing and catching and solving puzzles. They also benefit from projects they think up that engage them in inquiry (e.g how to make a bridge out of logs or put on a concert). Sometimes they are developmentally ready at this time to practise academic behaviours such as sitting at a table or desk to finish 'seat work', listening actively and following instructions or replicating demonstrations they have observed.

Variety in play

When play is active, voluntary, and meaningful, children are more likely to be challenged to try something they have neither tackled nor mastered earlier. Although play may be purposeful, it should not always require a specific end-product or a completed process, certainly not one decided upon in advance by someone else. Play may be planned ahead by the child or spontaneous. When play is symbolic and intended to represent what the child has seen or heard, he can entertain possibilities beyond the here and now. This is called "non-literal" (pretend) play as the players understand that what they are dramatizing is not what it appears to be, for example, when children pretend that they are rowing to a new part of the world. [11]

Children who experience a full range of play styles during the preschool years may already be skilled players by the time they reach kindergarten. As play styles and social contexts for play progress, children become increasingly sophisticated players. When children's toddler and preschool play experiences are limited, they may have some catching up to do in kindergarten. The task for parents is to encourage a range of play styles at home, but expensive toys and spacious indoor playrooms are not a prerequisite. Access to outdoor play with natural play space to move and be active, small places to explore indoors (like a sewing cupboard or toolbox), and outdoors (Dad's storage shed) all offer learning opportunities. For children to have a variety of things to explore safely, anything unsafe should be removed. Parents can usually cope with some mess here and there knowing how fleeting but important these early years are.

When home does not offer sufficient space and resources for play, there may be access to community resources such as drop-in centres and toy lending libraries. Rural areas usually provide easier access to safe outdoor space where children can explore naturally occurring phenomena that offer endless fascination. Families who live in high-rise buildings face the most difficult challenge. That is why developers of high-rises and other densely-populated family neighbourhoods in Scandinavia were required by law to provide shared, common areas outdoors (e.g., a total of 30 square feet of recreational space per residential unit) that is safe, well-maintained and resourced. Parents, educators, and child advocates should expect building requirements like this to be supported by local politicians, urban planners and developers but this expectation still does not register in many Canadian towns and cities. This is a regrettable omission in our culture and another issue for parent advisory groups to address.

Why is play-based learning important for kindergartens?

The young child is typically programmed for exploring, imagining, and creating. Connect these natural childhood drives with our nation's urgent needs for creative thinking and innovation, and with the kindergarten mandate to nurture children's curiosity and learning potential, and one can understand that play-based kindergartens are relevant to the original thinking, innovation and productivity challenges our nation faces today. The kindergarten is an incubator of children's curiosity and questions, an environment in which they uncover answers, and a social-emotional climate in which they are encouraged to try things out, test and overcome obstacles in play. Kindergarten is the right time and place to jumpstart children's creative problem-solving, their confidence to risk and the freedom to think novel thoughts. Chapter 9 emphasizes that it is essential to extend children's "creative orientation" into the primary years and well beyond.

Canada's future depends on how well parents, teachers, and education systems prepare children for a changing world. Perhaps the best way to prepare children for a future that has not yet been fully disclosed to us is to ensure that children continue to think creatively, learn to cope with uncertainty, maintain physical and mental health and an ability to imagine and aspire, and meet challenges with resilience and determination. Teaching children to cope with uncertainty and prepare for adversity is quite different from teaching them to anticipate college entrance criteria, achieve high grades and pick a financially secure career goal. The benchmarks of planning for success and a comfortable life for the future are quite different for children today from those experienced by their parents who believed they could chart a course toward prosperity and security through educational attainment. Education in the 21st century has a new mandate and an agenda that may point toward preparing children for self-sufficiency, creative and independent thinking, originality and invention, competent performance in all developmental domains, and realistic expectations.

The best of play begins with symbols and representation

Children use symbols as stand-ins for something else when they pretend. During the early stage of symbolic thinking (from age two) pretend play may involve imitating daddy going to work with his tool kit or mommy rocking the baby. As symbolic play evolves, simple imitation using language and action becomes more elaborate as two children dramatize something like "You be Elsa and I'll be Anna" or, "I'll be the conductor and you be the driver". Children gradually choose less realistic props for representing their imagined or remembered events and separate the meaning they attach to the symbol from the actual object they are representing. For example, a path becomes the river, and a twig doubles as a boat. As children act out an event such as going on a hike, they remember details from a hike as they dramatize actions and words.

Children who create an imagined environment for playing out an experience they remember or a fantastical story develop an ability to transcend the here and now in their minds and imagine what might be. This ability promotes flexible thinking and the mental freedom that allows them to abandon concrete objects as symbols; then, using mostly words and actions, they concoct a scenario in their minds, dream up possibilities and extrapolate scenarios. This level of play contributes to sustaining children's "creative orientation" and practice of the executive functions. The cognitive ability to project one's mind into a different headspace or environment is as important for mental health as it is for creativity and original thought.

Children's fluency with language grows as they are able to evolve a script that describes actions and events and, eventually, a scenario they have imagined and share with one another. As children create scenarios in their heads, without props, as in "let's pretend that our studio is on this carpet and the door is here", or, "let's rake some of the leaves into a pile and call it our mountain", they collaborate in planning and negotiating roles for a play episode that they sustain until they run out of ideas. On an individual level, the ability of a child to project herself into a different mental space without props also allows her to escape from the humdrum, think happier thoughts when sad or anxious, and create an imaginary world – think Anne of Green Gables! This ability to escape mentally, however temporarily, is good for mental health and a sign that a child can engage in representational thinking, an important kindergarten developmental task.

Children's ability to represent also becomes evident in their drawings, building and physical movements. In kindergarten, children build their own symbols that *represent* something they imagine, such as a house or the footprint of a fort perhaps outlined with the fallen leaves they have raked up. Their representations become more abstract as children try to understand how complex things work in the adult world such as "why did mommy and daddy fight this morning?" As children's experience expands, so also does their ability to engage in longer and more complex episodes of acting out remembered events and experiences. Their sociodramatic play episodes eventually become extended multiple-action sequences to which a larger group of children may contribute. At this stage, they have distanced themselves from the realistic props they needed earlier to get a play episode started. One may hear children say things like, "let's pretend this chair is in the spaceship and the blocks are on the moon, and let's walk like astronauts in space suits".

With practice, children evolve a script where their words, actions and ability to follow the cues of other players, share and collaborate become recognizable to an observer. They invent a script in their collective 'heads' and negotiate and change their plans as the play episode unfolds. They enlist other playmates, assign them roles and modify the script as they play, interrupt the episode to incorporate a new idea, and maybe renegotiate roles. If the play becomes bogged down – perhaps because the episode has become too ambitious – an observant teacher or parent may step in, ask pertinent questions that push the script a little farther, or step into the episode themselves to help the script along. The learning inherent in this sophisticated form of play is sufficient justification for an adult to use whatever time and ingenuity the situation requires in order to keep the play going for a while longer. There should be time set aside each day for kindergarten children to engage in sociodramatic play; it should not be used as a reward for finishing one's paper and pencil tasks, but an anticipated time for play that the children choose and concoct themselves.

The initiative, willingness to risk, and self-confidence that enable children to engage in sociodramatic play are richly rewarded as children acquire skills that may serve them for a lifetime. The determined focus and "volitional fortitude" to remain motivated to invent and continue an episode provides practice for many 21st century skills. [12] Negotiation, compromise, taking a perspective other than one's own, self-control and finding new ways to represent through action and words are social and leadership skills that are practised during this challenging self-directed play. [13] Making the transition from symbolic thinking to sustained representational thinking is linked to reasoning, concept formation, communication, and learning-to-learn skills. Sociodramatic play conjures a different world, catapults children mentally into another life, and fosters dreams and aspirations. This level of representational thinking helps children make the transition "from the purely situational constraints of early childhood to the adult capability for abstract thought".[14]

Representation relies on the lived experiences and imaginations of children and their ability to anticipate future events. The challenge, therefore, is for parents and teachers is to populate children's minds with a range of memorable experiences such as visits to museums, plays, galleries, farms and other community venues that provide meaningful reference points for children's fertile imaginations and memories. The uniquely human abilities to transcend time and space in one's mind, reconstruct past events, imagine a future and plan ahead are not a given for every child, or every adult. Some are able to distance themselves cognitively from the here and now; others remain tied to the present and do not venture into imagining a future, reconstructing an event, or asking "what if" questions. It is the nature of their daily environments and experiences that help children bridge the distance in their minds between the past, present and future, real and imagined. Children need time and lived experiences that allow them to distance themselves mentally and envisage what might be. Opportunities to recall past events and plan future ones encourage children to reflect back, plan in the present and anticipate the future. Becoming able to distance themselves from present reality through play may be unavailable to children without reflective teachers who learn how to facilitate sociodramatic play.

The social perceptions and social cognition gained from sociodramatic play

Sociodramatic play motivates children to stand up for themselves, adapt to a common goal, share ideas and information, provide and follow cues, and accept the legitimacy of another child in a role they might have coveted. This play style may ask children to shift attention among competing tasks and even refrain from an action if it is not helpful to the achieving the goal. Children have to hold a sparse script in their heads, share their intentions, *represent* using language, communicate their interests, muster their self-control over emotions, and exercise restraint. Sometimes, another child might take on a leadership role she wanted, or she might become tired and want to opt out but feels a responsibility to the group. Children learn to provide verbal cues to their playmates and negotiate changes with others whose vision of the plan and the script may differ. This play style helps children find ways to remain focused on the task at hand in spite of inevitable interpersonal hurdles and persist toward a satisfactory conclusion to their scenario. It has the capacity to transform their thought patterns and think on their feet. Does all that sound like practice for everyday living? It is the epitome of play - freely chosen by the children who also determine when the play episode is over. When children succeed in maintaining a narrative to a reasonable conclusion that suits the group, they have achieved important cognitive, emotional and social markers that all children should be able to practise. To sustain children's natural creativity beyond early childhood, to invent and begin to think abstractly, sociodramatic play offers opportunities and a boost like no other.

Too many children miss role play challenges because teachers fear they are unable to facilitate the play successfully. There are children who participate eagerly in sociodramatic play and make it seem easy, but there are also those (introverts are often an example) who seldom venture into what seems to them like insecure territory. Teachers need astute observation skills that reveal children's aptitudes and insecurities so they can detect which children might be enthusiastic leaders from those who may need coaching and support. Timid children often need a teacher or special friend to help them enter a play episode.

Teaching the way children learn relies on space design and organization

To keep designing kindergartens with tables and chairs in the centre of the room and shelves around the edges that store materials and supplies – i.e., a standard configuration – would be to force-fit traditional classroom organization into an emerging 21st century vision for early education. Children need freedom to move, not just now and then, but much of the time, and dedicated spaces for various play pursuits. The indoor and outdoor learning environments should be a microcosm of the world as children see it. A kindergarten that is beautiful, with soft artificial lighting and plenty of natural light, furniture in good repair, and clean floors helps parents rest easier about leaving their child for several hours a day. A positive social and emotional 'climate' motivates children to try new things, make friends, ask questions, and feel they belong. Noise levels should convey the sounds of active play and focused energy rather than disorganized exuberance, hyperactivity, or boredom and restlessness. The space should convey that it meets children's energy needs with nooks and cushions that allow them to retreat from mainstream activities for a few minutes. All children occasionally need to escape from the group to restore energy and some children regularly need these spaces.

Kindergartens today have many more mandates to address now than they did when their purpose was mainly to prepare children for schooling, groups, teachers and prescriptive tasks. New understanding of brain development, recognition that the years from two to eight are a critical period in learning and the challenges of the times we live in have added to the kindergarten mandate. Given the urgent need to recast elementary school education for an altered world, kindergarten is a good place to begin. Design and the organization of indoor and outdoor space should reflect the added mandates and learning outcomes instead of planning curriculum and daily programs to fit the available space. The kindergarten should be authentic, diverse and connect children's aspirations to learn how to do something with the guidance and resources to do so.

How to 'read' the kindergarten environment

Kindergarten classrooms are easier for parents to understand when they are organized into zones, learning centres, play stations, and visible pathways among the learning centres and zones. This approach to organization works best when teachers who plan the environment also observe the children's participation in the activities there; this knowledge helps them plan so that children may anticipate and engage actively in each learning centre.

Zones

Zones are large segments of space, indoors and outdoors, that visibly identify the category of play and learning anticipated in each zone, for example, zones for active play, quiet, focused play, or creative play, along with the relevant and accessible equipment, materials and supplies. Zones usually frame two or three learning centres. Once parents find the zones in the classroom, the next step is to locate the learning centres within each zone. This level of organization helps parents and others more readily discern how each centre contributes to the category of play and learning attributed to a zone.

The location of zones and space allocated to them are usually dictated by the shape and size of the room, sources of natural light, electrical and water outlets, pathways and traffic patterns, and teachers' decisions based on children's learning needs, interests and the curriculum. Many configurations are possible; the only requirement is that the teacher and ECE

communicate a clear rationale for the organization of the space.
The rationale for locating zones may be revised throughout the
school year as the children progress, seasons change, as projects of
some duration need dedicated space, and new conditions arise –
like the need for social distancing. A square or rectangular indoor
classroom with a visual perspective over the whole room allows
teachers and other adults to observe most learning centres from
anywhere in the room. L-shaped rooms require two clear vantage
points but they might enable a natural separation between the
active play areas and the quieter learning centres. Ideally, there
would be an enclosed observation room with a two-way mirror that
allows teachers, parents, health care staff, and resource teachers to
observe children unnoticed.

The typical zones for play in the kindergarten are often
designated for role play and construction, active play that also
accommodates music and movement, creative arts, science and
discovery tables; a protected area with boundaries on three sides
for unit blocks, and a quiet play area for concept learning that
includes table top activities for logical concepts and literacy
activities that allow children to focus. A library area stocked with
books is usually found in the quiet zone with shelves, tables and
chairs for reading-related activities in small groups and perhaps a
beanbag chair or small sofa. Well-defined zones for active and
quiet play, messy versus tidy play, and solitary versus
collaborative play are usually evident to the untrained eye. In
warmer climates, some learning centres would be located outdoors.
Space and weather constraints always challenge planning efforts so
common sense and good judgment have to prevail. Teachers learn
to hone their repertoire of activities so that they can quickly
replace activities on a moment's notice and know how to
improvise on the spot.

Pathways

Visible pathways between the play zones and fixed items
that identify pathways and mark a permanent footprint in the
classroom enable children to move from one zone to another
without disturbing the play in the learning centres or being
distracted along the way. Discerning what are likely to be the main
traffic patterns and pathways from one zone to another reduces
distractions children might encounter as they move from one zone
or one learning centre to another. The physical dividers that
separate zones from each other and protect the integrity of the play
there might be moveable storage cupboards or display racks that
offer flexibility when a learning centre needs to expand or contract
temporarily.

The teaching function of learning centres

When materials and supplies in each learning centre are
congruent, they provide messages to children about the options for
play there. The learning centres act as an organizing strategy for
using valuable space purposefully, ensuring that children move
around the classroom, and assisting teachers as they assess
children's participation and progress. The strategy should support
choice, children's interests and allow for a range of social contexts
- that is, noisier and more interactive, quieter and more focused,
task-oriented and individual. The number of learning centres the
kindergarten can accommodate depends on the size and amenities
of the room and, possibly, the amount of indoor space needed for
active play indoors on days when outdoor play is impossible. No
kindergarten should remain the same from September to June, and
if it does, that may be a sign that the program is not addressing a
full range of play styles, developmental goals and learning that the
curriculum intends.

Distinct learning centres make it easier for parents, volunteers and visitors to recognize the learning potential of the activities in each centre and in the whole classroom. Observers should be able to discern the classroom organization and so should the children. From month to month or more or less frequently, the equipment and materials will change and children will move on to another level of learning. As children learn skills and concepts at different rates, teachers and ECEs observe and record which children participate and consistently finish an activity successfully. Observation data determines when an activity may be replaced or augmented to ensure that children keep moving forward at their own pace. For children who take longer to master skills or concepts, the activity, or an alternative that provides a fresh start and another path to learning, might be set up in a different zone or learning centre that allows children to continue practising skills they have not yet mastered.

The centre for active play and role play would likely be located in or close to a zone with enough space and equipment for climbing, building, music, costumes and dressup clothing and enough space for role play props. The creative arts and science learning centres might be compatible in a *creative discovery zone* where a water source and tile floors are helpful. When space in the creative discovery zone allows, it might also accommodate a project table large enough for a group of children to gather around.

The organizing strategy

Kindergartens should be organized to accommodate the learning centres and play stations that are most relevant to the current topics and learning focus. When space is limited, this strategy is more important than trying to fit all learning centres into smaller spaces. As environments change regularly during the school year, it makes sense when space is scarce, to change the learning

centres more frequently so that all can be accommodated once or
twice during a term as determined by the curriculum requirements
and program plans of teachers. Given their intention to recast
primary education, a good starting point would be for governments
to ensure that kindergartens are equipped to accommodate the
space and resources needed to address the kindergarten mandate
and facilitate children's learning achievement through play indoors
and outdoors. This strategy is consistent with optimizing children's
learning instead of expecting teachers to adjust the play and
learning program to fit the available space which often happens.

Play stations

Each learning centre usually has two or three well-defined
spaces called play stations for specific types of play activities. One
activity table might invite children to string coloured beads in self-
repeating patterns, play that also provides practice with eye-hand
coordination and pre-writing skills; a nearby play station might be
a table for cutting and pasting for collage, and another for tracing
and printing letters and number symbols. Observing play stations
like these reveals that the learning centre is dedicated to quiet,
individual play that emphasizes concept learning, fine-motor and
perceptual skills and pre-reading and writing skills. The play
stations in the quiet zone might change a lot or a little each week,
but the purpose will usually remain consistent with quiet play,
thinking and attending. A science learning centre might for a
period of time accommodate discovery activities with microscopes
at one table and a water table for measuring activities; later these
activities might be replaced by creative activities.

Background and foreground of the zones

The play zones and larger learning centres provide the
background for classroom organization while the play stations are

the foreground. Parent observers should accustom their eyes to what they are seeing when they enter a kindergarten by first trying to distinguish between the background and the foreground when they enter the room. To do so, they might focus their eyes on the play stations and what the children are occupied in doing at each station. This advice is useful when entering the classroom or observation room as the eyes try to sort out what is happening there from among a busy, diverse panorama of things, people, sounds, and textures that bombard the senses when one enters the room. Even experienced observers need time to process the complex kindergarten background and the foreground activities where the play is occurring. The classroom for developing creative thinkers is designed for active, purposeful movement around the room so that space may be rearranged as projects and learning outcomes require, places to post signs and reminders about where to find resources, seating areas for collaboration, planning, and mapping out ideas, specialized surfaces for writing, drawing, and making things, and ready access to computers, cameras, projectors, and sound devices.

In the primary years, active, busy classrooms, choices of activities and projects for children, and play that facilitates learning do not spell the end of conventional learning tasks meant to teach literacy and numeracy skills directly which the 'back to basics' proponents tend to fear. Primary education can also address reading, writing, arithmetic, and problem solving in an active play and applied learning context. The result, in an active learning environment, is more likely to be learning that is remembered and endure while it builds a foundation for the next step in the child's learning journey.

Outdoor play and learning projects

Children are always curious about living things they find

outdoors and want to examine; they watch what happens under certain conditions and keep records of changes. Interesting natural objects for children's investigations are both animate and inanimate - insects, plants, sand and soil, rocks and stones, shells. These kinds of investigative projects conducted indoors might require terrariums, a water source and microscopes and lots of wipes and gloves, as well as printers, tablets and computers for keeping records.

Creating a garden in the school yard or in a nearby community garden plot is an outdoor project that is rich in learning for all developmental domains. Think of the opportunities for learning new words, reading and printing signs and tags, digging, pulling, raking, lifting, cooperating, conversing and collaborating, asking questions, measuring, counting, consulting books, drawing diagrams and maps, using computer software to plan and design, keep records and compare results.

Planning a play or a concert, making or learning to play musical instruments or creating a clubhouse outdoors with loose materials such as wood, branches, rocks, logs, and other items collected on hikes are interesting projects that appeal to children's interests. During pandemic times, gardening and other outdoor projects represent safer outdoor activities in which children each contribute to a project, work independently and practise social, physical and cognitive skills that are relevant for these times.

Prescriptive curriculum that outlines content to be "covered" and skills to acquire in a prescribed order and at the same time of year throughout the school system should become a relic of the past. Exciting learning through play, combined with visioning and planning is more engaging and child-centred than paper and pencil tasks at tables although there are times for these too. Opportunities to use computers in projects to accomplish what would otherwise be labour-intensive tasks encourage children to view technology devices as useful tools for research, communication, keeping track of data, reporting results and a host of planning and design functions.

The importance of time allocation in the daily schedule

An organized, coherent environment would be ineffective if the daily schedule intended to keep children on a time treadmill that does not allow them to choose an activity, start, follow through, overcome obstacles, and finish what they set out to do. Many good intentions have been thwarted by failing to allocate sufficient time for children to explore and complete what they started. This happens most often when programs are designed to keep all children doing the same thing at the same time. When daily schedules are tightly drawn, with short periods of time allocated for each successive activity to prevent boredom and hyperactivity, they contradict the play and learning intentions of the program and the development of learning-to-learn skills. Timing the flow of the day to provide short intervals of play interrupted by routines or to change the pace according to the clock will ensure that children develop short attention spans and miss the satisfaction of finishing what they start.

Schedules in which children have to change frequently what they are doing interfere with the learning process. When centres and play stations are set up each morning, children should take as much time as they need with each activity. The key factor is that teachers (kindergarten teacher and ECE) and education assistants know what each child is working on, their intentions, the approximate time they need to complete an activity or one phase of it, are aware of individual needs for coaching or input and to observe their progress. Two teachers, perhaps with an education assistant or a resource teacher in the kindergarten (depending on the presence of children with disabilities) with a group of about 20-22 children) is usually not expecting too much of teachers who are trained to implement this child- and learning-centered approach. Success relies on the organization of the classroom ahead of time. It also assumes excellent teacher training, mentoring for new teachers, adequate resources (materials and supplies), and ongoing support by school leaders.

Project-based learning

Children should learn to collaborate in cooperative play and projects throughout the primary years and beyond, starting in kindergarten. Kindergarten/primary teachers need ideas, planning skills, resources, and space to introduce, manage and support purposeful, interesting projects that address many skills and may unfold over time in several stages. Children collaborate when they exchange and share materials, take turns, share tasks, and communicate while playing. Collaborative play in projects also provide a foundation for sociodramatic play as children interact in small social groupings and help one another. Sometimes leaders emerge when one child encourages other children in the group to follow and accept a particular task or role. Picture five-year-olds who cooperate as they make a mural for a school wall, talk together with a teacher about what they want on a school mural, the tasks involved, and decide who takes responsibility for working on a piece of the project with another child or a small group or independently. Projects might involve planning a puppet show, or a concert in which children take responsibility for a part of a project – e. g. decorating a stage, planning the program, making the invitations and advertisements. Cooperative play that prepares children for project learning begins with short-term tasks in junior kindergarten that accustom children to working together toward a common purpose, experience that leads to more elaborate project-based learning in two or three stages over an extended period. [14]

Projects may be undertaken in several zones of the classroom and outdoors and should be attached to specific learning outcomes. They begin simply and gradually extend the number of stages and the timeframe, e.g., days/weeks/months, during which they evolve and finish. The location of a project depends on available space indoors or outdoors that is reserved for the project. Cupboards or storage bins nearby for tools, materials and supplies should be protected from the weather and disruption when children are not working on the project. Tables and floor space are needed for partially finished structures or artwork at various stages of completion. Space for hanging things might also be needed. Outdoors is often the best place to set up projects that require elbow-room and storage as long as they are sheltered from inclement weather. A dedicated outdoor space designed and constructed to protect children, teachers, and materials from the elements in most weather conditions would be an asset to schools and could be used by several classes and grades.

4

GOVERNANCE AND THE PEOPLE IN THE SCHOOL

"A new set of priorities is coming to the fore: put students first, democratize school governance, deprogram education ministries and school districts and listen more to parents and teachers." Paul Bennett. 2018. [1]

A child starting school is a significant event within a family; routines are altered, and the social circle expands beyond the home to include aspects of the child's school life. Having a child in school adds new parental responsibilities such as reporting when their child will be absent, talking to the teacher at appointed times and responding to school announcements and requests that usually include fundraising support. Parents' initiation into matters related to school governance and the obligations attached to schooling their children sometimes come as a surprise. This chapter provides information to help parents navigate the school system, understand how schools function now or should function, and introduces the roles of the educators and others on the school team who support children and the learning environment.

School governance

School boards

Elementary schools are governed by the ministry of
education in each province and territory which establishes laws
and policies related to the operation of schools, school boards and
education policy including teaching, curriculum, assessment, and
evaluation. Governments usually delegate to school boards
responsibility for establishing local policies and managing matters
related to the administration of schools in their jurisdiction. Boards
are composed of *trustees* elected by residents of their political
constituencies (*ridings*) who also govern related services such as
school buses, crossing guards, decisions to close schools and build
new ones, and education budgets for their jurisdiction. Board
trustees have no mandated role in the day-to-day management of
individual schools nor direct involvement in the curriculum or
classroom teaching. They exist to interpret and set local board
policies according to provincial law and are accountable for the
delivery of education services in their jurisdiction according to the
provincial education act. Boards are accountable to their provincial
government; they report to the minister of education for their
province, not to their local municipality.

School boards have been around for decades and large
municipalities have several, including one each serving public and
Catholic schools. Large, diverse cities like Toronto also have
French school boards. Together the school boards add considerable
costs to provincial education budgets that cover budgets for their
administrative personnel and staff – i.e., superintendents,
principals, consultants, health and mental health care workers, in
addition to paying their professional staff - the teachers and
principals - and support staff. Boards determine education budgets
for their jurisdiction and provide input to their municipalities
related to school tax rates that are deemed to cover the costs boards
have identified. School boards are expected to live within their
budgets; if they do not, the government is mandated to take over

the governance role of a board that exceeds its budget. When governments impose hiring restrictions, propose larger class sizes and make other demands on teachers that often lead to labour disruption, boards become a sounding board for local and provincial interest groups, but final decisions rest with the provincial government. Issues and problems related to the funding of education have been present for a long time, but few significant changes have been made to the delivery and funding of education services within the provinces for decades. Funding allocations to school boards from provincial coffers tend to vary from province to province. [2]

School board trustees receive a stipend for their role that requires them to attend regular board meetings, respond to queries from taxpayers and conduct themselves in a manner worthy of public trust. They are seldom held to account by voters who elected them and usually only in cases of flagrant abuse of power. Occasionally, there are calls to curtail the power of trustees or to abandon school boards altogether. Some educators and municipal governments have concluded that school boards should report to their municipalities on matters that directly affect the municipality such as school closures. Others suggest that school boards should be replaced by ministry-mandated central education committees that direct and oversee all provincial school jurisdictions. Nova Scotia took this courageous step in 2019 when school boards in that province were terminated by their Ministry of Education and the provincial government established one central authority that reports to the Ministry and governs and sets policy for all provincial schools. [3] Nova Scotia was preceded by New Brunswick, Prince Edward Island and Newfoundland and Labrador who took similar steps beginning in the late 1990s.

Re-thinking the mandate of school boards across Canada and examining whether they add value to education, especially given the considerable cost they add, is relevant when society needs and expects greater accountability for the quality and direction of public education, in times of societal stress, and when there are visible fissures between the skills of graduates and public expectations of their performance. All these factors are present at this time. Delivery methods and education services have been significantly challenged during the pandemic but finding solutions has been largely determined between the government and the local medical health authorities directly. Discussions should occur provincially about the value of school boards relative to their cost and the fact that they add another complicated 'layer' to school governance that seems increasingly extravagant. The following example seems relevant to this discussion.

Issues have arisen across the nation for nearly two decades related to school closures and the fact that school boards were, until 2014, under no obligation to consult municipalities before deciding to close a school. Now boards have been mandated to consult (minimally) with municipalities, but boards remain the decision-makers for closing schools and busing children to larger and more distant schools. School boards decide when older schools are too small to achieve economies of scale and too old to refurbish to today's technological and accessibility standards. It means that children no longer walk to school and the neighbourhood loses not just the school, but also its vitality and often its viability. Revised laws, reporting relationships and governance strategies are needed to update and clarify the roles, mandates and relationships among school boards, municipalities, schools, and the public. Increased government funding of education throughout all provinces and territories has been needed for decades to enrich the quality and performance of Canada's human resources, improve our nation's productivity, and regain our former stature in the world.

The disappearing neighbourhood school

School board overreach is cited in the many conflicts that
have risen over the closure of elementary schools in established
neighbourhoods, frequently those close to downtowns. This issue
has influenced the survival or demise of communities, where and
how families live and how they relate to their schools. The sweep
of the New Urbanism movement in North America early in the 21st
century introduced significant new demand for complete
neighbourhoods where families live, work, do business, and
recreate. The rapidly increasing population in towns and cities saw
more families settled on the suburban edges of towns and cities
where there was space for residential development, a factor that led
to declining school enrollments in inner-city neighbourhoods. The
first decade of the 21st century saw the closure of many older
schools and the construction of larger schools on the fringe of
communities to accommodate new residential development plus
larger numbers of children who are bused from inner city
neighbourhoods and sometimes from small bordering communities
and rural areas as well. The new normal has become, over nearly
two decades, children bused from the inner cities and towns to
large schools on the outer urban fringes – a phenomenon that led to
the term 'edgucation'.

Driving children to school has substantially altered the
relationship of children and parents to their schools. The
neighbourhood school used to be a local hub that families could
reach by walking. This issue has had an enormous impact on the
survival of communities, where and how families live, and the
relationship children and their parents have with their elementary
schools. Children who bus to and from school are restricted in their
participation in after-school play and extracurricular activities;
their inability to walk to and from school has an impact on their
fitness and health. Neighbourhoods have life cycles as children
grow up and leave home and older parents eventually sell the

family home. Another cycle of young families moves into the neighbourhood and the child population increases again - this time without the advantages of the former local school. The trend in cities for families who moved close to the central core brought older neighbourhoods that had been largely abandoned back to life again, but the local school had long since disappeared.

Although school boards claim they consult with communities before closing a school, in fact, the board-directed 'accommodation review consultation' (ARC) process has been pro forma, rigidly structured, as short as possible, and input from parents and the neighbourhood has seldom received serious consideration at decision time. [4] In 2014, the Ontario government reduced the timeframe for school boards to consult the public around school closures and allowed boards to impose further constraints on the input they would seek and from whom. Municipalities are given limited time to respond to the new proposals but are still excluded from the reconstituted ARC process. School boards continue to argue that upgrading old schools to meet new technological, health and security standards or to repurpose them is too costly.

Municipal governments have been largely silent in the face of widespread school closures even when closures void the projections of municipal official policy plans and undermine decisions related to housing development, the location of services, and urban renewal. Municipalities are beginning to argue that provincial governments should enact legislation to ensure that the official municipal growth plans of towns and cities are given the consideration they deserve before decisions are made regarding the fate of an old school and the location and size of a replacement school. Parental support for municipal and neighbourhood interests should have a large impact on decisions related to school closures but these decisions currently remain the exclusive domain of school boards.

The impact of demographic changes on schooling, families, and children

As home ownership in large cities becomes beyond the reach of many families, more children are being reared in high-rise dwellings. Health experts have highlighted what happens to children when they are physically removed from regular, vigorous play outdoors and miss the freedom and exhilaration of daily contact with the outdoors. Children need regular access to natural areas and spontaneous interaction with others outdoors and at school. Their sphere of activity outside school today frequently revolves around school-age childcare programs, pre-arranged playdates supervised by parents and an outdoor play schedule that depends on the timetables of adults. Some architects advocate the benefits of inner-city high-rise living for children who, they claim, thrive by living close to local parks and resources such as museums and stadiums. Their argument fails to acknowledge children's urgent needs for daily outdoor play and physical exercise that are vital to good health including mental health. [5] The case for outdoor learning environments in the schools has, therefore, become a pressing challenge.

The school – indoors and outdoors

School buildings have evolved from the two-storey structures of the early 20th century to the sprawling one-storey complexes of the 1960s, to a current trend back to the two-storey schools on smaller tracts of land. Smaller space dedicated to school grounds limits children's access to outdoor space and too often reduces time for outdoor recess and lunch periods in order to accommodate children outdoors in shifts. [6] Some say that the tradeoff is larger, newer schools fitted with elevators and ramps for

improved access, substantial investments in technologies and
larger gymnasiums to make up for the loss of outdoor space for
playing fields. The financial savings attributed to reduced outdoor
space in schools have not yet been weighed against the human
costs related to children's reduced outdoor play and daily contact
with nature.

Locating the kindergarten in the school

Kindergarten classrooms are usually located in the lesser
traffic areas of schools to reduce risk to young children. They
should have direct access to the playground that is sometimes
shared with other kindergartens and primary classes. Playgrounds
require space that is sheltered in part from direct sunshine and
some covered and paved space that allows children to be outdoors
in most weather conditions. Some schools are increasing the
natural features of playgrounds by adding grassy areas and
shrubbery along with naturally occurring tree stumps, logs, and
wooden benches. The best playgrounds include a partitioned space
with loose materials for projects and building such as bricks, logs
or lumber pieces, and branches. Schools should avoid replicating
the typical classroom outdoors, especially if this outdoor space still
envisages children seated and inactive for long stretches of time,
which is one more way of trying to fit a new idea into an old-
school framework. Children today need access to space for
experiential learning outdoors in natural areas.

Gardens in school grounds are ideal projects for children
that promote interdisciplinary learning. Consider the learning to be
acquired by young children, while they plan, plant, tend and harvest
a garden, in terms of communication and language, counting,
sorting, measuring, record-keeping, and reporting on the garden's
progress, as well as the physical skills involved in gardening.
Consider also the social advantages for families who live in

apartment buildings, contribute to garden maintenance and who may harvest the crop in the summer and meet their children's school friends, parents and teachers over collaborative jobs. [7]

The people in the school

Administrative staff

The administrative staff of schools includes the principal who is head of the school and vice-principal (for large schools), both of whom are former teachers who lead the professional staff. The school administrative assistant is usually the first person whom parents meet on entering the school; the custodial staff are well-known to the children who see them in action looking after the school building each day. Administrative and maintenance staff are the support team for teachers who are the front-line professional staff. The difference between a school that views teachers as valued, trusted professionals with influence over how the school is managed, versus the school where the principals and administrative assistant dominate, may be discernible from the moment one enters the school. The social-emotional climate of the school is usually revealed to visitors who experience how the staff treat them and their helpfulness in responding to parents' requests.

The way administrative staff members address teachers is one measure of the trust and teamwork among the teaching and non-teaching staff all of whom are responsible for establishing a positive and supportive environment for learning, belonging and community outreach. The school principal sets the tone that should suggest a climate of warmth, caring, and teamwork. Occasionally, a principal might see her role as keeper of the peace and monitor of protocols and rules, and the school system's first line of defense against the community, but, fortunately, this authoritarian stance is rare these days. The men and women who undertake this leadership role are expected to see themselves as team leaders, support systems for teachers, defenders of the education mandate, and, above all, champions of children's learning needs and their overall wellbeing within the school.

Recently, as a grandmother, I visited a school during an open house day for kindergarten. The principal offered to walk me to the kindergarten classroom, introduced me to the teacher and early childhood educator, then toured the learning centres with me, explained what occurs at each learning centre and outlined the play and learning goals. He queried the teacher when necessary, who supplied any details he was missing. His pride in the kindergarten, the children's achievements, and in the teachers, was evident; the relationship between teacher and principal was warm and informal while the information provided was specific and insightful. He addressed many of the children by name and the children responded accordingly. I left the school quite certain that children in this school are valued and important, teachers are trusted and appreciated, and the school sees itself as an integral part of the community.

Children often bring home stories about school custodians who tend to building maintenance, keep the school clean, and also contribute to the social-emotional climate of the school through kindness to the children and helpfulness to staff members. A cheerful custodian often indicates a school that functions well – one where the education support team believes in the importance of its role in the interests of children's comfort, safety, and learning. Years ago, my son came home one day from grade two and happily informed me that he was going to be a custodian when he grew up. When I asked why, he replied: "Mr. Sabia can fix *anything!*"

Other members of the education support team go in and out

of schools regularly; they represent the government, municipality
or school board in roles such as curriculum consultant,
superintendent, or the local health authority. It is not unusual for
parents to encounter these education professionals who have
specialized expertise and a unique mandate, interpret ministry
policies and regulations to the education team and provide
curriculum support to teachers. Health professionals provide
services to children in matters related to mental health, learning
disabilities, and health care. Some large schools provide permanent
office space dedicated to intermittent use by these itinerant
specialists who move from school to school during the week.
Large schools may hire resource teachers, psychologists or child
and youth workers as permanent staff who serve children with
learning disabilities, mental health or child guidance.

The team of educators

When children recall their school years, it is nearly always
the teachers they remember, usually for positive reasons. During
school terms, teachers spend almost as much actual time with
children as their parents do and they get to know the children in
ways that parents regularly underestimate. The fact that teachers
are positioned become familiar with each child's preferred styles
and performance within the group makes the teacher-child
relationship unique among all other relationships in a child's
growing years. Teachers observe how the child relates to other
children, his special interests and talents, the development and
learning areas where more attention and time are needed, and the
social context in which he is most comfortable such as whether he
prefers solitary play and needs to be coaxed into group activities.
The kindergarten teacher often becomes so important to the young
child that parents may envy their child's expressions of love and
admiration for the teacher whom few children ever forget. This
new person in their early lives often becomes a benchmark against

which they evaluate later teachers.

Teachers regularly recall relationships we developed with
many children as the most rewarding relationships in our
professional lives. When children grow up, they often
acknowledge similar feelings: that is, a teacher "changed the
course of my life" or a certain teacher is "the reason I am where I
am today". Parents often wish they could share the unique
perspective that the teacher has of their child and his relationships
within the class. As teachers gain experience and self-confidence,
they appreciate their privileged role and status in a child's life. It
should be a relationship based on mutual trust, respect, a genuine
desire to support and guide the child, and love, compassion and
understanding.

As parents and teachers share an interest in the child's
development and learning, kindergarten is a time when parents
should embrace a partnership role with the teacher. Likewise,
astute teachers should be attentive to parents' concerns and strive
to reassure them. When a partnership with parents is sensitively
cultivated during the kindergarten years, parents are positively
initiated to an ongoing relationship with their child's teachers that
can lead to their active support of the school and their trust in
teachers throughout their children's schooling.

Teachers are professionals

Primary school teachers are professionals with
postsecondary education credentials that include at least one
undergraduate degree and usually a bachelor's degree in education
(B.Ed.) with a significant child development component, from a
university faculty of education. Intermediate and senior division
teachers also have a one- or two-year B.Ed. degree that follows
graduation with a bachelor of arts or science degree. In some

universities, a B.Ed. may be awarded concurrently with B.A. or
B.Sc. studies following four or five years of concurrent studies in
Arts or Science and a Faculty of Education. Concurrent BA/BEd
programs are offered by some universities in collaboration with
college ECE programs. The B.Ed. training component includes
several weeks of practice teaching experience with master teachers
in the school system who have been selected to help train student
teachers in their classrooms. Practice teaching experiences in
Ontario are linked to the two divisions the student teacher chooses
at the outset of the training program; i.e. two of: primary (K to 3),
junior (4 to 6), intermediate (7 to 10), senior (11-12) divisions. In
some provinces in recent years, the post-graduate faculty of
education program following a B.A. or B.Sc. was raised from one
year to two years for a B.Ed. degree. This addition was
encouraging and necessary, but it further complicated the variation
among the provinces and territories in the duration of teacher
training, program quality and program and course content.

New teachers who have completed their pre-service teacher
training programs have to complete either a "teacher induction
program" or a probationary program depending on the
province/territory. Permanent certification is granted after the
teacher has successfully completed a period of teaching during
which he has been evaluated at regular intervals by a supervising
teacher, principal or other official. At times when the employment
prospects for graduate teachers are not robust, some graduates
decide to pursue a master's degree in education or another
academic discipline to potentially improve their chance of landing
a full-time teaching position. Certification standards vary across
the nation; they are governed by provincial/ territorial ministries of
education and, where they exist, are administered by a 'college of
teachers'. [8]

Pressures have mounted in recent years for faculties of

education to augment the content of courses, practice teaching
expectations and performance outcomes to accommodate
curriculum changes and responsibilities associated with larger
numbers of children with disabilities in their classrooms and, more
recently, curriculum revisions. The addition of one year to a
faculty of education program should offer additional time for
courses related to the nature of children's learning, child
development, and active, play-based learning strategies and
teaching methods that have been under-represented in training
programs for primary division teachers.

Faculties of education are beginning to catch up to the need
for specialized kindergarten teacher training related to the play-
based kindergartens. Much more content should be added related
to physical education, creative thinking, observation, assessment,
and individual education plans for all children. The use of
technologies in the classroom and, for some, remote teaching,
especially in intermediate and senior divisions, should also
command greater time and attention within training programs to
ensure that they are implemented in ways that buttress children's
learning, application of learning and practice opportunities. More
improvements to teacher training across Canada are long overdue
and should be included in all negotiations between teacher unions
and governments at contract renewal times.

Teachers are registered professionals with their ministries
of education (or provincial college of teachers in Ontario) which
regulate certification, and they are members of a teachers' union.
Dismissal or resignation by a regulatory body following a two-year
probationary period is not common, but it can happen when
teachers are deemed unfit, show insufficient interest or
professional growth during the probationary period, or are
incapable of fulfilling their mandate. In these cases, it is usually
the teacher who concludes that they cannot handle the emotional

demands, time commitment and standards of practice required by the profession and they leave voluntarily or are counselled to do so. It is rare for teachers with permanent status to be fired for anything less than egregious malpractice which usually involves proven instances of child abuse. Other instances of malpractice and abuses of the teacher's role must be reported to the regulatory body that arbitrates and determines the teacher's status going forward.

There have been instances in the past of teachers who ended up in the profession after sampling other vocations that didn't work out for them and teaching seemed to be all that was left. Job scarcity and the heavy professional demands of teaching made that situation an increasingly rare occurrence in recent years. The requirements of the teaching profession these days are usually such that a teacher who is not dedicated does not last in the profession and opts out. Teachers typically remain in the profession because the rewards of teaching tend to outweigh the demands of time, energy, professionalism, and mental and emotional stamina. I look forward to a time in Canada when the teaching profession is accorded the respect, professional regard, and appreciation it deserves. That time is more likely to arrive when the profession agrees to a formal teacher performance appraisal system mandated by ministries of education in which most teachers would demonstrate conclusively that they are professionals who make an incomparable contribution to the society they serve.

Teaching children is much like parenting; it is a relationship that can be hazardous to one's self-esteem, self-concept and mental health when that relationship goes off the rails. I vividly recall feelings of personal failure as a young teacher with a class of 40 fifteen-year-old girls in a grade eleven course in Ancient and Middle Ages history who refused to do homework assignments, chatted throughout the class and laughed at my overly

earnest attempts to engage them in this fascinating subject.
Fortunately, my department head offered to observe my encounters
with this class and pointed out behaviours of mine that irritated this
group. The girls were collaborating to induce me to put my hands
on my hips and raise my voice to try to attract their attention,
whereupon they would laugh and whisper gleefully to each other,
as in, 'got her again'! When he reported his observation back to
me, my first challenge was to avoid putting hands on hips and
speaking loudly. I began to talk in a normal voice, smiled more
often, made a few jokes about my not having lived during the
Middle Ages, and tried to look relaxed. I also changed my lesson
plans to make them more meaningful to teenage girls. Gradually,
they responded to my questions and participated in the experiential
learning activities I planned for them. Simple enough,
perhaps…but not so simple to me at the time, as it was clear that
my behaviour had provided an embarrassing sign of my insecurity,
inexperience, and lack of self-knowledge. After a period of
transition, teaching those 15-year-olds became a favourite class in
my long day of seven classes and the girls began to learn
something about ancient and medieval homes, clothing and how
women worked and lived during those periods. I felt indebted to
my department head and the experience certainly made me sharpen
my act.

Teachers who are new to the profession often see parents as
potential critics of their work and feel threatened by parents who
challenge their judgements, underestimate their expertise, express
unreasonable expectations, and then criticize their performance.
Young teachers usually struggle with immaturity, inexperience and
ego issues and find parents unduly demanding. Experience enables
teachers to feel the confidence that comes from working closely
with children who usually give authentic feedback. When parents
approach teachers in an adversarial manner before they hear the

teacher's perspective, it takes self-awareness, generosity, and maturity for teachers to sustain the criticism and repair the relationship. Parents can and do sometimes come on strong with a teacher, make unreasonable demands and try to undermine her authority. As with all partnerships, parents also have to learn how to conduct themselves within the partnership, examine their own emotions, and extend to the teacher the same consideration they expect from her in order for the teacher-parent relationship to proceed smoothly.

Whatever the dynamic between teachers and parents, it is usually the principal who eases a potentially difficult relationship by seeing an issue from the perspective of both the parent and the teacher. Parents can be confident that the principal most often sees their side of the issue even though she would likely support the teacher if there were meetings together with the parent and teacher. Parents don't need to know what goes on behind the scenes between the teacher and the principal as she works through the issue with the teacher, nor should they. In most cases, parents should simply state their case to the teacher as tactfully as possible, and perhaps later with the principal if nothing changes. I found that the principal usually became my mentor as I worked through issues with parents. As I matured in the profession, I had many occasions to refer back to the lessons my principals taught me, the guidance they provided, and their wise perceptions related to the complex human dynamics involved in parent-teacher relationships.

There may be no other profession that is more hazardous than teaching to one's self-esteem at certain stages in one's career. The daily contact with students over a considerable period provides ample time to publicly expose teachers' frailties which heightens their vulnerability. Parents often view their child's performance in school as a reflection of their parenting, and even of them as persons, and that makes them feel vulnerable, too, in

their relationships with teachers. Successful teachers learn to
absorb rather than deny their hurt or embarrassment when
criticized by parents, learn from their missteps, adjust their
behaviours, and become more human in the process. Success in the
humbling journey of learning to manage one's ego is fundamental
to maturing as an adult and one of the great rewards that becoming
a good teacher – and a good parent - brings.

Early childhood educators (ECEs)

Teachers are accompanied in kindergartens by the early
childhood educators (ECEs) who work closely with the teacher to
translate the curriculum into daily program planning, classroom
design and organization and activity planning. They are also
involved in group learning and individual interventions with
children. In Ontario, ECEs are registered professionals who are
accredited by their College of Early Childhood Educators (RECE).
[9] Sometimes, the ECE may meet with parents on routine matters
but preparing and communicating the assessment reports on
children's development and learning progress is usually the
teacher's responsibility. Data for the assessment reports is based on
observations and concrete evidence of children's progress such as
their productions. In kindergartens, the caregiving routines, group
activities, and the regular human dynamics of the kindergarten all
contribute to perceptions, factual information, and anecdotal
evidence for the data-gathering process involved in assessing
children's developmental and learning progress.

Early childhood educators are professionals who have
completed at least a two- year college diploma in early childhood
education; increasingly, they also possess an undergraduate degree.
ECEs in kindergartens maintain the play-based focus of the
program, a role that capitalizes on their specialized knowledge of
play, activity planning, and child development and guidance. ECEs

are trained in classroom design and organization and curriculum
planning that promote play-based, hands-on learning. They match
play materials with activities to promote specific developmental
objectives, set up the learning centres, and guide children's
interpersonal behaviours and challenges. They need more training
in how to observe, report, and implement KIEPs that individualize
curriculum for children.

Managing the relationship and division of labour between
the teacher and the ECE in the early stages of their partnership
sometimes involves the principal who understands the different
training and experience each professional brings to the
kindergarten classroom and is alert to potential areas for conflict.
A wise principal usually establishes a positive and respectful
collegial relationship between the teacher and the ECE and
encourages them to negotiate who does what in the classroom. The
teacher is ultimately accountable for the effective functioning of
the kindergarten and the assessment and reporting of the children's
individual learning and developmental progress.

Resource teachers and other professional staff

Several professionals may be permanent or transient
members of the kindergarten education team. Schools may assign a
resource teacher who is a specially-trained professional to work
closely with a child with disabilities on a regular or part-time basis
and follow the child's individual education plan (IEP) or revise it
as needed. Resource teachers or other specialists describe the
child's disability, recommend specific interventions, provide for
additional resources as needed, and identify the developmental and
learning outcomes that the child is likely to achieve. When the
child's challenges are intermittent, especially if there is an
education assistant, or a regular visit by an itinerant resource
teacher, the child with disabilities may be integrated effectively

and function well without full-time, additional professional
support.

The professionals who support children with disabilities in
kindergartens, and often throughout their school years may be
resource teachers, child and youth workers, health care
professionals, speech and language therapists, psychologists, and
social workers. These professionals move in and out of classrooms,
meeting with teachers and ECEs, and sometimes with parents, to
develop a special program or curriculum for a child, adjust the
physical environment to better accommodate the child's disability,
observe and assess the child's progress, recommend additional
resources, and help teachers manage behaviour issues. A recent
addition to teams of specialists in schools is the mental health
worker who assists teachers in the observation, recommendations
and interventions for a child who may be suffering a significant
loss, mental illness or high levels of anxiety and stress. The fact
that a mental health worker is becoming a fixture in many schools
is evidence of the high levels of stress in the lives of many more
children, their inability to cope with adult problems that are thrust
upon them much too early, and increasing incidence of
pathological symptoms. These conditions raise alarm and signal a
need for specific and rigorous interventions to help a child as soon
as a problem is identified.

Education assistants

Education assistants are employed by schools to assist
teachers in classrooms where class size might be at, near or over
the student-teacher ratio mandated by the ministry of education.
Education assistants are needed on a regular basis in classrooms
that have a larger than usual number of children who need
additional care, guidance, or extra support. An education assistant
may help to maintain the play environment, set up of activities,

assist with lunch and snack times, and dress children for outdoor play. This staff member is usually a paid employee, increasingly with a college certificate or diploma or a former teacher who is no longer registered as a professional. Colleges frequently offer training programs for education assistants and this trend is likely to continue. All professional and volunteer personnel who are deemed eligible to work with children are required to produce a Criminal Record Certificate (CRC) obtained from the police that verifies that they do not have a criminal record.

Parents and volunteers

Schools are busy places with volunteers to assist the school, staff, teachers and children on a regular basis. Most schools have parent advisory committees (PACs) that have replaced the home and school associations of past generations. Given today's scarcity of resources for schools caused by government 'austerity', one role of the parent advisory committee is to recruit parent volunteers to assist in fund-raising for the school. Increasingly, these funds are used not just to purchase extras for the school but also to provide resources that are essential to the curriculum. This is not as it should be, but it has become a fact of life in Canadian schools. Parents who volunteer time to the PACs are often busy working parents who feel a commitment to the school, the community, and the children. Typical fundraising events include school sports and game days held on a Saturday, events for parents such as casino nights, concerts or lectures, raffles, and events for children such as holiday parties. Parent volunteers are valued and essential members of the school community who are usually members of the school's PAC. This group would be well-positioned to host focus groups that involve parents in raising issues related to education reform and provide input to consultations that should be conducted locally, organized provincially and sponsored nationally.

Visitors and guests

Years ago, I undertook a study tour of schools in
Scandinavia and visited a number of childcare, kindergarten, and
elementary schools in Norway, Denmark and Sweden. One of
many memorable aspects were the beautiful features of the school
interiors, especially the classrooms, but also the playgrounds where
children played and learned outdoors every day, rain, or shine.
Schools even provided showers at the entrance to the playground
for children to shower away mud and grit from their full-length
waterproof raincoats and rain hats (sou' westers) on wet days. Our
visits were anticipated, but the warm welcome and homelike
atmosphere of the school as well as the openness of the teachers
were enlightening. A lasting impression was of friendly, open
schools that reinforced the parents' and guests' right to be there.
Approaching our schools can be more like entering a fortress, with
their locked doors, an intercom to talk with someone inside, and a
wait to be allowed entry. On entering, there may be more
requirements. The intentions are good and the safety of children is
paramount, but, in Canada, we should find ways to make our
schools welcoming rather than formidable.

The expanding school learning environment

Governments and the tax-paying public should understand
that spending and investing in schools to promote the learning
potential of all children is a crucial investment in the future.
Chapter 3 described the features of classroom design, organization
and provisioning for learning through play. Having visited
kindergarten classrooms in several nations as well as in Canada, I
would describe many of our kindergartens as "make do"
environments that give the impression of being under-resourced
and cobbled together. Kindergarten classroom space may be
cramped and tired looking and walls are sometimes a cluttered mix

of random pictures and outdated notices to have meaning for children or purpose for anyone else.

Compelling arguments are made that a 21st century educational system should be relevant to global and domestic cultural, social and economic challenges. At a time when business and economists call for creative thinking and innovation to maintain our nation's prosperity and influence in the world, education systems should recognize that creativity hardly ever develops in an atmosphere of standardized learning and testing, outdated delivery systems, protection of the status quo, and make-do environments. To prepare children for creative and higher-functioning performances, the venues for learning should represent a positive vision, creative design, and environments that represent our claim that we value children and childhood. Most important of all, creative design, welcoming and well-provisioned environments demonstrate to children that they are important and valued.

Diverse resources and sufficient space for the essential resources allow children to move around and they accommodate divergent learning activities with broad appeal to children. The physical organization of school environments requires thoughtful design that supports projects, fascinating resources to explore, and ideas for experiments and testing. Investing attention, energy, and funding in re-visioning kindergarten/primary environments to nurture children's imagination and creative thinking abilities is a good place to begin an essential reform of education. Schools should automatically include space for outdoor learning and shared, common-use areas where children can tackle projects that lie beyond their immediate experience (like gardens for city-schools or making model cities for rural schools), and indoor and outdoor space to develop their bodies at frequent intervals and in all seasons. A vision for kindergarten/primary learning environments should include the use of community spaces such as libraries and recreation centres, parks and conservation areas, and regular access to large muscle play spaces and gymnasiums. Education environments should regularly expose young children to real-life contexts and experiences that bridge the gap between learning about something (i.e., knowledge) and developing 'know-how' by observing, being there, practising and doing. It is remarkable to observe, as one example, the undivided attention that children give to whole-class experiences in art galleries where they sit on cushions on the floor to sketch a painting they admire, or visit exploratoriums to take apart and rebuild an airplane or model car.

Children in the primary years enjoy outings where they experience acting on things they have not seen, held or experienced before; for kindergarten children, learning about nature and natural things outdoors is memorable and rich in sensory-perceptual learning. Ready access to conservation areas, natural parks and visits to local farms and gardens could be made available in many more communities. Exposure to direct experience in a variety of environments for learning, including the outdoors, should be a regular feature of primary school learning. The more often children are taken into the community to visit and use resources, the more we populate their minds and memories with dreams of what is possible and motivating.

The kindergarten is a laboratory for learning; the classroom and playground for the primary division should offer children optimal opportunities for exploration, interesting challenges, satisfying group times with peers, and new connections to make. It should provide time for children to choose, begin and finish activities and engaging enough to move children steadily and securely through new ways to view and think about their environment and their place in it. Parents should anticipate that their child will be supported by a teacher who cares about their children's individual progress as she navigates with them what Montessori called this "sensitive period" in learning. Tackling real-life questions, finding solutions, and having authentic learning experiences sharpens children's observation and research skills, and helps them make choices based on their experiences.

5

SOCIAL AND EMOTIONAL READINESS FOR LEARNING

"An educational system isn't worth a great deal if it teaches young people to make a living but doesn't teach them how to build a life." David Suzuki

Curriculum discussion in this book begins by focusing on children's social and emotional readiness for learning in the kindergarten/primary years. In times when anxiety levels are high, children's social-emotional wellbeing deserves centre stage in education because it influences their motivation to learn and how effectively they do so. Chilling data related to children's mental health, even in a nation as privileged as Canada, raises questions related to their emotional stamina and ability to cope with ongoing stress and remain positive. Children who are fearful and preoccupied with concerns way beyond their years are unable to release themselves to play, let their imaginations flow and commit to a goal; stress is simply a roadblock to learning.

It is harder today to predict the future, riskier to rely on past practice, and naive to assume that Western society can continue along its former growth-driven economic trajectory at a time of dire threats to the planet. Parents yearn to know how to nurture hope, resilience, empathy and motivation in their children for a world that increasingly appears to be "in disarray".[1] A social and emotional curriculum that frames kindergarten/primary education should foster and support mental and physical health, character-

building and sustain children psychologically, emotionally and
spiritually. The importance of civil social discourse, character and
empathy has been brought into sharper focus as families deal with
uncertainty, the upheaval of institutions they used to depend on,
and preoccupation with staying afloat and living as normally as
possible. This time appears to be right for education to focus much
more on preparing children to become responsible citizens and to
develop their potential in all domains instead of planning for future
vocations that have not yet been defined.

Schools already address skills associated with social
interaction and social responsibility but psychological health,
empathetic connection with others, and character building have not
been spelled out as outcomes for kindergarten/primary curriculum.
In a time when lifelong learning dispositions and skills, novel
thinking, seeking creative solutions and invention have been
identified as essential educational priorities, it is important to
understand the natural links between these priorities and children's
social and emotional wellbeing that affect all aspects of their
childhood and future lives.

A social-emotional agenda for 21st century schools

The developmental tasks of the social-emotional domain
may be understood according to many categories, but I have
chosen five broad areas: *psychological health*; *social cognition*;
social relations; *social perceptions*; and *moral behaviour*. A
social-emotional curriculum may be framed in many ways; parents
should be consulted and their input factored into decision-making.
Pertinent questions parents might ask themselves as they begin to
generate their own questions on this topic might be: How can
families and schools prepare children for a future for which there is
no reliable roadmap or navigator? To what should children be
encouraged to aspire? What values would serve children best in

times of environmental threats and social unrest? How should
children be educated so they can find meaning and purpose in lives
that may be lived largely outside traditional workplaces and
occupational roles? How can adults help children frame hopeful
visions of the future? How do we guide children to discern right
from wrong and develop the courage to act accordingly?

Education is called upon to listen to the input of parents in
order to evolve a viable social-emotional agenda for children. This
quest relies on empowered parents who are actively involved with
the schools during their children's educational journey. Parents
should ask questions that are informed by their own experience
rather than by trends and biases. They should expect a decisive,
rational response from the educational system and be ready to
actively support their children's social-emotional and character
development at home. Public education systems should no longer
duck a leadership role or blame outside influences or the potential
threat of litigation for the systemic failure to impose clear
sanctions for unacceptable behaviours such as bullying, cheating,
disrespect and racial, ethnic and gender intimidation tactics.

When public education systems fully understand and
communicate their mandate, values and mission and assume
responsibility for carrying out their mission, there will be less
dissembling and avoidance related to their rightful role and
obligation to promote societal progress. There are many reliable
reference points that may guide this challenging quest that should
draw upon the collective wisdom of Canada's philosophers,
scientists, historians and spiritual and cultural leaders. A national
discussion of this kind is demanding but it is one that has never
been undertaken and is profoundly important at this juncture. An
over-riding question is, 'what values should a Canadian education
represent'?

Psychological health

Psychological health with reference to young children addresses personality development that includes forming bonds and attachments to others, trust, self-concept and self-esteem, ability to act independently, empathy, and emotional self-control. Becoming able to identify one's own negative feelings and find acceptable outlets for fear, anxiety, anger, and other powerful feelings depends significantly on an ability to express oneself through actions and words. Many branches of psychology believe that the roots of lifelong psychological health are established in the early years, at home and at school, that are considered 'prime time'.

Forming attachments, bonds with others and trust

The infant's earliest social-emotional experience begins with mother-child bonding and expands to attachments with other caregivers and members of the family sphere. The infant learns gradually to separate from principal caregivers for brief periods and gains independence physically and emotionally as he learns to trust that mother will return, familiar faces will reappear, and his basic needs will be met. He develops a sense of separateness as he becomes mobile and gains confidence and satisfaction in his own achievements that motivate him to take further risks. The toddler seeks greater autonomy that leads to his sense of identity. If the conditions are right, he overcomes hurdles and challenges as they appear, feels proud of his successes and receives feedback from others that all contribute to his concept of self.

Self-concept

Self-concept and self-esteem are both important to the healthy development of the personality but they differ in terms of their origins and emphasis. When children have opportunities to react, risk, regulate their own behaviour, and to respond, connect, and separate from others effectively they acquire self-concept based on authentic evidence. Whereas self-esteem is largely achieved through recognizing one's own success in meeting challenges, self-concept depends more on feedback from others. Self-concept develops by comparing oneself to others, through interactions with others and formal and informal feedback that help children construct an accurate picture of themselves.

Kindergarten children want to be liked and accepted by peers and teachers which makes fours and fives particularly endearing children to teach. Healthy personality development in the early years depends on developing confidence in one's own abilities and feeling positive about oneself. An important kindergarten task is to help children achieve a realistic self-concept that is closely related to ego identity, (a sense of "I" in the context of "we" and "us"). A healthy self-concept promotes children's ease in social situations, a sense of humour, and an understanding of the purpose of limits and rules of behaviour. Helping children feel positive about their own body image also supports self-concept and enables them to adapt to changing physical demands, set realistic physical goals and strive to achieve them.

To be truly "comfortable in one's own skin", children, like adults, have to learn that their individuality brings with it special talents and positive character traits, as well as personal weaknesses that define them for others regardless of how actively they might try to deny or hide them. Parents and teachers nurture the child's self-concept by helping them sustain a flippant comment or occasional joke played on them, and by recognizing their unique talents, personality traits and achievements. When adults demonstrate active interest in what the child is doing, what interests him and the struggles he is dealing with, they provide a powerful boost to the child's ability to accept himself for who he is. When children are encouraged to recognize and express interest in the struggles and successes of others, they learn to empathize with the challenges that others face, a recognition that also contributes to their self-concept.

Self-esteem

Values, behaviours and attitudes evolve over time and seldom endure intact for more than a generation; they tend to follow trends and cycles. The collective spirit and will that motivated people to build a future for North America over more than two centuries, by the 1970s and early 1980s had evolved into a preoccupation with self that characterized the so-called "me-generation". This preoccupation helped to drive self-esteem to the top of many lists of emotional strengths to actively cultivate. The notion that teachers and the school system should "dispense" self-esteem to children became endemic in North American education systems for more than two decades. Schools began to promote children to the next grade whether or not they had achieved the learning related to their grade level, ostensibly to protect their self-esteem and keep them with their age cohort even if they had not yet acquired the foundation they needed to succeed. This practice frequently compounded children's learning difficulties. The assumption was that they would either catch up to their peers or fall behind. Privileged children were able to take advantage of private tutoring or help from parents and catch up to their grade level. Others fell behind especially in subjects where learning is cumulative such as mathematics, and schooling became an ongoing struggle to succeed in something. In the worst cases, these "casualties" of the system were unable to enjoy any aspect of school, got used to failing in important subjects and the negative impact on their self-esteem often became a lifelong impediment.

The importance attributed to self-esteem for its own sake, without a foundation provided by the child's own successes to moor it, had a significant impact on education standards and evaluation of children's performance. Boosting children's self-esteem through praise and positive feedback, irrespective of their performance, became a regular practice whether or not a child had

demonstrated effort and progress to merit the positive
reinforcement. Children who were praised for indifferent effort and
mediocre achievement learned to over-estimate their status as a
learner. Education systems began to accept wide variation in
performance as good enough and started to devise tests and
calibrate scores and grades accordingly. Grade inflation was one
result and appeared at all levels in the education continuum
through to postsecondary education.

When children's meaningful achievements are recognized,
however long and whatever paths they take, children are
encouraged to link their goals to behaviours such as persisting,
overcoming challenges, delaying gratification and achieving
success. Making these links contributes to self-esteem which is an
inner sense that they have achieved something worthwhile usually
through effort and perseverance. Self-esteem is not a plaster that
can be applied by others to make children feel good by bestowing
praise that is disconnected from the child's performance. Self-
esteem develops when children feel gratified by what they perceive
to be their own success based on their own efforts.

Parents and teachers who set reasonable goals and
expectations for children understand them, their limitations and
strengths. When they guide children to overcome hurdles, revise
goals or find alternative pathways toward achievement of goals
parents and teachers are being authentic and honest. Giving
children praise and positive reinforcement thoughtlessly and
without evidence of effort are hollow gestures when they
underperform; from this behaviour children learn that any
performance will do and there are few expectations or standards
they should meet. Mindless praise leaves them wondering, "is
there anybody home?" and does little to encourage self-discipline
and effort. Authentic praise for something well done is durable and
motivating and helps them gain confidence to tackle other

challenges.

Self-esteem is achieved when children meet challenges that
are intrinsically motivated, such as "I really want to climb that
tree", and extrinsically motivated, such as "the teacher says I have
to speak in front of the class like everyone else" and finally does so
despite their fear or shyness. When children develop healthy self-
esteem, they not only build an inner sense of self-worth, they also
appreciate the achievements of others and recognize their
strengths, make healthy and honest comparisons of themselves
with other children, and set realistic goals. Self-esteem is a crucial
ingredient in the development of positive dispositions for learning
that motivate children even in spite of limitations. These children
become the 'over-achievers' who surprise themselves and
everyone else, or the 'under-achievers' who may eventually learn
that hard work pays dividends.

Empathy

The development of empathy builds an important
foundation for psychological health and emotional intelligence that
influences social perceptions, social cognition, social relations,
moral understanding and character. When children put themselves
figuratively in the shoes of another child to understand what he is
feeling, they demonstrate empathy especially if they have
experienced a similar challenge. Babies demonstrate a kind of
empathy when they reach out to pat the head of an upset child.
Empathy is the ability to relate to the feelings of another and act
accordingly by expressing understanding and helping others who
are in distress. As children develop empathy in the company of
other children, the kindergarten/primary years are prime time to
foster children's kinder, gentler perceptions of others.
Psychologist Daniel Goleman uses the term *emotional intelligence*
to describe the internal awareness and self-knowledge sufficient to

govern one's emotional responses, empathy and behaviours. "Our
emotional capacities are not a given; with the right learning they
can be improved." [2] Goleman sees emotional intelligence as a set
of abilities that includes self-motivation, self-awareness, ability to
deal with anxiety, and being able to detect social cues.

Emotional self-control

Self-control is associated with exercising self-discipline,
understanding that actions have consequences and responding to
the dictates of one's conscience. It is learned over time and usually
in small increments. Four and five-year-olds are challenged to find
acceptable outlets for fear, anger, anxiety, and other powerful
feelings they do not yet fully understand. As self-control is also a
key predictor of success in school and in life as a whole, children
should begin early to practise this disposition in an environment
like kindergarten with dependable routines, orderly space, and
observant teachers who notice behaviours and intervene when a
child wanders aimlessly or loses control. When young children do
not learn emotional self-control, they often face behaviour issues
during middle childhood and adolescence. Helping young children
achieve small victories as they learn to contain or express their
emotions appropriately makes it more likely that self-control will
become a habit, a disposition to call on when confronted by
challenges and a lifelong character trait.

Aspects of self-control such as an ability to share, wait
one's turn, delay gratification, regulate impulses, and exercise will
power are subject to beliefs and behaviours that may change from
generation to generation and are culturally driven. Try comparing
and contrasting families of the Victorian era with families who
raised children in the 1960s and 1970s, versus today's generation
of families. One sees significant differences between the Victorian
obsession with discipline, coercing children and preaching the

virtue of self-restraint, and the permissive child-rearing practices
of the "me generation" of the 1960s and 70s. Then compare both
of these child-rearing styles to today's "helicopter" or
"snowplough" parents who are sometimes criticized for being
excessively protective, program their children's lives to reduce
ambiguities they may encounter, keep them busy much of the time
to avoid risk, and make decisions for them. Wise parents strive for
a healthy balance between steering their child in a positive
direction and trusting them to act accordingly, versus regularly
intervening to reduce the risks and bad choices their child might
make. It is always a difficult balance to achieve but children can
learn from their mistakes, failures and bad choices and need a
reasonable measure of freedom to practise navigating for
themselves.

Learning to control one's emotions, actions and choices is
associated with success in school and in life. When parents
regularly give in to their child's demands and never say no because
they fear she may act out, the child learns she can manipulate
others in order to achieve what she wants. A failure to "parent"
almost always ensures that children will not learn to control their
emotions and will have difficulty accepting denial of any kind. To
learn self-control, young children need opportunities to accept that
they cannot always be first in line, have an extra cookie, or watch
another movie before bedtime. They need time to reflect on their
choices and accept the consequences of their actions and decisions.
Children learn gradually to accept their limitations after encounters
with failure and to appreciate their strengths and unique talents
when they compare themselves to the other children in the group.
As with so much of learning, it is easier and more efficient to do
things right the first time instead of having to unlearn a bad habit
and learn a new one. Self-control is harder to achieve during
middle childhood and adolescence than it is during early

childhood. When positive dispositions and habits are not encouraged and practised early while the brain is developing rapidly and personality is being shaped, they are harder to acquire later after habits, behaviour patterns, and dispositions have become ingrained and personalities further developed.

Self-expression

By age four, the child has usually learned to express immediate needs verbally and is increasingly using symbols and media such as role play, song, words, or movement to display feelings and perceptions. Self-expression is a developmental task of the preoperational period that is in full flight during the kindergarten years. As the child's vocabulary expands, he uses more mature syntax and longer sentences in speech, his drawings become more recognizable and expansive, and he expresses himself through movements to music, singing, sociodramatic play, and exuberant physical activity such as climbing walls and ladders.

The important developmental task of learning to appreciate one's achievements is encouraged when children are able to choose their own medium for self-expression in their self-directed play. Kindergarten environments should provide an abundance of media, props, space, materials and supplies from which children can choose. The emotional climate should invite them to take advantage of their newly-acquired independence from home to express their positive and negative feelings in a range of acceptable ways. The child who responds to social and environmental challenges appropriately within a supportive kindergarten classroom and learns to express feelings without fear of shaming or rebuke starts to build a foundation for psychological health and wellbeing. Robert Fulghum's book "Everything I need to know I learned in kindergarten" was right on in so many ways. [3]

Today's epidemic of mental illness among young people is evidence of the urgent need to guide children toward hopefulness instead of futility and initiative rather than despair. Mental health implies an ability to make viable choices, form healthy relationships and accept the commitments that accompany significant decisions. Physical health relies on good nutrition, fitness, constructive and meaningful lifestyles, and life-sustaining recreational outlets. All of these requirements should be represented in school and extracurricular school programs, not treated as frills to be available as time and resources permit, but stable components of education programs from kindergarten through secondary school.

Social cognition

Social cognition includes social relations, social perceptions, adapting to changing social demands, reasonable respect for social norms and conventions, feeling comfortable about one's gender and positive about one's ethnicity, race and language, and feeling they belong and can identify with a group. From birth, children begin to develop their notions about other people, to interact with others and observe what they do and how they respond. Social cognition is a broad subject that ranges from knowing the self and others, showing interest in human beings and what interests them, and seeing oneself in relation to others. Neuroscientists have concluded that humans are wired to connect with others and these connections influence how we view ourselves, how we relate to others, and, ultimately, how we choose to live our own lives. (4)

Social intelligence examines how individuals connect with each other, form relationships, interpret social cues and filter our responses. Daniel Goleman (2008) included empathy, social cognition and *social facility* (the ability to pick up on social cues

and influence others) in his definition of social intelligence, as well
as *social awareness* that also includes empathic reactions and the
ability to express concern. All these social skills contribute to the
trajectory of growth and learning that occurs while learning to get
along with others. [5]

Social relations

Kindergartens support children's development of social
relations by placing a high premium on learning to care, help
others and feel empathy for those who are sad, lonely or need
something. Healthy peer relationships are established in a
kindergarten that supports individual needs, helps children act
independently but also to function successfully as group members
and enable the group to achieve its goals. Group times generally
encourage friendliness, sensitivity toward others, and humour; they
redirect aggression, competition, and overbearing assertiveness.
They respect individual rights and help children learn that others
also need the teacher's attention, deserve to be first in line now and
then and be recognized by the group. Healthy family relationships
receive attention in the kindergarten as children hear about various
family customs and celebrations, the extended family relationships
in other families and the various roles that family members play in
their households – all important learning for them.

It is a tribute to parents of the current generation of
children that Canadian children are generally tolerant and open to
multiculturalism and cross-cultural friendships. Observing the
cultural diversity among children's friends, in large cities
especially, shows progress in addressing several goals of
multiculturalism although we still have farther to go. Another
aspect of visioning a future for education is to rethink whether
education should prepare children for a world where they can stand
out, lean in assertively, be independent, compete vigorously and
gain advantage. It is more consistent with social justice and equal
opportunity to promote values related to the public good and

collaboration in order to succeed as a nation. Nations like Norway seem to have integrated these values and are beacons of light in a troubled world. We may have reached a time in history when we should contemplate not how to prepare children to compete in a world of continued economic growth, but rather to conserve, share, cooperate and collaborate. In a world that will only protect and sustain human life if we take meaningful, difficult steps now to protect the environment, children today should be encouraged to expect and live with less, and to help generate and share the world's life-sustaining resources.

Social perceptions

Social perceptions include understanding the self in the context of others and how we perceive others. This aspect of social cognition relates to feeling positive about one's gender, race and ethnicity, demonstrating ease in social situations and respect for the law, viable rules and conventions. Social perceptions also rely on one's self-concept and self-esteem, self-respect and humility, all factors that contribute to personality development and psychological health. Supporting children's development of social perceptions is another important mandate of the kindergarten.

Social perceptions that are authentic and honest enable children to approach new social situations with ease and confidence. Sociodramatic play provides practice in remembering and portraying children's perceptions of real-life behaviours and roles they have observed. They use their perceptions of the memories and experiences of other children to assign roles and tasks and learn who to count on for coming up with a new idea. Their sociodramatic play allows parents and teachers to observe how children perceive adult actions and behaviours.

When children closely observe older children and adults,

they develop their perceptions of gender, ethnicity, language, and
race and are influenced by what they perceive about people closest
to them. Their perceptions are often played out in their role play
episodes which is why teachers should view this play style as a
fruitful way to observe children's acquisition of social perceptions.
Children sometimes need the support of an alert teacher to help
them reconsider their perceptions of situations, roles, and
behaviours they might have observed and to propose an alternative
and more authentic perception. There are times in their role play
when teachers might need to intervene to provide an alternative
perception. There is usually no harm done to the integrity of the
play episode if a teacher intervenes (perhaps by assuming a role
himself) to help the children reframe a script that becomes mired in
inaccurate information or perceptions children might have
acquired. [6]

Ability to act independently

As the kindergarten child gains greater independence, she
expresses curiosity about other people. Who are these children here
with my teacher and me? Can I do what they can do? How do I
find out more about them? When time is set aside during the day
for group learning, children have to manage their own interests in
the context of those who have other interests. They practise
expressing themselves and try to satisfy their needs for recognition.
The observant teacher can be an influential role model for children
as he responds to each child in turn, allows him or her an
opportunity to speak and be heard and acknowledges the
contribution of each member of the group.

Gender issues

Children's development of self-concept and self-esteem is essential to being able to identify with one's gender, develop respect for the gender of others, and observe that there are behaviours, emotions and aspirations which are common to both genders and often interchangeable. Perceptions of gender and gender confusion should be sensitively handled so that they promote healthy relationships between girls and boys, help them accept ambiguities they may perceive and reject rigid definitions. If respect for all children is nurtured and modeled by the adults in their lives, respect for the gender manifestations of all persons becomes a deeply entrenched part of the child's personality. The enlightened attitudes we want to cultivate in children, and the respectful relationships we want to promote, make this agenda item particularly important today for girls and boys. The anticipated outcome would be children who are sensitive, appreciate, support and reach out to each other, see gender differences as complementary and not competitive, and sometimes ambiguous rather than clear-cut.

Kindergarten children usually develop perceptions of each gender based on their home experience which means that they may absorb a wide range of differing perceptions. Children acquire stereotypes at an early age if that is what they see and experience around them. When girls tell boys they can't come into the housekeeping area and play with the dolls, they are usually acting on stereotypic perceptions of behaviour they see at home that do not always lead to positive perceptions of male-female relationships. When boys exclude girls from the block area, they demonstrate that this activity does not fit their idea of what girls should do. Teachers usually find ways and appropriate times to encourage boys and girls to engage each other in their favourite play activities. Gender-related preferences are real and undeniable, but the stereotypical gender preferences do not fit all or very many children. [7] Encouraging interaction between boys and girls in activities that both can enjoy together establishes a foundation for healthy relationships, reveals the strengths each possesses and is an appropriate first step in the elementary school sex education curriculum.

From an early age, boys face unique challenges at school that can have long-term consequences. Some of their challenges relate to their developmental timetable which tends to be different that of the girls. Our feminized elementary school system has for decades favoured the behaviours more often exhibited by girls that include eagerness to please, conform and follow rules. Boys need to be active yet are expected to fit a school system that has promoted physical restraint and sitting still, and not the motion and robust physical actions and interactions boys often need and crave. [8] A way to even the playing field is to ensure that the daily timetable includes an hour of physical activity, indoors, outdoors or both, that is planned and implemented by teachers and consistent with the aims of physical education curriculum. This active time should have a permanent slot in the kindergarten/primary day and include physical activities that involve tasks like problem solving, measuring, counting and forming sets, using new words, remembering and responding to music, singing, and games. Physical programs are addressed in Chapter 6.

The data on the rate at which boys drop out of school in their teens, leave postsecondary programs before graduating, and generally rank behind girls in academic achievement confirm that schooling should fit boys, as well as girls, rather than force-fitting boys into schooling. [9] Changing the delivery of education to make it easier for boys to succeed and flourish from kindergarten on does not imply that the comfort levels and developmental needs of girls are less important. The fact is that the primary and middle school grades face a special challenge to engage boys, address their developmental needs, and improve their motivation to learn and enjoy school. Treating traditional perceptions of boys as boisterous, hard to harness, and less engaged, as if these were choices they made, and finding ways to stifle their natural exuberance has, over decades, derailed schooling success for many boys. [10] It is long overdue to start demanding that schools become as relevant to boys' developmental timetables, interests, and energy levels as they are to girls. Once a fair balance is achieved in the interests of boys perhaps more of them will go on to higher learning and succeed at the same rate as the girls do.

A good starting point is to understand that boys learn in their own ways and their brains are wired differently from girls. [11] Boys respond to active play and hands-on learning - another rationale for play-based kindergartens. Activity planning to attract boys and keep them interested should involve them in movement and action for a significant part of each day. Transforming the education environment and activity planning to capture the energy of boys as well as girls does not mean retreating to common stereotypes. Boys sometimes like quiet play, are not constantly in motion and enjoy creative arts. They enjoy resource books about science phenomena, magic and monsters of almost any kind, joke books, and computer games that often involve reading, memory, imagination, communication and math concepts.

Girls also need and enjoy physical activities and active games indoors and outdoors. They like to create their own versions of sociodramatic play episodes. They sometimes require encouragement to engage seriously with math and science activities and their interest in both should be captured in kindergarten. One solution to broadening the activities of girls and boys is usually having at least one significant class project underway either indoors or outdoors at all times. Projects typically

include several stages and cater to a range of learning preferences,
with plenty of tasks to keep all students engaged in a task that
interests them. They also encourage boys and girls to collaborate
and achieve an outcome they can all appreciate.

Cultivate positive feelings about ethnic and racial identity and
heritage

Today's parents grew up when multiculturalism was
already a significant factor in Canadian culture so most have some
understanding of the social attitudes and behaviours that contribute
to equity, tolerance, and fairness that they pass on to their children.
New challenges have emerged, however, that call for awareness
and support for children and families of racial, ethnic, and religious
communities that are still surrounded by suspicion, ignorance, and
fear. The kindergarten/primary years should be laboratories that
model peaceful co-existence, interdependence, mutual respect, and
friendship among the children who are usually blind to skin colour
and ethnicity when they are permitted to make their own choices.
Their natural interactions model for adults the behaviours that
should be extended toward the diverse range of families in our
communities. Schools promote a positive multicultural mindset
when they facilitate children's learning about their own culture and
extend it to learning about other cultures and family
configurations. Planning social gatherings and celebrations for
families to come together to share food (or plant gardens in the
school yard) can be a welcoming, exciting and uplifting way to
begin.

An impediment to turning schools into a multicultural
meeting places for families is the large composite elementary
school that is increasingly located on the fringe of a community
after the neighbourhood schools have been closed. Parents don't
gather at the school and visit at the end of the school day as they

collect their children; buses bring children to school and home
again. The distance to travel to their children's school limits
parents' interactions with teachers and other parents and may offer
a reason for not participating in the life of the school. Being able to
interact with other parents is, for immigrant families especially, an
important introduction to community life, and perhaps to a new
language and social customs within their adopted country.
Engaging them in school projects is a way for teachers and parents
to mingle and contribute to school life and a practice that makes
their young children happy.

Moral understanding and character development

Guiding children's moral development and character has
been treated as the domain of parents and family; this attitude has
apparently made it tricky for public education systems to navigate
in Canada's multicultural context. The education system has
tended to steer clear of "morals" teaching in schools because they
see morality and religious affiliation as two sides of one coin even
though many moral teachings are essentially human and non-
denominational. Ethnic and class biases are more likely to drive
values and moral standards that each culture wants to inculcate in
their children. Multicultural societies accept that cultures and
religions have a right to decide, within the bounds of Canadian
law, the moral priorities and attributes of character they want their
children to adopt at least until the power of the peer group and the
dominant culture begin to take over.

In the past decade and more, some intractable social issues
have demonstrated that education should more vigorously protect
children and intervene immediately in harmful and sometimes
deadly encounters in schools that involve widespread bullying.
School boards have been urged to frame and enforce policy with
respect to prevention and sanctions related to bullying, violence

and intimidation, bringing weapons to school, racist remarks and behaviours, alcohol and substance abuse, and sexual harassment. Where policies exist, they are often not enforced by school management or boards.

Few families across all socioeconomic sectors manage to escape situations whereby their children are threatened physically, bullied, or persecuted during their school years. Bullying, intimidation and violence are perpetrated by children as early as kindergarten and is more common than school officials are ready to admit. It often involves the covert actions of a child who persecutes and stalks a vulnerable child who is perceived to lack power and connection with someone who might protect him. Children fear reporting incidents to parents or the teacher because of threats of reprisal. Girls are often innocent victims of aggression by another child – a girl or a boy who holds power over them because of size or popularity, a disposition to torment and hurt, or to intimidate someone who appears unable to fight back. Decisive and immediate intervention is essential to protect and reassure children; otherwise, they learn that the school officials will look the other way and fail to deal with the perpetrators.

School boards and schools should be active partners with parents in the moral development of children by teaching and modeling behaviours and concepts related to conscience, moral behaviour and character. Curriculum should introduce developmentally appropriate discussion related to the impulses that perpetrate hate, persecution, ostracism, and shaming. The incidence of unhappy children whose fear goes unaddressed by adults they depend on is an important moral issue of our time. Schools are obligated to respond openly and forcefully to acts of aggression and hate when they occur, communicate forthrightly with parents, talk with the perpetrator, apply meaningful sanctions as necessary, and work persistently to ensure that the climate and culture in the school remain healthy and positive for all.

Conscience

Children begin to develop a conscience during the
kindergarten years. Conscience governs people's choices and
actions and how we behave irrespective of whether our actions are
observed by others. The ability to empathize with others helps
children understand the difference between right and wrong
actions. Conscience reinforces the ability to self-regulate when
confronted by unmet needs, hostility, jealousy, selfish desires, and
feelings we know we should suppress. By the time children enter
grade one, they are ready to understand a set of simple personal
standards that should govern their behaviour. Simple rules such as
"don't hit; take turns; share; play fair" (Robt. Fulghum) are among
the first rules for interacting successfully with others that should be
practised in kindergarten. When behaviours occur in which a child
hurts another child physically or with words have immediate
relevant consequences, children begin to understand the
importance of self-control and they draw a link between cause and
effect that is absorbed by the emerging conscience.

Children should recognize early their obligation to follow
simple rules even when they have a choice and there is no one
around to check. They should also learn that following simple rules
and treating others respectfully is not just a matter of avoiding an
undesirable consequence. Conscience plays a key role in good
citizenship, social justice, morality, and ethical behaviour
throughout life; its ongoing development and sustainability is a
lifetime challenge. When the conscience is under-developed,
children's tendencies toward aggression and anti-social behaviour
remain unchecked. A positive kindergarten/primary environment
provides a supportive climate in which to help others, be
considerate and exercise kindness. These habits of mind and

dispositions are reinforced in a context of kind words and actions, reasonable and clear rules for behaviour, empathetic supervision, and unambiguous, conscientious adult role models. David Brooks, author of the book, "The Road to Character" (2015), referred to a paper by William James (1877) entitled "Habit". "When you are trying to lead a decent life", he wrote, "you want to make your nervous system your ally and not your enemy..."You want to engrave certain habits so deep that they will become natural and instinctual" and never allow yourself to make an exception "until the habit is firmly rooted in your life". [12]

Parents and society in general need help from the schools in addressing the urgent social, environmental and mental health issues that have resulted in an epidemic of anxiety, depression, violence, substance abuse, and despair among children and teens. Schools are in a better position to influence children's moral development as parents often do not have as much leverage to make as large an impression on children. Schooling molds children's character in countless ways and schools should become more active participants in children's moral development and character-building. "Parents as partners with teachers" has been a rallying cry in educational circles for many years, but this suggestion is too passive to generate the action needed today to improve school life and secure a safe present and future for children. When parents resist the urge to threaten schools with lawsuits and instead convince schools and school officials to establish and enforce policies that build and protect children's conscience and character, children's moral development will have become an important education priority and not just words.

Cultivate a "rich inner life"

Modern democracies are increasingly threatened by foreign and domestic forces that sabotage technology networks and social

media in order to divide citizens, stir hatred along cultural, political
and class lines, and break down consensus on the values a nation
represents. The pervasiveness of depression and anxiety among
teens and young adults is sufficient reason to draw urgent attention
to children's emotional resiliency and character-building in early
and middle childhood. Children should feel secure and able to
aspire to a secure future but conveying this message to children
today is a much greater challenge than in decades past. When
adults turn away in the face of the outrage of "kids killing kids",
bullying, hatred and racism, they exhibit a moral disengagement
that is the opposite of maturity, courage, personal integrity, and
good faith that their children may emulate. Children need to see
courageous role models in order to process what is right as they
observe the adults around them acting responsibly and taking
action when confronted by evidence of the injustice a child suffers
or of physical or psychological harm.

Child psychiatrist Bruno Bettelheim (1976, 1987) used the
term "rich inner life" to describe a human condition he believed to
be fundamental to children's mental health, sense of wellbeing and
moral courage. [13] A rich inner life provides a buffer against
despair, anxiety, loneliness, alienation, and an absence of meaning
in life. It can also enable people to rise above retaliation, hatred,
and intolerance. A rich inner life can be an antidote to the moral
disengagement that allows adults to excuse themselves from taking
action even when they are obligated to do so. Some adults fear
retribution for taking a stand and defending what is right, and
thereby fail to protect and parent the young responsibly. A "rich
inner life" provides a fertile base for developing the conscience
and moral sensibility that are nourished by positive experiences,
insightful coaching and uplifting examples. Teachers, principals
and parents have to exercise the courage to take stands and act on
their obligations to support others who do the same so that children

have more positive examples to emulate.

A rich inner life occurs in the context of meaningful life experiences. Participation in sports and fitness activities, appreciation of music and dance, regular and sustained contact with nature, and creative pursuits add meaning and texture to life. A rich inner life encourages children to reach beyond the mundanity and the routine of everyday living and become involved in activities that inspire and provide nourishment for imagination and dreams. In the midst of today's abundant choices, people often make less effort to identify and dedicate time to pursuits that foster inspiration and they resort instead to easier choices and immediate satisfactions. So many mindless distractions make it harder for children to achieve a "rich inner life". School timetables at all educational levels should provide time and resources each week for children to explore learning pursuits they might not otherwise access such as music, sport, and immersion in nature, all of which mitigate stress, instill hope, and help children think good thoughts.

A rich inner life is derived from feeling a part of something larger than oneself. It comes from pausing to reflect on one's own life and participating in activities that challenge, create wonder and cultivate an inner harmony that is a manifestation of psychological health. Time to contemplate one's choices, habits and use of time and energy contributes to an inner life that prioritizes self-improvement. Currently, more than one generation of children has already spent a large share of their life on technology devices, staring passively at screens even while they crave meaningful and rewarding activities that nourish insights and self-awareness. Children who claim to have insufficient leisure time can usually blame their "addictive use of communication devices" and "overly managed lives" that keep them occupied but not motivated or inspired. [14] Bettelheim's work reminds us that what sustains human beings in times of uncertainty, anxiety and stress is a life of

148

meaningful experiences they can build on, positive memories and creative ideas to explore.

Nurturing a "rich inner life" should be an explicit goal of elementary school curriculum (and secondary school curriculum too) that cultivates values that guide and affirm the sanctity of life. Social media and films (often violent and mindless) desensitize children to bullying, brutality and persecution of others. Some parents debate how best to help children develop commitment to humanitarian principles and their relationship with nature. Apathy is easier than commitment, but disengagement with important issues and challenges fosters futility and despair. The obligation to commit to something larger than oneself is understood by adults who have discovered how difficult it is to find hope and fulfillment within a neutral socio-moral environment that makes few demands and offers no promises. Education leaders should concern themselves with the social and moral environment of their schools or their schools will fail. [15]

Moral intelligence

Borba (2001) cited seven essential components of moral intelligence: empathy; conscience; self-control; respect; kindness; tolerance; fairness. [16] Introducing children to these moral concepts is developmentally appropriate for children as early as kindergarten. Moral development in the early years is mainly about following rules, respecting limits, sharing, and taking responsibility for one's behaviours. Young children can learn that being "good" includes knowing the difference between right and wrong, whether or not they can recite the specific rule or anyone is watching.

Daniel Goleman used the term moral intelligence to describe the dimension of human personality that notices how people relate to each other, considers issues that affect humanity in general, and exhibits behaviours that reflect respect for human principles. Kindergartens usually emphasize functional rules such as "put things back where you found them", "wash your hands before you eat" and "tidy up your own messes" but young children also understand more abstract rules such as caring for others including pets and reminding others to be kind. Later on, we want children to understand that being successful in learning and living are mutually interdependent. Timeless rules for children such as share, follow rules, and don't push are no longer sufficient to equip children to sustain the pressures of 21st century life. Sociomoral and character strengths that children need today to feel that life is meaningful, rich and worth living are more complicated. Amid the confusing array of behaviours, attitudes and choices children see around them, it is harder for them to resist empty distractions. This is an essential challenge for education today.

Building Character

In times of relative peace and prosperity such as the period Canada has experienced since WWII, character has been perceived for the most part as relative and abstract. "Character in what context" may be the response to questions about character. Treating character as "relative" makes it difficult to identify the behaviours and human qualities that define it and too subjective to be a goal of education. Entitlements and rights now appear to out-rank the obligations and responsibilities of character, good citizenship, and moral responsibility.

Nonetheless, there remain some prominent thinkers who believe that character-building is and always has been an important component of childrearing and education. They believe children build character when they are faced with adversity of some kind such as the experience of failure, deprivation that they can overcome with effort, and challenges that demand they improve themselves. [17] When we have few expectations of children,

protect them from all risks, and clear a smooth path for them to
follow through life, we interfere with character building. Angela
Duckworth sees habits and character as the same, suggesting that
when children work to acquire good habits, they build character.
[18] This belief is supported by Kronman, "Character is an
ensemble of settled dispositions – of habitual feelings and desires."
[19] Character becomes apparent in the predictability of a person's
behaviours, commitments and attitudes gleaned over a
considerable period of time.

The recent pandemic brought some traditional ways we
used to measure character back to our attention. People became
aware that the power of nature is greater than the ingenuity and
foresight of human beings to stall and control it. The world rallied
for a time around the people who mattered most in the world
during the pandemic – the nurses, physicians, caregivers, and
others who performed essential services in spite of the serious risks
they faced. Character was on daily display in hospitals, grocery
stores and families where people had to care for loved ones and
comfort the dying and bereaved. Out of this tragedy, character
traits we recognized, such as courage, commitment and self-
sacrifice, came into sharp focus in the context of real-life risks
people from all walks of life felt obligated to face, and did so, in
order to help others. Instead of defining character as variable traits
relative to individuals and their context, character was increasingly
demonstrated as an essential core of behaviours that define who
one is – that is, the internal discipline and drive that cause some
people to rise selflessly to the call of duty and persist to the end.
People reflected on the commitment it takes to live according to
one's values and obligations that turned some, especially essential
workers, into beacons of light in a dark time. We should all ask
questions about the conditions and contexts in which these
qualities may best be taught and practised. Answers may include

moral instruction that is personalized, more rigorous parental guidance, and the conduct and commitment of the education system. Education systems should step up.

Components of a new vision for education

A new vision for education should encourage children to consume less and be resourceful instead of anticipating their entitlements in a world of ongoing growth. At a time when security and survival may depend more on sharing and generosity and less on zero-sum attitudes of we-win-you-lose, the education of children should reflect the altered world we now inhabit, its fragility, and our obligation to preserve human life on this planet. A visioning process might predict which collaborative actions, attitudes and skills would encourage generativity instead of consumption, sharing instead of accumulating, and equity rather than oppression. If schools were to prioritize enabling all children to achieve their human potential, society might become more productive and fulfilling for the benefit of everyone. In this revised context, psychological and social health would be viable aspirations and outcomes. Conscientious leaders, teachers, parents, and business and government representatives who participate in a visioning project would be called upon to decide what values should be cultivated in a revised agenda for educating children in the 21st century.

Education needs a vision and a coherent plan that would incorporate relevant values of the past and be proactive and responsive to the realities the globe faces; that is, the vision and plan should venture where no education system has gone before. When the future is unclear and existing accommodations are being severely tested and found wanting, visioning tasks and values clarification become monumental challenges. A visioning process might begin with fundamental truths about the essential conditions for human survival and a world where more people thrive. If we were to translate these conditions into a plan that addresses current challenges, we would likely talk more about releasing human potential, new venues, methods and resources for learning. We would re-think the recruitment, training and certification requirements for teachers, and use formative systems for the assessment and evaluation of children's progress and performance that would inform the next steps in their learning journey.

The psychological, social-emotional and mental health outcomes that a reframed education system would prioritize should not steal time and resources away from curriculum that must also address the intellectual, academic, vocational, and generic skills that are essential to liberating individual potential and high levels of human performance. By teaching subjects in interdisciplinary contexts rather than in subject silos, and integrating social, emotional and moral curriculum into all aspects of schooling, education would emphasize the holistic capabilities of individuals to enhance quality of life for all. Teaching across the curriculum would enable better integration of knowledge, concepts, skills, attitudes, dispositions and performance and more relevant applications of learning to living. Learning outcomes that integrate traditional subjects – language, reading, math, social studies, physical education and health, social and emotional intelligence, music and arts – could be addressed, practised and learned using interdisciplinary and experiential activities such as project-based learning in the classroom and outdoors, in the community and at home. Technologies would be used more judiciously to provide practice opportunities, conduct research, enhance productions, gather and tabulate information, and assist in the generation of solutions, ideas and creative applications.

It is not a huge stretch to envisage, for example: music and movement and physical education that incorporates logical

concepts; science investigations that use math and engage critical
thinking; reading and writing activities in arts, music and social
studies; learning to learn and executive functions that are part of
every project; traditional lessons for teaching essential knowledge;
and community-based learning experiences. The wide expanse of
social and emotional intelligence along with the promotion of
conscience, moral development and character building can and
should be infused into schools and all learning venues and
activities.

6

PHYSICAL LITERACY

**"A stronger adult emerges from a childhood in which the
physical body is immersed in the challenge of nature."**
Richard Louv [1]

Physical literacy involves the ability to move one's body
competently and with confidence and participate actively in the
exercise, physical skills, and sport one enjoys most. As physical
development and movement skills are closely related to cognitive
development and emotional wellbeing, a physical curriculum and
program should be an important mandate of kindergarten and the
primary years. Regular physical programs are instrumental in the
development of healthy habits of exercise, fitness and outlets for
stress and anxiety; they energize, enhance mental alertness, and
motivate. Although parents are usually tuned in to the value of
physical exercise, they might not have made the connection
between physical and cognitive development and children's habits
of mind and dispositions for learning. During a pandemic or other
extended school closures, physical programming for children is an
accessible and enjoyable way for parents to engage their children
in learning activities that are fun, energetic and rich in learning
skills, knowledge and concepts, indoors and outdoors.

The physical fitness of Canadian children has been in sharp
decline for over two decades as childhood routines have changed
dramatically since the turn of the century. Tax incentives intended

to encourage parents to enroll their children in extracurricular
physical programs never compensated for the reduction of school-
based physical education as they largely benefitted families with
the means to support the full costs of participation and did little to
change children's physical outcomes overall. [2]

Physical development supports children's learning in all domains

Young children are physical and sensory beings whose
image of themselves and the world around them comes largely
from their physical and perceptual experience in the concrete
world. Physical development influences development in all other
domains; the child's body, mind and social-emotional wellbeing
are closely intertwined and develop together. In kindergarten,
children learn to execute fundamental physical movements such as
jumping, hopping, throwing a ball without falling, and skipping in
a cross-lateral fashion while they also learn to classify, remember
simple songs, solve puzzles, and recognize numbers and letter
symbols. As they refine their coordination abilities and locomotor
skills, they also recognize words, print their names, speak in full
sentences, and link number symbols to the number of objects being
counted. Skilled movements, such as ability to dodge and
manipulate sticks and bats about ages five and six improve along
with the ability to classify, put things in sequence and seriate, and
understand the constancy of number. The simultaneous
development of cognitive and physical skills supports the viability
of interdisciplinary learning in early childhood.

An indoor and outdoor physical program in kindergarten
would ensure that children practise the skills and behaviours that
contribute to a lifetime of good health, physical fitness and
competence in individual and team sports and facilitate children's
progress in the cognitive, social and emotional domains. Body
awareness (e.g. self-concept), basic fundamental movements (e.g.

marching, jumping, skipping), physical-perceptual skills (e.g. differentiating sounds and moving in time to a rhythm beat), and physical abilities (e.g. balance, agility, strength, endurance) support cognitive skills such as speaking, listening, remembering, "feeling number" and classifying. Children who are slow to use language often speak more fluently in the context of physical activity; they also develop social and emotional competence as they cooperate and coach one another, form teams, and choose partners.

The current reality is that teaching cognitive skills occurs mainly during seatwork or circle activities that leave little time for physical programming let alone activities that promote learning in both domains simultaneously. Physical programs have been threatened or reduced in schools because they were deemed "non-essential" when, in fact, many kindergarten outcomes may be practised effectively through physical programming. indoors and outdoors. Denmark, Sweden, France, and other countries provide physical activities with cognitive components that occur outdoors each day, rain or shine. A few Canadian schools have been mobilizing to do the same.

Activities that promote fundamental movements influence social development as children cooperate, take turns, and motivate each other during games and active play; emotionally, they relieve stress, require practice and persistence, and promote movement while learning. Think of the learning that takes place, for example, when children are challenged to run an obstacle course - they bend, climb, stretch, jump, and roll and build muscles and motor skills. They learn directional prepositions such as around, above, below, estimate space and distance relative to their bodies, attend to the teacher's verbal instructions, and follow pictorial and word signs at each station in the obstacle course.

All kindergarten/primary division teachers should be trained to plan and implement indoor and outdoor physical curriculum that addresses learning outcomes in all domains. Children speak and learn language best in the context of physical activity which means that a physical program is also helpful to children who are learning English or French as a second language. Number concept is experienced physically when a child estimates how many jumps and hops they need to reach the gate. Literacy is stretched when children are asked to move their bodies according to verbal commands or learn a new word for a block structure a child is building when someone says it looks like a "condominium" to me. Language fluency is linked to physical movement and words heard in the context of physical, active experiences are seldom forgotten.

Self-concept is related to children's perception of their physical characteristics that makes them vulnerable to criticisms or mockery of their physical abilities or appearance. A child who is able to move his body skillfully is usually admired by peers, a factor that contributes to a positive sense of self, whereas a child who is overweight may feel self-conscious when he cannot bend and stretch as well as other children. Whether competently executed or not, physical exercise permits emotional release and channels pent-up energy and should always occupy a generous portion of the school day.

Role of teachers and parents

Children who do not master basic movements and cannot keep up with their peers soon lose enthusiasm for physical activity. When a child feels that her body is awkward and does not function as well as that of other children, feelings of inadequacy can lead to withdrawal and shyness. From an early age, children need encouragement to develop physical skills they can be proud of and to accept that there may be some physical skills they cannot perform as well as other children do. They also discover the ways their bodies perform well; for example, children who are wheelchair bound may develop exceptional upper body strength and children with visual impairments sometimes exhibit particularly acute hearing skills. Parents and teachers typically help children accept physical limitations by reinforcing their progress and capability in performing physical skills or tasks that are unaffected by disabilities.

Although children develop physically through casual play indoors and outdoors, they need to attempt and persist with challenges they might not otherwise try. Without regular, school-based physical programs, children who experience space limitations at home and have only irregular access to the outdoors have fewer opportunities to develop a full range of physical skills. Body build, weight and muscular control may also affect a child's ability to meet all physical outcomes equally well; therefore, it is important to emphasize activities they perform well and enhance self-concept and enjoyment of fitness exercise and recreational sports.

Key elements of physical curriculum

Physical education in the kindergarten/primary years should include skills in body awareness; fundamental movements; perceptual skills both sensory-based and cognitive-perceptual, physical abilities, and skilled movements. During these years, social and emotional factors begin to determine the number and nature of the risks a child will take physically and psychologically. Whether the child seeks fulfillment from physical activity and is willing to venture and risk often depends on how she perceives her place within the group, how easily she interacts with others, and the importance she attaches to feedback from peers. Physical growth and development affect children's progress in all domains. When children move efficiently and freely their bodies respond to physical demands, their progress is concrete and directly observable to themselves and others. Satisfaction experienced by performing well physically leads to a general sense of wellbeing, self-worth, and competence. The child's control over his body and senses provides a vehicle for self-expression, an outlet for feelings, a visible sign that he is making progress, and appreciation of the aesthetic quality of well-executed movement.

Body awareness: body image, spatial awareness, laterality, directionality, temporal awareness

Body image

The child is sensitive to his perception of what his body can do, looks like, compares to the bodies of others, and enables him to achieve goals, so acquiring a healthy respect for one's body is essential. *Body science* teaches children to respect all body parts and keep their bodies healthy as they will likely have these body parts all their lives, marvels in medical science notwithstanding. In kindergarten, children learn about hidden internal organs such as the heart, lungs, stomach, and brain and some of their functions. They compare differences in bodily shape, colour, size, strength, height, and weight. One child might wonder why he can't make his ears wiggle, and another might envy the curly red hair of her friend and wonder why she can't have curly red hair too. *Body image* influences children's perceptions of the uniqueness of their own bodies and praise does not compare with the pride a child gains from recognizing firsthand that his arms are stronger than his friend's as he lifts a box his friend can't lift, even though his legs are shorter and he cannot run as fast. Children feel proud of their unique physical achievements that are gained through observation as well as authentic feedback from others at relevant times.

Spatial awareness

Spatial awareness involves ability to move the body in a confined space such as making it smaller to fit the space, and projecting and controlling the body in space by leaping and not bumping into things. The child who masters somersaults learns how much space he needs to do four somersaults in a row before rolling off the grass and onto pavement. Children learn to locate objects in space in relation to themselves and in reference to other objects; for example, a short child stands on a stool to reach the snack plate on the counter. Spatial awareness involves forming mental images of objects in space, remembering the images, following a path in one's mind, and remembering the relationship of objects to one another. How capable are most adults at giving others verbal directions to a familiar place when they have no map in front of them - and even then?

Laterality

Laterality, or sidedness, is an internal awareness of the symmetry of one's body and its quadrants – e.g. left and right sides, above and below the mid-line. Laterality is linked with "coordination" as it involves ability to move each side of the body consecutively - first one side, then the other, and to repeat these movements in smooth succession, that is called *alternating laterality*. Children perform *cross-lateral* movements by moving the left arm and right leg in forward movements and repeating on the other side of the body as in marching, then skipping, usually by age five. Cross-laterality is important in cross-country skiing, dancing, gymnastics, climbing or scaling a wall. The grade one child who has not mastered cross-laterality is unable to run fast, march and skip and when he cannot keep up to his friends, his deficit is visible to all, including himself. He may see himself as clumsy and physically incompetent, a perception that can lead to avoidance of sports and games, not to mention its impact on self-esteem.

Children practise performing one action with one side of the body and a different action with the opposite side as in rubbing the tummy and patting the head, a skill called *integrated laterality*. The child who paints with one hand while guiding the paper with the opposite hand, or executes a smooth throwing pattern which uses each side of the body differently has mastered integrated laterality, a skill that is important for art, sports, games, driving, and needlework.

Directional awareness

Laterality and directionality both relate to *directional awareness,* a sense of the body and its parts and their relationship to objects in space; these skills depend on maturation and experience and are important for games with rules, team activities, reading and writing skills. Directional concepts relate to learning that letters and numbers have their own direction in space such as b,d,p,q. 6.9.7. Ability to recognize the correct directional configuration of symbols can be improved by practising laterality and directionality activities that may help children overcome reading difficulties that are perceptual in origin.

Temporal awareness

Eye-hand and *eye-foot coordination* involve ability to link sensory messages, timing and body movements in order to execute an accurate, smooth motion. The development of *temporal awareness* is related to concepts of space, direction, laterality, and timing in the context of movement. Music and movement activities are especially helpful practice for timing and movement coordination. Physical programs should always take advantage of music to help children learn to move in rhythmic patterns, observe musical stop and go signals and musical directional signals.

Basic Fundamental Movements

locomotor skills; non-locomotor skills; manipulative abilities; fine
motor skills

Basic fundamental movements are prerequisites for skilled
movements that involve complex combinations of fundamental
movements. Children learn these skills in much the same way they
build the mental structures necessary for learning logical-
mathematical concepts. The interrelationship of physical and
cognitive abilities means that, whenever possible, activities should
combine cognitive and physical skills as in moving to musical
commands. Children who do not acquire fundamental movements
in early childhood find it harder to learn skilled movements later
on; therefore, physical curriculum should introduce basic
movements in an order and at a pace that works for the individual
child.

It is risky to involve children too early in contact sports
such as hockey and soccer that require performance of skilled
movements until they have mastered the fundamental movements;
otherwise, children risk overextending their muscles and bone
structure, and acquiring incorrect skilled movement patterns.
Trying out for team sports before they have mastered fundamental
movements may jeopardize children's chances to fully participate
in sports, games, and precision activities later. Primary school
physical programs should aim for children's mastery of
fundamental movements in preparation for learning and using
skilled movements. There are always exceptions to a
developmental timetable for learning these skills; some children
acquire them seemingly effortlessly and at an early age. Children
usually master fundamental movements when they have access to

regular practice opportunities while their bodies are naturally supple and motivation to be active is at its highest.

Locomotor skills

Walking; running; jumping; hopping; galloping; marching; skipping; climbing

Locomotion involves projecting the body into space and includes walking, running, jumping, hopping, galloping, marching, skipping, and climbing, in which children cover a space from point A to point B. From age three, children develop mature walking patterns, coordinating their legs, trunks and arms and eventually march to a rhythm beat and music. *Running* is a motor progression of walking in which, at the mature stage, the arms move in opposition to the legs, the body is in full flight with feet leaving the ground for an instant, while the length of the stride increases. Mature running involves moving in a straight line, changing direction quickly to dodge and stop, racing, running on different surfaces, and running to imitate others and animals.

Jumping is a two-foot take-off from a squat with arms forward to back and a spring up and landing on two feet. It is the first stage in a motor progression that includes *hopping* (one- or two-foot take-off), *leaping* (a long running stride from a standing position), and *galloping* (a leap and a hop with one foot taking off in a leap and the other hopping with the body weight remaining on the same side). As children learn to shift body weight from side to side, they *march* with the right leg and left arm moving in a *cross-lateral* pattern. The next stage in the progression is *skipping,* which is a step, then a hop on the same foot, with arms swinging in opposition in a cross-lateral pattern and the body shifting weight from side to side. Mastery of these locomotor skills prepares children for sports and performance-based skills (martial arts,

dance, and games) that may begin about age six. Although many
adults believe that locomotor skills come naturally to most
children, I was always surprised to find so many students who, in
their late teens and twenties, were unable to perform fundamental
movements such as galloping, skipping, catching and balancing,
even dancing.

Climbing is a locomotor movement whereby the body
weight is pulled by the limbs, usually with the arms and legs
working together, first using one side to pull the body against
gravity, then using the other side, in an alternating fashion. The
upper and lower parts of the body may be used simultaneously, or
in an alternating sequence, depending on the terrain or the object
being climbed like a ladder or mounting a pole. Climbing requires
confidence in one's judgment and physical prowess, trust in the
teacher and oneself, and courage to face fear of heights and falling.
Chances to practise these emotional skills – self-confidence, trust
and courage - enhance self-esteem because of the satisfaction the
child feels for having met a significant physical challenge.

Non-locomotor skills

swaying; curling; stretching; twisting; twirling; swinging; lifting;
reaching; pushing

Non-locomotor movements are *axial* such as *swaying,
curling, stretching, twisting, twirling, swinging, lifting, reaching,*
and *pushing* while the body remains largely in one spot. These
movements are also components of skilled activities and sports,
such as soccer and basketball, in which the common element is
stability, the ability to maintain one's relationship to the force of
gravity. Combining non-locomotor skills with fitness exercises
helps develop physical abilities as well as rhythmic movements to
music.

Manipulative skills

propulsive: rolling; throwing; kicking; punting; striking; bouncing; volleying

absorptive: catching; trapping; ball handling; stick handling

Gross motor (large muscle) manipulative movements refer to contact with bats, balls, racquets, and hockey sticks that require stability, strength and the ability to move the body in space. *Propulsive actions* give force to objects and *absorptive actions* receive force from the objects. Mature manipulative abilities involve combinations of movement and require time and practice to execute proficiently. Engaging children in playing with balls is especially valuable throughout childhood, first by rolling large and medium-sized balls and eventually tossing gently and then throwing smaller, denser balls. Practice and individual coaching help children progress beyond the initial stages. Ball throwing and catching also exercise *eye-hand coordination, ocular-motor skills, directionality, spatial awareness; fine motor skills, locomotor* and *non-locomotor* skills; and physical abilities such as *agility* and *flexibility*.

Fine motor skills

eye-hand coordination; hand control; pincer movements of thumb and index finger; finger dexterity; grasping; tracing; crushing; arranging objects; shaping and folding; filling and pouring; bending and folding; juggling

Fine motor abilities use the smaller muscles of the body, often in combination with hand-eye-foot coordination and with *gross motor* (large muscle) movements. Fine motor skills are important for drawing, painting, printing, and writing that also facilitate academic and sport-related skills. Children fine-tune their

fine motor skills in finger plays, puzzles, and table-top block play
and as they fasten buttons and zippers. A favourite activity for
developing eye-hand coordination has always been "colouring
inside the lines" but there are more creative activities for
developing fine motor skills that also allow for artistic self-
expression such as free-hand drawing and stringing beads in
various self-repeating patterns.

Sensory-Perceptual and Cognitive-Perceptual Abilities

visual perception; auditory perception; haptic, gustatory, and
olfactory perception; spatial awareness and kinesthetic
discrimination

As young children learn through their senses, their
competence depends on the acuity (accuracy) and physical
responsiveness and processing of the messages received through
their senses. Physical and cognitive behaviours are stimulated by
sensory input and *sensation* (ability of the sensory receptors to
accurately detect a stimulus in the environment) and *cognitive
perceptual skills* such as organizing, interpreting and processing
physical sensations accurately. Cognitive perceptual processes
include detecting the direction a sound is coming from or
understanding or interpreting the meaning of a signal they hear but
cannot see. Sensory-motor competence refers to processing
information or directions coming into the central nervous system
through the senses and making appropriate motor responses. Many
of these skills are addressed during outdoor play.

Physical programs that emphasize perceptual skills are
especially important for kindergarten children with perceptual
delays or deficits that may be preventing them from making
progress in letter and number recognition and later on in reading
and writing. Children who suffer delays or malfunctions in

sensory perception or sensory-motor competence may also
progress more slowly in language development and
communication skills that sometimes signal perceptual delays.
Many of these early problems are quite amenable to practice and
small interventions can make a big difference when they are started
early. Children with speech and perceptual acuity delays should be
assessed by a qualified health professional. When a teacher
suspects a perceptual delay, often the sustained attention of the
teacher, parent or assistant who works with the child and provides
additional practice activities may be sufficient to help the child
overcome the delay without further significant intervention; these
activities should be guided by a KIEP. Kindergarten/primary
teachers should all be trained to design and implement a KIEP and
observe and assess children regularly. Physical and perceptual
delays and deficits are harder to overcome as the child matures
which makes it essential that they be identified and addressed
before she starts to experience reading difficulties that influence
other learning and dispositions for learning.

Teachers should understand the discrete skills that
comprise *visual* and *auditory* perception and processing in order to
match play activities to individual needs for sensory-perceptual
and cognitive-perceptual development. A KIEP for all children
ensures that delays or deficits are noted early so that remedial help
and additional practice can begin right away. A child who fails to
respond to the plan and practice activities contained in a KIEP
should be referred to a health care specialist to ensure that delays
or deficits are addressed before they impact overall development,
learning and wellbeing.

Visual perception

form discrimination; depth perception; figure-ground perception;
ocular-motor skills, such as accommodation, fixation, pursuit,

tracking

Vision is the dominant sensory system in most humans and develops rapidly from three to five years of age. *Visual perception* refers to the accuracy of messages children receive via the eyes which affect pre-reading skills. Nearly all visual-perceptual skills are learned more readily when they are practised during outdoor activities. As with auditory skills, visual skills involve both the accuracy with which the child receives the sensory image (vision) and his ability to process (i.e. respond appropriately) to the message received

Form discrimination

Form discrimination is the ability to detect differences in basic form (shapes, forms, symbols), to see straight, curved or dotted lines, and to detect size differences, all of which develop as the sensory receptors (eyes, ears) mature. Children gradually recognize similarities and differences in one- and two-dimensional form and shape in the everyday environment, such as a clock or TV screen, and shape symbols such as a stop sign and a yield sign. As children perceive colour earlier than form, colour is often used to help children recognize one characteristic of a form at a time. The ability to recognize shapes also depends on perceiving the constancy of shape; that is, circles, squares and triangles belong to those shape categories regardless of their size, colour, texture, medium, or the perspective from which they are viewed. Form discrimination is an early step in children's recognition of same-different and matching which makes it both a cognitive-perceptual ability and a physical-perceptual skill.

Depth perception

Depth perception is the ability to judge relative distances in three-dimensional space when children are jumping, bowling, target tossing, walking a balance beam, and climbing. Depth perception has important links to child safety as it affects the child's judgment when deciding whether to jump from the climber to the ground, or how high to hold the milk jug when pouring into a tumbler. The ability to judge depth and respond accordingly also makes depth perception both a sensory-perceptual and cognitive-perceptual skill.

Figure-ground perception

Figure-ground perception is the visual ability to select a limited number of stimuli (figure) from a visual field or ground even when the figure and the field keep changing. The stimuli selected by the child become the figure, such as picking out the small mouse on the busy page. The remaining detail on the page is the background or the field. The child's ability to look at only one part of a scene or a field and ignore the other parts is essential for reading as the child needs to focus on the words on a line and not the lines above and below. Children's figure-ground perception is honed by activity books such as "Where's Waldo" and the Richard Scarry books. [3] Children use this skill when they try to find a special friend in a busy playground or mommy in a department store. When children are developing figure-ground perception, it is wise to limit the number of stimuli in the background and add them only gradually. Children should initially focus on the selected stimuli, move their eyes through the visual field, and locate objects on command that are in the field of vision.

Ocular-motor skills: accommodation; fixation; pursuit; tracking

Ocular-motor skills refer to the movement of the eyes which should work together and be constantly matched and balanced. Eye movement control is another prerequisite for reading and children need practice with activities that challenge their eye movements.

Accommodation or near-far focusing adjustment is the ability of the eye to make adjustments in order to focus on objects at a distance and then objects close at hand. Problems with accommodation can be detected by watching the child's pupils closely. The pupils should enlarge as she focuses on the distant object and smaller when focusing on the near object. Excessive blinking and jerking of the head are clues that a child may be having difficulty adjusting her focus. One-on-one practice with a teacher or parent may help the child overcome accommodation difficulties. Playing catch with a ball or beanbag are playful ways outdoors to practise near-far focusing adjustment.

Fixation is the ability of both eyes to look simultaneously and accurately from one target to another and to control eye movements by holding eyes steadily on a figure until the child is ready to move on. Children who have fixation difficulties have darting eyes that cannot rest on a figure long enough to collect the needed information. The child who experiences immature fixation moves his head to make the eyes move to each object in the field and back again. The child should be able to move his eyes without moving his head as each figure is called and hold his eyes steadily on the figure until the next figure is called. Outdoor target toss, T-ball and playing catch help children with fixation skills.

Pursuit is the ability of the eyes to follow a moving target without moving the head. At three years, the child is likely to move her head; at four, the child begins with practice to follow the target without moving the head, and at five she can usually pursue a moving object with the eyes only. Taking children to watch the airplanes landing and taking off, playing catch, and following birds, butterflies and clouds in the sky are outdoor ways to practise this skill. Playing catch with a child is a particularly fruitful activity that addresses many perceptual and fine-motor skills.

Tracking is the ability of the eyes to make a series of
saccades, or long sweeps, smoothly across a page, board or screen
with the eyes moving slowly or quickly as needed and back again.
Children practise this skill when they look at picture books and
posters, scan a page to find an object, and play *connect the dot*
activities.

In helping children develop visual-perceptual skills, the
usefulness of computer software should not be underestimated.
Video games and educational software suitable for young children
are widely available but should never replace play activities in the
concrete world. Well-chosen computer activities can reinforce the
skills children acquire through play with puzzles and games. The
variety and rapid change that screens can deliver makes the
computer a powerful tool for practising perceptual acuity and
processing skills.

Auditory perception: listening; auditory discrimination; auditory-
motor integration

Auditory perception refers to the accuracy (acuity) of
messages children receive via the ears and includes skills such as
hearing sounds (listening), selecting and labeling one sound from a
field of sounds (auditory discrimination), and moving to sound
cues (auditory-motor integration). When children attend to verbal
directions, move to music, and physically interpret various sounds
through movement to music, they develop auditory perceptual
skills.

Listening: identify sounds; be aware of sound sources;
follow the direction from which sound comes; respond to auditory
instructions; discriminate between auditory cues; respond
efficiently to auditory cues

Listening ability plays a crucial role in learning at all ages; it involves the ability to hear (acuity) messages and the cognitive ability to understand, attend to and respond to what is heard. The cognitive and physical components of listening are mutually interdependent as they are with visual perception. Listening includes the ability to identify sounds and be aware of sound sources (what is making the sound). Children should identify the direction from which sounds are coming and follow the direction to find the source of the sound. Indoor and outdoor activities require children to follow sounds and find an object and include "find the ticking clock", "say after me" and statue games. "Simon Says" provides practice responding to auditory commands. Musical games that link the sound of an instrument to a specific movement, such as stomp to the sound of the drum, spin to the harmonica's sound and jump to the sound of the piano help children recognize auditory cues and link the verbal command and action to each sound cue. These skills also involve both the perceptual acuity and processing skills.

Auditory discrimination

Auditory discrimination is the ability to hear differences and similarities in sounds and tones and to detect one specific tonal quality and frequency within a complex mix of sound stimuli (auditory field). Identifying specific instruments within an orchestral piece is an auditory discrimination task. Familiar recordings such as "Peter and the Wolf" provide practice linking the sound of the instrument to the character in the story. [4] *Auditory rhythm* involves being able to repeat a regulated series of sounds interspersed by regulated moments of silence. Activities such as clapping in unison with the group, or "clap the beat after me" provide practice in both the sensory-perceptual and cognitive processing skills.

Auditory-motor integration

Auditory-motor integration is the ability to move the body
according to sounds on command of the auditory stimulus. A sense
of timing, hearing acuity and linking verbal commands to motor
activities are involved. Tape-recorded stories, musical instruments
and games with musical cues promote development of these skills.
Children who can execute basic fundamental movements but are
unable to integrate their movements with verbal or auditory cues
require individual attention and planned practice opportunities.
Teachers and parents should speak slowly and distinctly to
children at their levels and in a natural rather than a heightened
volume that may distort what is said and confuse the child.
Children should be able to see the adult's lips moving while she is
speaking and maintain eye contact.

Olfactory, gustatory, and haptic perception

Olfactory (sense of smell), *gustatory* (sense of taste) and
haptic (sense of touch) perception develops along with visual and
auditory abilities during early childhood. Their development
follows a pattern similar to vision and hearing. Children first
identify simple cues (i.e. activities that ask children to identify a
specific taste or flavour) and discriminate simple cues within a
more complex field. Later, children may be asked to rank flavours
in a range from sour to sweet, or textures from soft to rough. This
task asks children to classify (sort) sensory cues according to their
specific characteristics, sequence (put in graduated order) and
sensory cues according to their level of intensity, e.g. from loudest
to quietest.

Spatial awareness and kinesthetic discrimination

Spatial awareness is the ability to perceive one's own body
in relation to the surrounding environment. It is linked to sensory-

perceptual skills, body awareness and directionality but also involves depth perception, estimating distance of self from objects in the environment, and the relationship between one's body and the surrounding space – for example, how to stop before hitting the boards when skating. Spatial skills involve making one's body adjust to space in the environment by turning, dodging, stopping, crouching, balancing, and slowing down or speeding up. These skills are essential for playing tag, soccer, baseball, and many other games.

Kinesthetic discrimination refers to awareness of speed in relation to distance, mainly reducing speed as one approaches barriers or to stop or increase speed in order to win or escape. These skills are prominent in individual and team sports such as hockey, track and field and basketball and are practised in races and relays, musical chairs, tag, and statue games.

Physical Abilities

physical fitness: muscular strength; muscular endurance; flexibility; cardio-vascular endurance; circulatory-respiratory endurance

motor fitness: static and dynamic balance; coordination; speed; agility; power

Physical abilities refer to physical and motor fitness that affect coordination, endurance, and the smooth execution of skills. Many children today have an indoor lifestyle; therefore, they may have little or no regular, spontaneous contact with the natural world to build physical abilities casually in their outdoor play nor freedom to roam the outdoor environment. Safety concerns are the reasons parents often give for children's indoor lifestyles. [5]

Along with lifestyle constraints, there is an alarming

increase in obesity rates, mental illness and early onset of adult diseases in childhood; these are serious safety and health concerns that should be factored into decisions about children's access to outdoor play and regular physical programs in schools. [6] Poor diet, parents' busy lives, too much screen-time, and fewer opportunities for outdoor play are among the causes of the ongoing decline in children's fitness and health.

Physical fitness: muscular strength; muscular endurance; flexibility; cardio-vascular endurance; circulatory-respiratory endurance

Muscular strength

Muscular strength is being able to exert a maximum effort and force against an object external to the body as in swinging on monkey bars, tug-of-war, and climbing a rope. Girls and boys gain from programs that build muscular strength. Intensive training for sports, especially those involving bodily contact, is not recommended while children's bones and muscles are forming.

Muscular endurance

Muscular endurance is being able to perform a movement task over an extended period of time as in skipping rope and push-ups several times in succession. Children who engage in active physical play for sustained periods every day usually acquire muscular endurance without adding activities that specifically target endurance.

Flexibility

Flexibility refers to the ability to move limbs through a full range of motion using the joints – shoulder, knee, elbow, wrist. It is necessary for successful performance in swimming, gymnastics, and ballet. As flexibility requires regular exercise and decreases

with age, specific activities that promote flexibility are an
important component of physical programs for children who start
out naturally flexible. The emphasis is always on maintaining and
retaining one's flexibility.

Cardio-vascular endurance

Cardio-vascular endurance is an aspect of muscular
endurance related to the heart, lungs and blood vessels; it involves
ability to perform numerous repetitions of a stressful activity such
as running on the spot, shoveling snow, or skipping rope that put
pressure on the circulatory and respiratory systems. Aerobic
capacity develops early in life and depends on individual
tendencies toward either an active or a sedentary lifestyle. Children
who spend most of their days indoors do not have sufficient
opportunity to develop their aerobic capacity during play and
benefit from planned fitness activities that are part of a daily
physical program. Health and fitness education for young children
should make their hearts work hard for a while to exercise the
vascular system.

Motor fitness: balance - static and dynamic; coordination; agility;
force of movement: speed, power, stability

Motor fitness influences the control and force of movement
and includes control factors such as *static* and *dynamic balance*
and coordination. Force of movement factors such as *speed, agility*
and *power* are more relevant for children six to eight years.

Balance - static and dynamic balance

Balance is so important to overall functioning in daily life
that it should be a significant component of physical education
from preschool on. Balance is influenced by the inner ear, vision,
and the muscles of the body that control posture and stability.

Riding on a wheeled vehicle requires the balance needed to sit on a
tricycle with pedals, steer the vehicle with the hands and use the
legs to push pedals and move forward without falling over.
Children are generally able to ride a tricycle successfully at three
years; at four and five years, they begin to ride two-wheeled
bicycles that involves practice using the body for different actions
above and below the body's mid-line. Learning to skate at ages
three and four is a useful activity for developing balance and
usually begins by holding onto a chair or prop that may be
discarded quickly once children get the feel of the ice under them.

Static balance is the ability to maintain equilibrium while
motionless and is influenced by the child's ability to "right
himself" as he spins around. Activities that call for quick turns,
swaying, standing on one foot, and spinning should be part of the
physical curriculum. *Dynamic balance* involves being able to
maintain equilibrium while moving as in hopping, bouncing,
skating, dodging, skipping, and riding a bicycle. Balance beams
ensure that children practise dynamic balance moving forward,
backward, and sideways, in a heel-to-toe fashion.

Coordination

Coordination is the ability to integrate smoothly all motor
systems and sensory-perceptual abilities and move efficiently. It
involves streamlining the movements of body parts and is linked
with balance, speed, and agility. Rhythmic, synchronous
movement in a timely sequenced pattern relies on coordinated
movements of the eyes and hands, eyes and feet, head, and trunk.
Physical programs that include balance, speed and agility goals
help children become well-coordinated.

Speed

Speed is acquired through practice running, skating, and

skipping to promote strength, endurance, balance, and muscular
control. Reaction time, or the time it takes for a child's body to
respond to a "go" signal, is an important factor in speed.

Agility and Power

Agility is efficient movement of the body through space as
fast as possible while changing direction quickly to execute
dodges, stops and turns - movements that are important
prerequisites for sports. Agility activities challenge children to
make quick changes to their body height, change direction, and
adjust the force with which they propel themselves forward. *Power*
refers to a combination of the speed with which the muscles
contract and is sometimes called "explosive strength" or the ability
to perform a maximum effort in a short time. Games such as
baseball - throwing, batting, quick takeoff from standing or
squatting; hockey, and track and field call for a sudden burst of
power to facilitate the ability to cover distance quickly.

Stability involves the ability to right oneself against a force
of movement when the body is placed in various positions. It
allows the body to compensate rapidly and accurately for changes
in balance and to stabilize oneself in relation to the force of gravity
by altering the movements of the body. Stability is required in
racquet sports such as tennis and badminton, volleyball, contact
sports such as hockey, and for skating and dancing.

Skilled Movements

Young children who have access to planned physical
programs typically acquire enough confidence and body awareness
to take minor risks, pursue challenges, and achieve their own
objectives. By age six or seven, those who have played actively
indoors and outdoors have usually acquired the skilled movements
they need for non-contact sports such as skating and gymnastics.

They are also more likely to have the confidence to pursue dancing and swimming lessons, play gently competitive games and practise skilled movements related to team sports such as soccer and baseball. Kindergarten should focus on the fundamental skills that prepare children for skilled movements in the primary years. Some children may be ready for advanced skilled movements in grade one such as jumping on trampolines and maintaining balance, but care should be taken to ensure they are physically prepared. Throwing a ball with wrist and finger release, hitting a ball with a bat, and playing modified versions of T-ball and soccer are useful ways to begin to play team sports and games with rules.

<u>Healthy Habits and Attitudes</u>

Children need to play outdoors

Decades ago, children played outdoors during much of their out-of-school hours, in all seasons, and developed strong bodies without significant intervention. Things have changed dramatically in recent years. Children who play outside alone or with others are usually more physically active than those who are constantly supervised. Children today do not spend much time outdoors and, when they do, their freedom to play vigorously and take mild risks is often curtailed by the supervising adults who have overly-protective fears for their safety. Regular school-based physical programs helps to address children's need for vigorous outdoor activity that stretches their bodies and minds while, at the same time, "teaching the way children learn".

In addition to building strong bodies and healthy minds, active play in childhood is insurance against many health problems that arise in adult life. More children today than in previous generations show evidence of diseases that normally afflict adults such as heart disease, high blood pressure, and Type 2 diabetes which is related to obesity. Factors like these may contribute to risks that today's children face that their lifespans might be shorter than those of their parents. An organized, daily, health and physical curriculum throughout the elementary school years is essential.

Canada currently lags behind other nations in the attention paid to promoting and facilitating healthy activity levels for children. Only seven percent of 5 to 11-year-olds meet the recommended guidelines of 60 minutes of moderate to vigorous activity daily. [7] The World Health Organization stated that 80% of young people are not getting enough exercise. Children's indoor lifestyles, too much time spent looking at screens, the elimination or reduction of physical education programs in schools, and fewer children who walk to school are identified as factors. [8] Intervention in children's physical development is an urgent issue and another reason for parents to act together to insist that schools include regular, planned physical programs in the elementary school curriculum. To achieve this goal, teachers should be trained to plan and implement physical education programs in elementary schools as part of their pre-service training and certification requirements.

Issues in the physical development and education of children

Children's safety is not the only concern

School boards and schools have made it a priority to respond to parental concerns about child safety and they fear litigation whenever a child has an accident. This fear has led to policies and practices that have increasingly limited children's freedom to engage in healthy, active play. [9] Some schools removed slides, trees, bushes, and natural areas from playgrounds to improve visibility over children's play, banished play with balls,

and shortened recess and lunch periods to keep children safe
indoors. Some communities adopted policies to prohibit
tobogganing and require that skating rinks be open to children only
when they are supervised by an adult. No one argues that children
need secure environments, but realistic measures in playgrounds
that meet safety standards can still offer choices that do not stifle
children's physical activity, inhibit their access to outdoor play,
avoid moderate risk-taking, and derail the development of healthy
bodies and minds.

A significant impetus for outdoor play and contact with
nature was motivated by the book *Last Child in the Woods: Saving
our Children from Nature-Deficit Disorder (2008)* by Richard
Louv who coined the term "nature deficit disorder".[10] This
seminal book attracted attention to the physical, spiritual and
health benefits of children's contact with nature and revealed that
children who play regularly in "green" outdoor environments, even
in inclement weather, have better motor coordination, and ability
to concentrate, as well as greater respect for nature. Better vision
may also be attributed to playing outdoors, as daylight is good for
the eyesight. Natural play space outdoors engages children's
imagination and creativity and encourages them to take mild
physical risks that ultimately make them stronger and better able to
recognize and resist real danger.

Regular contact with nature and physical exercise improve
children's mental health

A devastating effect of inactivity in childhood is its impact
on children's mental health that includes a significant increase in
anxiety as early as kindergarten. Children who are encouraged to
be irrationally cautious and avoid all risk tend to view the world as
a fearsome place. Regular physical activity changes moods, boosts
energy, and enhances self-concept. It keeps emotions in check and

diverts energy from repetitive, unhealthy mental patterns that dig deep into the psyche. Increasing evidence of mental illness in young children is like the canary in the coal mine; it is a sign that something present, absent or both in our social milieu are toxic to health, peace of mind and motivation. They subtract from children's natural ability to meet physical challenges, take risks, and achieve physical goals. These warning signs lend urgency to the need for daily, planned physical programs and physical curriculum in schools.

There are also concerns about the extent to which children are prescribed powerful drugs to manage emotions and behaviours so children can "fit" school environments. It should be the other way around; schools should fit the natures, health needs and best interests of children. The primary years are a time to establish healthy habits and attitudes that promote respect for one's body, teach children why they should avoid toxic agents and make connections between healthy food, exercise, outdoor play, and mental health.

Physical development is a kindergarten/primary curriculum priority

Physical exercise, movement activities, games and sports contribute to children's ability to attend to the task at hand and stay at an activity for a sustained period. Being able to move with grace and precision and experience the satisfaction of mastering complex physical skills add zest to life for children just as they do for adults. For all ages, physical activity elevates mood, induces a positive mindset, supports optimism, and improves resilience. As children's early development in all domains are intertwined, physical development outcomes should be treated as equally important to outcomes in all other areas of curriculum.

It is a concern, therefore, to observe the experiments in some schools to create 'outdoor learning classrooms' that resemble the indoor classroom by creating seating areas, tables and partially-enclosed spaces outdoors, especially those that expect children to sit and listen much of the day. This is another example of a good idea in education, i.e. outdoor learning, that would be derailed unless principals and teachers understand that healthy outdoor venues for learning should provide opportunities for children to learn differently than in classrooms. Until children are trusted to learn and be active at the same time, 'outdoor learning' policies and practices may imply 'outdoor classrooms' and become another passing fad that claims to be 'real change'. It might disrupt conventional classroom-based learning for a while, raise hopes and add cost but little value.

The planned physical program should be scheduled for a time of day that children can anticipate eagerly; it can be effective at the beginning or the end of the school day as children arrive for school, or prepare to leave for home, or in the middle of the day. Assessment becomes easier when children are guided at certain times toward specific physical activities so that the teacher knows immediately what she is observing and is better able to note children's participation and progress. ECEs and education assistants are often eager to lead physical activities and coach or intervene to assist a child. Physical programming and leadership should be a curriculum and practicum requirement in all ECE training programs.

Physical programs in Canadian schools are subject to weather conditions that often make it necessary to move physical activities indoors in extreme cold, heat or precipitation. French kindergartens (the ecoles maternelles) solved this problem by designating a classroom, a wide hallway or foyer for the physical program when outdoor space or a gymnasium was unavailable.

Their programs are about an hour a day in length and combine physical and cognitive learning tasks and plenty of social interaction. The programs are taught by the classroom teachers who are trained to teach the physical programs using indirect and direct teaching methods. [11]

Gender differences

The physically competent girl and boy are more likely to enter middle childhood with greater resilience and ability to deal with failure, lose gracefully, and be a team player. Girls and boys who play easily together during the kindergarten/primary years learn about each other in ways that make it more likely they will continue to be at ease in mixed company. Boys who learn early that it is okay to welcome girls' participation in their activities are more likely to respect girls' strengths and appreciate the ideas that girls bring. Girls learn to challenge boys' exuberance and believe that they are equal though different. These early mixed-gender physical programs go a long way toward enhancing respect and enjoyment of each other's companionship in gender-neutral activities.

Teaching and the Physical Curriculum

Physical education training should be a core feature of teacher preparation programs at the faculties of education. Literacy (reading and writing), and technological literacy have been hard-wired into school curriculum and teacher training programs evolved accordingly. The urgent need now to restore a serious physical curriculum for the primary division (and throughout elementary school) should significantly change the duration, curriculum and learning outcomes of teacher training. Parents have hitherto borne much of the criticism for children's indoor, inactive lifestyles, but the education systems are also to blame. Adding a rigorous, daily physical curriculum to the primary grades (K to 3) would offer lifelong benefits for children. To optimize the investment of time and resources for regular physical programs, primary teachers should all be trained to plan activities and implement physical curriculum just as they are also trained to plan and implement KIEPs

Implementing a physical curriculum requires planning that accounts for individual differences and disabilities, and introduces new physical challenges when children are ready. Parents should advocate for a physical curriculum and reinforce teachers' efforts and successes with their children. No one expects teachers to teach everything equally well, but many teachers, myself included, have been surprised by our own progress when we have risked teaching physical education (with only self-training) that combines physical activities with practising literacy and number skills and problem solving at the same time. When teachers take the risk and overcome some reluctance, the regular physical program often provides a break in the day and results in fun and growth for children and teachers alike.

School systems are misguided if they believe that physical programs rob the academic curriculum of precious learning time as the physical curriculum also facilitates cognitive and affective learning. Continuing to deprive young children of their native right to be active much of the day is a throwback to a time when educators believed that primary schooling should contain children's robust energy, encourage passive behaviours, and teach them the 'lessons' of physical restraint and self-control. Physical activities are, in fact, a powerful medium for enhancing all learning.

Pedagogy for physical curriculum

Direct and *indirect teaching methods* are options for implementing physical curriculum. In kindergarten, indirect methods work well when children are playing a game, exploring equipment such as climbers or balance beams and having fun with materials such as bean bags, beach balls, or hoops. Direct teaching methods are teacher-centred and focus on guiding children through a series of exercises to practise skills such as learning physical fitness techniques or teaching children the various moves in a sport. Indirect teaching methods usually require setting up the environment for play and allowing children to explore the equipment, materials and other resources. While groups of children play freely, the teacher is freed to provide individual support and coaching to a child, or observe and record children's engagement with the equipment. In these roles, the teacher is alternately a planner, leader, coach, instructor, and observer of children's progress. These roles may be daunting at first, but like most learning, the results are satisfying, and the teaching experience becomes familiar and natural and adds fun and value for teachers and children alike.

Physical curriculum and project learning

Projects such as planning a parade with costumes and musical instruments or building a path through the woods include many physical abilities, perceptual and motor skills, as well as cognitive and social-emotional skills. Projects provide an interdisciplinary pathway to learning skills in all domains. A creative challenge in teaching is to generate ideas for projects that address children's expressed interests or introduce something novel to tackle over an extended period that combines aspects of several curriculum areas. For example, reading and writing practice may be needed to make the signs and symbols for large

murals. Physical and cognitive skills such as stretching and
bending to measure and estimating and predicting whether plans
and resources will fit the available space are natural components of
gardening, construction and woodworking projects.

Transformative change is needed

It has been four decades since research in education
confirmed the close relationship between physical and cognitive
development and the positive impact of physical exercise on
learning. In the intervening years, school intramural sports
activities have been reduced or eliminated and physical activity has
been limited to recess times that are often controlled and short.
Children's overall health has deteriorated and obesity and adult
chronic diseases are appearing in childhood.[12] For how much
longer will public education that is mandated to serve children's
best interests, and governments that are mandated to serve the
society they represent, continue to ignore evidence that the system
no longer meets children's needs nor those of our society.
Transformative change demands that education systems emphasize
children's development of their physical potential and acquire
dispositions, habits and skills that would enable them to learn and
perform effectively throughout their lives. A physical curriculum is
central to curriculum redesign and education reform for the
primary years. What is needed is vision and the will to change
course now before it is too late for another generation of children.

7

LANGUAGE AND LITERACY

**"More than the foundation for school success, fundamental
literacy is critical for full democratic participation and the
exercise of other fundamental rights."** Julia O'Sullivan, 2020.
[1]

Literacy involves reading and understanding written
materials and an ability to speak and write with sufficient fluency
to enable full participation in society and enhance one's potential
for lifelong learning. Literacy skills start from an ability to decode
written words to understanding sentences, then to comprehending,
interpreting and evaluating complex texts later on. Becoming a
literate person takes place over time with appropriate role models,
practice and the motivation to read, speak and write proficiently.
The early development of literacy skills is an important mandate of
the kindergarten and one that resonates well with parents.
Kindergartens generally focus on the language arts of *listening,
speaking, recognizing and forming letters* that prepare children for
reading and writing instruction in grade one.

Language and literacy used to be the "crown jewel" of
schooling and people's main claims to being "educated". The
ability to speak fluently, convey complex thoughts in complete
sentences and read comprehensively were markers of one's
educational status and social class. Literacy was the prized
outcome of a sound education. The fluency, clarity and accuracy
with which human beings communicate and receive information
have always influenced progress in school and one's capacity for
lifelong learning. Clear verbal expression of ideas and information
that is persuasive, timely and reflective, using language that is
understood and relevant to one's audience, continue to be human
assets but many expectations of spoken and written language have
changed. To be deemed literate today depends on the acquisition of
communication skills at better than functional or basic levels.

In recent years, the term *literacy* has been expanded to
define competence in other endeavours that are also deemed to be
respectable measures of educational status. Numeracy (e.g. to work
successfully with numbers, formulas and models to gather data,
analyze and reach conclusions based on evidence), technological
literacy (e.g. use of computers and other devices as tools for
design, writing, storing information and problem solving), musical
literacy (e.g. recognize, remember and replicate notes, pitch,
rhythm and melody), physical literacy (e.g. use the body
competently in all its potential functions) and cultural literacy (e.g.
awareness and knowledge of one's own and other cultures), are all
deemed to be viable literacies for today. Language literacy has
long been considered the standard for children's performance in
school, perhaps because the fluency, clarity, and accuracy with
which human beings communicate, influence our capacity for all
learning and what matters most to us in life. Literacy in the 21st
century enables us to be "attentive to addressing important social
issues and being alert to the responsibility of deepening and

expanding the meaning and practice of a vibrant democracy". [2]

Current student literacy rankings in Canada and their impact

The 2018 results of the standardized international tests of student performance conducted by the Organization for Economic and Cultural Development (OECD) in language literacy demonstrated that our students were performing well relative to other nations. Overall, Canadian students ranked seventh in the world, with Alberta, Ontario and Quebec ranked first, second and third among the Canadian scores. The Canadian Council of Ministers of Education (CMEC) [3] concluded that greater focus should now be on students who have not developed literacy skills at the baseline literacy level. Douglas Willms, a Canadian expert in literacy and human development, agreed that instead of dwelling on the overall rankings, students who do not meet the benchmark for "basic literacy ... especially in the early years of schooling" should be the new focus of language and literacy education in Canada". [4] He cautioned that performance at what is deemed to be the basic literacy level is insufficient for today's complex world. Up-dated literacy standards should reflect the skills and performance criteria that are essential for developing learning potential, lifelong learning, self-expression, and physical and mental health. This emphasis should begin in kindergarten and continue to grade three. Dr. Willms' emphasis on the needs of children in the primary division who do not meet basic language literacy benchmarks also relate to learning to read data presented on simple charts and graphs as well understanding the messages contained in stories and poems.

Children who are slow to read sometimes experience physical and cognitive perceptual processing deficits. If these go undiagnosed, they can negatively influence their image of themselves as successful learners and their progress in other

literacies. The difficulties some children experience in learning to
read and write, and being left behind their peers, can become a
liability from which some do not recover. Failure to assess and
identify perceptual processing problems early enough that they can
be corrected or remediated is an omission that could have long-
term consequences. Parents sometimes complain about the lack of
individual attention their children receive when they experience
reading difficulties at school and many undertake to remediate
their children's reading practice at home. Less fortunate children
flounder on their own. This chapter outlines what parents should
expect from the schools related to language literacy and how
teachers are well-positioned to observe and report potential
obstacles children face as they learn to read.

Literacy begins with learning language

Most children learn their first language naturally at home.
Learning language in infancy is a receptive, inner process whereby
the child focuses and observes people and events around them,
listens intently, and eventually coos softly in response. The first
recognizable sounds infants utter are often the murmurings of
mama, dada; then they may utter a word in the context of
something that they are doing and say, "button" while trying to
fasten a sweater. Babies and toddlers learn much more about
language than we might think before they utter sounds and words
we recognize.

Language development is a social process that relies on
children's perceptual skills as the infant observes lip movements
and hears sounds. Responding to the infant's (birth to about 18
months) cues when he cries or smiles is a parent's earliest
language interaction with their child. A caring, warm relationship
between infant and parent nurtures language development that
begins as a receptive process and becomes more expressive as the

toddler (about 18 to 30 months) begins to imitate what she hears and sees. Facilitating language development right from the start is relatively straightforward: talk and read to your child; listen; and respond to his babbling, immature speech. As the child begins to speak in short phrases, ask questions regularly and often throughout the day that require him to respond in many contexts.

When children hear language that is clear and spoken in positive tones, they gradually learn what they hear. When children are read to regularly they learn protocols that accompany reading - cuddling on a lap, turning pages, moving the lips and murmuring sounds as pages are turned, and moving the eyes and head from side to side on the pages to look at the dazzling array of colour and symbols. Most parents remember watching their toddler choose a book and sit on a cushion, turn the pages one by one, and babble quietly to herself. These early behaviours demonstrate that the child is acquiring important physical and perceptual skills for language and reading and that she remembers the protocols.

Symbolic thinking and language development go hand-in-hand

Language is a system of symbols that children typically develop naturally and rapidly. The preoperational period, from age two to six or seven is prime time for the development of language and communication; this period covers the symbolic phase from two to four years and the intuitive, representational phase from four to seven. Language development during the symbolic phase enables the child to describe an object or an event that is no longer present with words that let them express what they want to communicate. For example, she may represent an event with words such as "mama gone" or a single action like waving bye-bye. In junior kindergarten, children use full sentences to convey what they need or have experienced and can tell a simple story. Symbol recognition is an important pre-reading skill that involves

recognizing and naming objects and sorting words according to
their similar sounds, e.g. cat/hat/bat. Magnetic boards and
formboard puzzles are materials that encourage children to arrange
letters into words and practise the directional positioning of letters
and numbers.

The child's growing language fluency becomes his ultimate
tool for representing what is going on in his mind. Few things
make children prouder than to communicate and make themselves
understood. Using language is such a pleasurable experience for
them that they repeat themselves, learn and sing to communicate a
feeling, recite rhymes, carry on conversations with themselves, and
dramatize a pretend conversation. The child learns to communicate
actions that will occur in the future such as "the dentist will check
my teeth" and they may over-generalize during the later symbolic
stage, as in my daddy carries a briefcase to work - therefore, all
men carrying briefcases must be fathers.

Language and exercise

Recent studies show that brain plasticity and learning
language improve in the context of physical exercise that changes
the brain to "make it more malleable and receptive" to new
learning. [5] Parents who are concerned about their child's
language development usually find that their speech flows more
spontaneously and the words come more readily when they are
engaged in any active play. As the brain and the body are
connected seamlessly, parents who want to facilitate their child's
language development should take him to a playground or a nature
area where he can run freely; this motivates him to speak, say new
words, recognize and label symbols, and read signs.

Theories of the relationship between literacy and thought

Literacy development involves connecting the content of

what one is saying, the thought one wants to convey, one's choice and use of words, and the construction of full sentences. Jean Piaget [6] believed that the child's active physical interaction with concrete objects in the environment build the knowledge and mental structures she needs in order to acquire the content for thought that is the foundation of language. Children are quick to learn the language they need to express the thoughts they have in their minds. The cognitive scientists in the Constructivist tradition supported Piaget's findings that the child finds the language he needs to express what he is thinking, as language is the expression of thought and not the other way around. [7] Constructivists believe that thought precedes language and that language is a product of general cognitive abilities and active interaction between children and their environments. When they have many opportunities to manipulate concrete objects, children see relationships, make connections and develop concepts that they can think and understand without language, although language may support and shape their understanding and reinforce it.

Lev Vygotsky, who is also identified with the cognitive scientists, held a different view. He claimed that language leads thought and that language and thought develop separately and independently in the early years. In other words, children need language to have thoughts. For Vygotsky, labeling things and attaching words to actions helps children understand concepts and events. He believed that language learning depends on social interaction and that the social and cultural setting in which language is learned is important. [8]

Behavioural scientists suggested that language learning is largely an imitative process acquired through imitation of the language the child hears and positive reinforcement by adults that firms up the link between the word and the object or event. Noam Chomsky [9] believed that humans are pre-programmed to use

language due to innate and universal language abilities that are
hard-wired into the brain along with a "universal grammar" that
children absorb as they hear and use language. Other theories
propose that language is socially driven, and the child learns
language according to the incentives they receive from the
environment and interactions with others in groups. [10]
Neuroscience continues to propose explanations that are still being
investigated which suggests that language acquisition theory still
retains elements of an unsolved mystery.

I like Lise Eliot's conclusion even though her approach
does not solve the mystery either: "The capacity for language may
be genetic, and our grammatical rules may be limited by universal
features of human brain hardware, but the particular language a
child masters, and the way he ends up speaking it, are largely a
function of experience". [11] The remarkable thing is that babies
learn language at all given that they are born not knowing a word
of what they hear around them. In three years, without direct
teaching, they will usually develop an extensive vocabulary, talk
incessantly, display proficient sound patterns, and demonstrate a
basic command of the grammar of the language. [12]

Emergent literacy

The term "emergent literacy" describes the child's growing
ability to use language fluently in many contexts. Reading has
traditionally been considered the first important academic skill for
children to acquire starting in grade one. Preschools and
kindergartens emphasize children's acquisition of emergent or pre-
reading skills such as the conventions of print; phonological
(sound) awareness; phoneme correspondence (rhyme); and
pragmatics (using words in the right social context).

Learning to read is largely a perceptual process that

depends on the ability to see (visual acuity), hear well (auditory acuity) and cognitive- and perceptual-processing skills. Children who master the perceptually-based pre-reading skills may become early readers before they begin grade one. It is important that teachers have the skills they need to identify children who are likely to fall behind in reading. Indicators of potential reading problems that can be detected early are delays or deficits in children's sensory-perceptual acuity – i.e., the acuity of their vision and hearing - and their cognitive-perceptual processing skills that indicate whether children receive messages and process them accurately. [13] Kindergarten children who spend enough time on activities that emphasize practice of the full range of physical- and cognitive-perceptual skills that relate to reading may learn to read with little instruction. Those who also receive adequate phonics instruction may become independent readers seemingly effortlessly.

Nurture the reading and literacy skills

Teaching children to read should begin with a comprehensive program that promotes the full range of perceptual skills outlined in chapter 6. Reading also depends on the development of hand control, eye-hand coordination, and ocular-motor skills as the child learns to scan a page, recognize, and name symbols and focus on the words on a page. Reading is also an imitative function as children try to emulate the tonal quality, register and pace of the reader as they read out loud. The importance of linking reading with experiences that are pleasurable, reassuring, and nurturing for the child should not be underestimated.

Learning to read is not confined to the book centre or the puzzle area. The skills for reading are practised in all learning centres, on the playground, at home, and wherever children are exposed to print, language and opportunities to listen, respond, and express themselves. Literacy development occurs whenever children are exposed to interesting and varied print materials and opportunities to interact with them and with other children. Classroom activities that require children to plan and represent what they are thinking, as in doing project work or visiting someplace new, such as a post office or fire department, also promote literacy and language development as new experiences add new content for thought. These are all important activities and practise opportunities that parents may provide to support reading and other literacy skills.

The technicalities of language and reading

Literacy development is a combination of perceptions, receptive and expressive language, and interest in doing something that has pleasurable connotations for the child like being read to. Fostering literacy development involves components of: *learning language, phonology, phonetics, syntax, word meanings, vocabulary,* and *pragmatics.*

Phonology is an awareness that words consist of separable sounds; it refers to the organization and pattern of sounds that include tone, register, pitch, rhythm, rhyme, and emphasis. Phonology also refers to the variety of speech sounds, even among speakers of the same language, including differences in pronunciation called "accents". *Phonics* is an approach to teaching reading by linking letters or groups of letters to specific sounds. *Phonological awareness* is a predictor of children's reading skills; if they can recognize words that sound and look alike, detect and make words rhyme, and segment the sounds in words, children usually become proficient early readers who are able to advance somewhat effortlessly to higher reading levels.

Approaches for teaching children to read have been through
a number of pendulum swings over several generations. "Whole
language" was a teaching approach that became popular during the
1980s but was later held responsible for the reading deficits of at
least one generation of children whose inability to write
grammatically and spell accurately adversely affected their reading
and written language throughout their schooling. [14] This
approach dismissed the importance of phonetics instruction in
learning to read. In some education jurisdictions, teaching phonics
is still considered to be "outdated" by teachers who were trained to
believe that. Today's kindergarten/primary teachers mostly adopt a
balanced approach that emphasizes oral language, whole word
recognition, enables children to identify and manipulate phonemes
(phonemic awareness), teaches children to sound out words
phonetically, understand word meanings (semantics), and use
words in the right context.

Peterson, Shelley Stagg and Jang, Eunice 2012. Knowledge skills
related to learning to read Early Literacy Development. Ontario
Public Libraries. pp. 9-10.

Vocabulary development – learning meaning of words,
understanding concepts and context for words.

Print motivation- recognizing and identifying new letters and
words and sounding out printed letters and words, recognizing
orientation of a book.

Phonological awareness- repeating sounds and finding rhyming
words, singing words in songs, and reciting rhymes.

Narrative awareness- responding to questions about stories they
have heard, predicting endings or how stories will evolve.

Cognitive and Physical Perceptual skills involved in learning to read- recognize letters (visual acuity and cognitive perceptual skills), sound out simple words phonetically (auditory skills and remembering the sounds of letters) match consonant sounds with sound patterns and figure out simple words by sounding them out (visual and cognitive-perceptual skills) recognize spoken words (auditory skills) and written words (visual-perceptual skills) move and scan the eyes steadily from left to right on a page and keep the eyes focused on one's place on the page (ocular-motor skills) copy numbers and words correctly (visual and physical perceptual skills) find words in a passage and connect words to pictures (visual-perceptual skills)

Spoken language

Oral language (speaking) connects with learning to read, listen well and write. Sociodramatic play encourages children to practise oral language skills, listen actively, use new words, and link words to actions. In sociodramatic role play, children develop memory, use symbols, plan collaboratively, respond verbally and physically to visual and auditory cues, elaborate on and follow a script, and begin to think on their feet. Outdoor play and almost any form of physical activity are particularly useful contexts for children to develop their expressive and receptive (listening) language skills.

Pragmatics involves learning to speak and converse fluently, follow social conventions (when to listen, when to speak and taking turns) and use language to influence others. Language is largely a social enterprise that connects people in ways that are difficult to achieve without engaging in verbal communication that is accepted and understood by others. Language used properly has the power to persuade and elicit feelings. Used improperly, or without due consideration of the rights and interests of others,

language can distract to the point that the listener disengages.
Using language in socially skillful ways facilitates explanations,
getting things done and finding meaning. The skilled use of
pragmatics in conversation and formal speaking exerts power and
can clarify and change minds. In the broadest sense, pragmatics
refers to the rules and conventions of communication that depend
on the social context and purpose.

Children four and five years of age who already have some
command of oral language are usually ready to practise the skills
of pragmatics. Their ability to adapt to the conventions of language
is also related to their social and emotional competence and
cognitive maturity. The simplest rules of conversation are: listen,
speak when no one else is already speaking; wait your turn to
speak; don't interrupt. How many adults demonstrate that they
have learned these rules? Learning and following them takes
practice and is, for some, a monumental lifelong challenge.
Following the conventions of conversation influences social
relationships, the ability to learn and understand, and how one is
perceived by others. Learning to use language is another example
that reinforces Fulghum's message, "Everything I need to know, I
learned in kindergarten". [15]

Children are able to learn how much to say before letting
someone else speak, to try not to dominate the conversation, and
practise saying what they want to communicate clearly and
concisely. The integrity and manner of what they say are also
important, i.e., what you say should be true, unless you let others
know that it's not and why. The way we speak, i.e., tone,
orderliness and staying on topic, usually determines whether others
keep listening. We use words that are polite and agreeable to
others. We repeat what we have said if others are unable to hear or
do not understand. In group times, teachers coach children on
language conventions, using simple terms such as "say whether

you liked the story and why in one sentence". Group time is a valuable opportunity for children to practise pragmatics while talking and responding to others about what they enjoyed and accomplished that day.

Parents and teachers sometimes discover belatedly that being too demanding and picky about how children speak can be overdone and discourage children from speaking. Interrupting children to correct how they have said something is a quick way to discourage speaking, not to mention curbing their natural eagerness for self-expression. When children feel coerced to follow all the rules when speaking, words may fail them, and they stumble over words they understand. Correcting children's speech is best achieved by repeating the correct version back to them without mentioning the child's earlier error – that is, by simply providing a correct model. Most children should leave kindergarten being able to speak clearly in complex and compound sentences of 8-10 words. Children who demonstrate worrisome speech delays or impediments should be referred to speech therapists who can diagnose the problem and provide timely interventions.

Neuroscientists have found that the brain map is dominated by the language of its culture and reading changes the biological structure of the brain. [16] In fact, every new medium has the capacity to reorganize the brain. Becoming literate in the early years depends on the acquisition of a range of cognitive skills, dispositions to use language effectively to make oneself understood, willingness to use language to connect with others, and the motivation to read. Kindergartens try to instill these skills and motivations in children as preparation for grade one.

Cultivating lifelong literacy habits

Reading and writing skills transcend other educational outcomes largely because they serve as doors that open the mind to most other forms of knowing and understanding. A key goal of kindergarten literacy curriculum is to motivate children to read and read widely; it is also important to learn to write. The age at which a child learns to read and write varies according to the child's experience and maturation; therefore, the range of play activities should engage each child at his own level. Literacy activities should be accessible to children over sufficient stretches of time to allow children to achieve the learning outcomes. Teachers should monitor and note the activities each child has participated in and mastered; they select new activities when he is ready to take the next step. Teachers know the developmental continuum in learning to read and write so as to exploit a range of play materials in timely ways. An individualized kindergarten/primary program implies that the teacher has an agenda for each child each day; she maintains careful records of the pre-reading skills already mastered and provides new activities when the child is ready. The individual attention children need when learning to read calls for high adult-child ratios in the primary division to ensure that children build a strong foundation in reading that is the child's window to many other kinds of learning.

Many physical activities lend themselves to listening, speaking, reading and writing, and physical programs may include activities that promote all four. Traditional childhood games such as 'Simon Says' and 'I Spy' promote listening combined with motor activity and visual perception; small groups of children building with blocks accelerates vocabulary and communication as well as creativity, fine motor and gross motor skills; and treasure hunts require children to read signs, signals and clues. Collaborative projects encourage literacy skills such as communication, sharing ideas and tasks, finding and reading

resource books, displaying and disseminating results (data) using
bar graphs, and explaining to classmates verbally the outcomes and
products of the project.

Literacy depends on enjoying books and language arts:
word plays, rhyme, poetry, songs, and stories. Declining readership
of newspapers and magazines gives cause for concern, but giant
bookstores are still filled with books that captivate young and old.
Many more people nowadays are interested in writing books and
speaking out through memoir, biography, opinion pieces, and
sharing information and ideas through social media. The fact that
some writers of novels are now trying their hand at short-story
writing may signal that literature might, in future, be delivered in
increasingly abbreviated formats. The popularity of Twitter and
short clips of news on the media suggests that people increasingly
like to receive information and communication in capsule form.

Parents and teachers grapple with how to introduce and
maintain children's interest in books and reading. Reading to
children from infancy and even after they have learned to read for
themselves is a tried-and-true approach. When young children
become registered library users, they cultivate a time-sensitive way
to start and finish the book within the borrowing period. The real
challenge today is not how to access books, but how to instill a
love of books and reading in children whose lives otherwise
become dominated by screens. Another way to encourage reading
is to introduce books that can be read in daily action-packed
instalments, much like the draw of televised series that build
anticipation of what is ahead. Children similarly enjoy reading and
hearing short stories read to them, an approach that can offer
excitement and encourages them to reflect on the events just past
and discuss how they felt. The remarkable success of the Harry
Potter series is a testament not only to the enduring attraction for
children of weighty books and a good story about a worthy role

model; they also build anticipation for the next book in the series. It seems unfair to deny children the excitement of reading these books and developing their reading skills by letting them see the films before they have read the books.

Books that contain beautiful illustrations hold endless charm; children return to them throughout childhood and save them for their own children; for many, their proudest possessions are the books they own and will cherish forever. The best way to keep children reading may be role models at home – parents who always have a book on the go, talk about it at the dinner table and refer to it at relevant times. Films and videos may inspire a love of media and provide passive engagement but they stimulate the senses simultaneously and lay it all out, leaving little to the imagination. Books, on the other hand, force children's imaginations to fill in the gaps that print leaves out. The printed words and illustrations on a page encourage children to conjure up an image, invent sounds and project the effects of various actions, all in their heads. The picture book artist/illustrator fills in the blanks that the print/author leaves out. The power and durability of books inspire a passion for inventing stories that other media do not. Parents are wise to promote books and reading over television and films because books feed the imagination, ignite a desire to express oneself through the printed word, and encourage children to create their own books.

Using music to promote language and literacy

A regular music program in kindergarten and the primary grades is a powerful way to introduce and play with words, associate them with sounds, and create rhymes. While singing, children practise listening, pronouncing and repeating words. They encounter new words in songs and tune their ears to replicate tone, pitch and timing. When children sing songs, they develop a sense

for rhythm, cadence, and rhyming that becomes more creative over
time. Songs introduce language, including new languages, expose
children to emotions, draw pictures in their minds, and evoke
memories. Similarly, music and movement programs are crucial
teaching tools for imitating beat and timing in dance and exercising
and interpreting melody through movement. Music has the power
to transport a child from the here and now, alter a frame of mind
and soothe the soul. A regular music program for children is a
powerful stimulant and an agent of hope, motivation, and
transformation.

<u>Learning to write</u>

Learning to write opens another window to self-expression;
as children usually learn to read and write at the same time, each
tends to strengthen the skills of the other. Writing is an
"intentional activity" in which the brain "converts the words -
which are symbols - into movements of the fingers and hands".
[17] The physical skills associated with writing are challenging for
young children to master – that is, grasp a pencil or crayon using
the fingers, not fists; control the wrist and forearm to write in a
straight line; guide the pencil to form legible letters. The first
writing task that a child performs is usually to print or write her
own name. The act of writing words and sentences competently
without copying is a harder task that requires knowledge and
cognitive skills such as: know the difference between lower- and
upper- case letters; write words by remembering the letters; and
know what one wants to say.

Children usually learn to print letters first which makes
fewer demands on the brain than cursive writing movements.
Children who experience reading difficulties are often identified
initially by their unwillingness to write in cursive; they develop a
preference for printing slowly that allows their hands and fingers to

keep up with the thoughts they produce. Most children learn to
write in grade one so issues or delays in learning to write may be
detected that soon.

Issues in teaching children to write

The purist's belief in the sanctity of conventional grammar and
spelling.

A common criticism of the school system is that children
do not write frequently enough and when they do, their written
work contains inaccurate spelling, misused words, and
grammatical errors. In spite of Canada's impressive record of
award-winning contemporary literature, print media sometimes
slips into awkward writing styles, inappropriate use of the
vernacular, unconventional grammar, and spelling errors (often
labeled *typo's*). The relaxation of rules related to writing
conventions is often praised for the freedom it affords writers for
self-expression, expanding the boundaries in literature, and
originality.

Many Canadian writers have taken full advantage of the
loosening of conventions and are recognized for the creative and
evocative ways their words and styles inspire and resonate with the
complexities of life and the human condition. The volume of print
material produced today has increased in proportion to advances in
word processing, but literacy standards are treated more casually.
Purists wish that writing standards would respect traditional
conventions, but languages, including our own, evolve over time.
Grammatical rules are readily modified to satisfy a range of tastes,
impact and clarity. Language adopts or discards words every day
and grammatical rules are increasingly traded off in favour of
economy instead of aesthetic quality. Writing today is largely
judged to be a matter of stylistic preference which makes it harder

to make a convincing case for teaching grammar in schools - although some of us keep trying.

The "be concise" refrain

Probably no one ever told the literary geniuses to be concise when they wrote the voluminous novels that likely represent the epitome of descriptive English literature. Technologies have had a significant impact on changing the conversation and conventions associated with writing styles. The key messages to writers these days are: get to the point quickly; forget embellishment and unnecessary words; avoid jargon and cliche; be considerate of the reader's time. [18] Writers are cautioned that the reader's time is in competition with other media and, if writing is not precise, the screen will communicate in a few images what took much longer to convey in words. These messages have filtered down to the schools and become part of the lexicon of new writing conventions for children in school.

To teach or not to teach cursive writing

The dominance of word processing software has made writing a simpler and faster task for writers-that is likely linked to the abandonment of teaching cursive writing in many school jurisdictions. There remains a strong case for teaching cursive in the primary grades although arguments against often win out. The case against is that children use keyboards and touch screens to read and communicate before cursive writing is taught in schools. Teaching cursive used to occur rather naturally in the continuum from learning to trace letters, printing words then to handwriting words in cursive which is faster and manages to keep up with children's developing thought processes. Defenders of cursive writing sometimes use the artistry of penmanship to make their case for retaining it in schools. Better reasons exist to defend cursive writing.

Neuroscientists have discovered that more connections are
made between the hand and the brain when people handwrite their
notes, thoughts and arguments. For example, taking notes by hand
is believed to facilitate greater retention of information and ideas
than typing the notes. This evidence may suggest that cursive
writing supports cognitive development. The act of handwriting
relies on fine motor skills and connects them to cognitive skills,
neuromuscular processes, and the language involved in writing.
Forming letters by hand in cursive writing engages the mind and
helps children focus on the quality of their written language. The
strokes of the hand promote the connection of letters into words.
Studies also show a relationship between better handwriting,
higher grades, and academic achievement. They also claim that the
act of reading is connected to the motor process of forming
letters.[19] Most evidence to date suggests that it may be
misguided to abandon the teaching of cursive writing in schools
because neural connections may exist between handwriting and the
stimulation of thought, memory and other cognitive processes.

Evaluating children's writing (and their art) may inhibit creativity

Today the thinking is that young children should first be
encouraged to express themselves in their writing without the
constraints of following grammatical and spelling conventions.
Freeing children from fear of judgment and knowing that their
writing will not be edited seem to produce the most creative
products while they are young. Even teachers and parents who
most appreciate the beauty, accuracy and precision of written
language often feel humbled when they read the compositions and
illustrations of young children who have been encouraged to
express what is in their minds and hearts. Researchers found that
children's natural creativity appears to endure longer, even into the

teen years, when they do not have to submit to judgement of the
value of their work. Children generally perform better on all
creative tasks when they know they will not be evaluated. [20]

The enterprise of learning to read, write and become literate
is a challenge that should be pursued individually by every child
every day. Just as important are the social, group-oriented learning
experiences because they provide opportunities for children to use
language, listen and practise the pragmatics of discussion. Most
important of all is to acknowledge that writing depends on thought;
it is difficult to write about something one has not thought first. As
Piaget found, children usually find the language they need to
express what they are thinking. [21] Thought is stimulated by
reading and by diverse and meaningful events indoors and in
nature that provide the 'food' for thought. Creativity, originality
and literacy in any creative medium derive from that "rich inner
life" described by Bettelheim (1987) that is nurtured by and within
the human soul. A childhood of meaningful experiences provides a
solid foundation for all the literacies.

Project learning promotes literacy

Using projects to facilitate literacy development is one of
the most effective ways to encourage children to listen, read, write,
ask questions and seek answers especially when the projects
emerge from children's own interests. The key to effective project
learning is choosing projects that clearly address a range of
learning outcomes that include specific skills, concepts, problem
solving and understanding that have been well defined and
embedded in the project. Creating effective projects requires
research, careful planning, thoughtful design, a range of interesting
materials, several steps, and the time children need to complete the
project. Effective projects do not materialize overnight and their
planning makes demands on teachers to think them through,

prepare all materials ahead, and define the steps and roles involved before the projects are introduced to children. Typically, children should be encouraged to provide some input into the planning process. Projects nearly always require children to be active physically and encourage them to seek resources they may need indoors or outside which is an interesting part of the planning. Children also enjoy participating in the planning, negotiating small changes to plans and offering ideas about what they want to achieve and learn. All literacy skills may be embedded in projects at various stages.

Multi-stage kindergarten projects usually involve a series of activities related to a common outcome for the whole class perhaps over several days. A project with several components might involve all children in every component or might assign small groups of children to take on responsibility for their part of the project and then connect the various sub-projects together at the end. Sometimes a project might include some 'stand-alone', mini-projects that attract the special interest of one or two children who work together or alone. Generally, projects involve several types of tasks that may be done over a period of days or weeks, indoors or outdoors. Increasingly, they involve the use of technological devices, e.g. camera, tablet, projector. Using technologies appeals to children who are attracted by the features that allow them, for example, to plan gardens or playgrounds using cameras or software, store project work on files and draw diagrams.-Technologies allow children to polish their product, file it so as to retrieve it and use it again, and find quick answers to questions, all of which are compelling reasons to ensure that children have access to various devices and learn how to use them effectively. [22] Project learning encourages children to collaborate, plan, anticipate, tackle diverse tasks and skills, and persist with a meaningful project to its conclusion. [23]

Project-based learning is a key strategy for teaching and learning

Young children respond well to projects that sync with their interests and let them apply skills they have acquired. Viable projects should have an observable end-product or result that they feel proud to display and talk about. Projects are useful for learning at every stage in schooling and for individual or group learning. The skills, knowledge and dispositions to be applied are usually embedded in the project as it unfolds instead of calling for direct instruction at the beginning. When they are well-introduced to children, projects are exciting examples of 'discovery learning' whereby new information, concepts and ideas may be 'uncovered' as children get deeper into the project. Almost any skill, knowledge or disposition for learning may be practised and acquired in the context of a project.

The fact that project-based learning can ease many of the constraints and limitations of schooling became more relevant during the pandemic as projects are adaptable to small groups and larger groups, indoors or outdoors, and usually involve active learning and movement in space rather than sitting. Projects may be conducted in 'pods' of children engaged in learning as a stable group whose membership is not expected to change during the confinement period. Project-based learning nearly always involves *interdisciplinary learning* that may address knowledge, skills and understanding related to curriculum learning outcomes for several developmental domains and disciplines. This is a preferred way to teach in the context of the learning-centred approach to education. (addressed in Chapter 10). Projects are also creative, motivating, fun, and remembered by children years later.

A kindergarten project usually has an established timeframe between starting and finishing - such as starting a seeding and growing project in time for spring planting in the school garden. Gauging the time various components of the project may take, anticipating the tasks to be completed and the order in which they should be tackled encourages children to estimate, plan, predict, gauge probability, and use time well. Kindergarten projects should start small; in the later years they expand to include several stages, various roles and tasks, and take longer to complete.

Projects work best when they contain some ideas put forward by the children; they are then researched and directed initially by the teacher who steers children in a viable direction and toward resources they will need and identifies the tasks, roles, skills and learning outcomes of the project. Projects offer opportunities to solicit parental input and help in gathering resources or demonstrating and teaching a specific skill (like cutting out fabric pieces, or using a small saw to cut wood). The social experience and literacy learning to be gained are so dynamic that there should be a significant project underway most of the time. Projects are an inclusive way for children to involve family members in helping their class, making new contacts and friends, and feeling part of the children's school life.

Technological literacy through project learning

Project learning provides an authentic framework for using technologies to expand children's brain development, cognitive skills, and knowledge. The variety of ways in which technologies may be employed positively in the kindergarten/primary years is setting the scene for a new pedagogy, one that relies purposefully on technologies to help and enhance learning but not replace active play with concrete materials. Children's purposeful use of technologies ensures that they begin to understand their many functions instead of passively watching screens. Primary classrooms that have access to a range of technologies enable all children, regardless of family resources, to experience equal

learning opportunities. When computers are productively
employed in the classroom, some of the teachers' time may be
freed to help children individually and in small groups. While
some children move on to other activities, software programs allow
children who need additional time for learning specific skills to
practise on computers or tablets on their own or with another child.
Computers and tablets are useful devices that respect children's
need to learn according to their own developmental and learning
timetable, at school and at home. This calls for a system that
encourages parents to borrow devices or purchase one from the
school at a modest cost when the home does not have one.
Purchasing and selling, refurbishing, or lending computers might
be another useful project for parent advisory groups in schools.

Technologies as an issue in literacy learning

Marshall McLuhan, an early Canadian communications
expert (1911-1980), believed from the early days of television that
each new medium reorganizes our brain and our mind in its own
unique way and the consequences of these reorganizations are
much more significant than the effects of the content or the
media's messages. McLuhan did not mean that every technology is
harmful to brain development; instead, he suggested that each
medium leads to a change in the balance of our individual senses
and increases some senses at the expense of others. He also
claimed that the harmful effects of television, computer games and
videos have the most impact on attention (attending skills) because
people become accustomed to more and faster transitions on
screens As screen watchers acquire a taste for rapid changes in the
stimuli that reach their brains, activities such as reading, listening
and conversation may become more difficult. [24]

Neuroscientists mostly agree that extensive use of
electronic devices rewire the brain. For example, people who

typically write fluently on a computer find it more difficult to
switch to writing by hand in cursive or by dictating "because their
brains are not wired to translate thoughts into writing or speech at
high speed".[25] Issues related to the amount of 'screen time' that
is appropriate for children at various ages tend to dominate
discussion about the viability of technology devices as tools to
promote learning. When technologies are used as assistive devices
to promote learning and provide practice, some of the issues
related to screen time tend to disappear. As a general rule,
however, the extended use of technologies for learning by young
children should be avoided especially in early childhood.

Second language learning in kindergarten and the primary years

The period from infancy to puberty is a critical period for
language learning. After this period, the ability to learn a second
language is limited as second languages are not processed in the
same part of the brain as the native language. On the other hand,
because the human brain is "plastic" during the critical period, if
two languages are learned at the same time, both languages are
processed in the same part of the brain – that is, after about age
three, usually in the left side of the brain. The age at which we
process a new cognitive skill influences the area of the brain in
which it will be processed throughout life. In a bilingual child, all
the sounds of the two languages share a single large map, a library
of sounds from both languages. [26]

Computers can be useful tools for children who are
learning second languages. Software programs assist teachers by
providing activities that introduce the second language, engage the
child in practising the sounds and vocabulary, facilitate the child's
social integration when he plays with another child on the
language-learning software, and contribute to the child's sense of
belonging in the classroom.

Home language

Home language is that which is spoken in the home by the child's family. When young children come to this country speaking only the language of their parents and country of origin, they face a significant challenge when they enter a classroom where the children and teacher are speaking English or French. Learning to count and identify number symbols which mean the same in all cultures can be a useful starting point for children. The daily physical program and the music program are nearly always the best contexts for an ESL or FSL child to try speaking or singing new words and songs while they are physically active and performing as part of the larger group. To welcome newcomer parents and children to the kindergarten classroom, posting signs in their home language, as well as in English or French, sends a message that they and their children are a valued part of the kindergarten/ primary school family which provides an important bridge between the home and the school. When the teacher labels certain play equipment and learning centres, in English or French, along with corresponding words in the child's home language, children feel that they and their language are valued.

Kindergarten classrooms where many home languages are represented are among the most exciting learning environments one can find in schools because they encourage the participation of family members in class events. When this happens, all children benefit from learning bilingual and bi-literate skills associated with the languages and the cultures they represent. [27] When the kindergarten teacher and ECE learn familiar words in the child's home language and the words to songs the child knows, they encourage all the children to sing them together. When resources related to home languages of children in the classroom are scarce, software programs can introduce them to their second language which enables the child to practise and learn independently and

potentially reduce the stress she may feel for a part of each day.
Teachers should not be burdened by insufficient resources as this
reduces their time for individual attention to children.

Bilingualism and immersion programs

A key principle behind language immersion programs in
Canadian schools is not only to enable children to speak both
official languages but also to fully exploit young children's native
receptivity to learning language. Chumak-Horbatsch cites research
that suggests understanding "language ecology" helps teachers
think of their classrooms as "linguistically complex ecosystems"
which is "healthy and good for ... the classroom environment".
Bilingual speakers learn to "language" differently than
monolinguals and find it easier to adjust and move between
languages or to "translanguage". [28] Some suggest that the
mastery of more than one language is also a component of literacy
as bilingual children are better able to understand what other
people are thinking and take perspectives other than their own.
[29]

Using the music program to learn and practise a new language

The kindergarten music program is a key tool for teaching a
new language and is often the first experience a child has to mouth
and speak words in the new language in a less-intimidating context
than trying to speak while others listen. When singing, all children
experience the sounds, catch the rhythm, clap along, and learn the
words to the songs even though the meanings might not be readily
apparent. Singing the words, noting rhymes and cacophonous
sounds, and catching the phonetic emphases in words all introduce
elements of a second language including new ways of opening and
holding the mouth to make the sounds and connect the syllables.
The music program should introduce songs to be sung in the

diverse languages represented in the class, a practice that helps children tune their ears to the unique sounds and increases children's acceptance of the different sounds. Singing songs in someone else's home language is exciting for all children and helps children lose their inhibitions about making the new sounds and experiencing a new language.

8

NUMERACY AND LOGICAL-MATHEMATICAL THOUGHT

"Not knowing how to think mathematically makes people, on average, less healthy, less financially secure, less innovative and less productive. Innumeracy damages the economy and degrades the environment." John Mighton, 2020. [1]

<u>Numeracy and logical thinking for the 21st century</u>

Children should achieve a level of numeracy that is relevant to their lifelong learning and competent participation in society, just as they are expected to read and write well enough to communicate capably. Essential life skills today include using mathematics to manage one's finances, plan and implement budgets, interpret data, and practise wise consumer habits. These competencies require an ability think logically and apply basic mathematics to everyday obligations. There is seldom a valid excuse while children are in elementary or secondary school for claiming "I can't do math" and dropping math courses before high school graduation. John Mighton [2] insists that even advanced math is accessible for most children and adults although he acknowledges that not everyone aspires to achieve the elevated levels of scientists, researchers, and mathematicians. But all children should become competent enough in math, as a condition of high school graduation, to function and be self-reliant with respect to the routine expectations of life in advanced societies (e.g., taxes, mortgages, budgets) that involve math. They should not require postsecondary remediation in order to learn the basics they should have achieved in elementary school in order to be successful in high school math and beyond.

The ability to analyze and make informed choices and judgements based on fact and evidence are 21st century skills that require rational, logical thought processes. At the turn of this century, it was estimated that many more jobs that require higher levels of numeracy, literacy and technological skills would become available and that schools should prepare children accordingly. Although that was a prophetic prediction, two decades later there are still not enough Canadians with the skills needed to fill the available high-performance jobs. [3] It is not postsecondary education that can miraculously attach these skills to the under-prepared students they receive from public education. Acquiring a foundation for high-performance skills should begin in the kindergarten/primary years where children build the intellectual capacity (mental structures), psychological stamina, resilience, and learning to learn skills they need to become capable in high school math, to solve the routine math-related problems of daily life and to cope with math in the world of work.

Logical-mathematical skills help children make informed choices for their future in a world of "mechanized intelligence that is increasingly dominated by machines and technologies... and the embedded thinking styles of logical thinking and disciplined problem solving that will be essential to life and work that involve intelligent machines". [4] Skills relevant to perspective taking, hypothesizing and scientific research, creativity and innovation are now on the list of employability skills for a much larger share of the labour market in Canada. Children should be competent in math from the primary grades on to be adequately prepared for a secure future.

Numeracy today implies that children acquire math skills

that prepare them to become self-reliant, productive and financially stable. In kindergarten, the journey toward competence in math begins as child's-play, but the play-based agenda is far from frivolous or casual. It begins by enabling kindergarten children to build, initially through play with concrete objects, the mental structures in the brain that lay a cognitive foundation for engaging with and understanding number and math-readiness skills. Kindergarten curriculum should emphasize children's understanding of the foundational logical-mathematical concepts and the development of a positive attitude toward number.

Myths about math

Conventional beliefs of the past held that the ability to think logically and grapple with math was associated with high intelligence and genetically endowed. This belief was typical of the *"fixed mindset"* that people only do well in math if they are "smart" and have a genetic predisposition for math.[5] Twentieth century educators sometimes dismissed the fact that abilities in math could also be taught, practised and learned like most subjects, and many parents dismissed that fact also. This 'fixed' mindset infected too many children who believed "I can't do math" and dropped math courses as soon as the system allowed or switched from academic math to applied, simplified courses for students who were deemed "not mathematically inclined".

Neuroscience began to change that fixed mindset early in this century as much more was learned about the brain. Research confirmed that although cognitive development occurs most rapidly during early childhood, the brain continues to develop and change throughout life. [6] "This is our famous *plasticity*: every human brain's built-in capacity to become, over time, what we demand of it. Plasticity does not mean that we are all born with the exact same potential...but, it does guarantee that no ability is fixed...plasticity makes it virtually impossible to determine any individual's true intellectual limitations at any age". [7] A *"growth mindset"* affirms that success in math also depends on

221

perseverance, a disposition to succeed through hard work and self-discipline, and a positive concept of self as a learner. [8] Children's confidence in their ability to 'do math' was, and still is, negatively impacted by those teachers and parents who tell them that "math is hard" before they even begin the journey.

People who possess "growth mindsets" believe that most learning is accessible to children who possess the habits of mind and dispositions for achievement. Capable teaching and presentation of the logical-mathematical concepts and pre-math skills in kindergarten lay the foundation for mathematical understanding. Most parents assume that primary division teachers have positive attitudes toward math and that their pre-service teacher training in math is sufficient for them to help children grapple with concepts and surmount hurdles in their thinking. The fact is that many teachers readily admit to 'math avoidance'. Upgraded teacher training and new certification standards that require teacher competence in math are essential to improving all children's math performance.

Studies show that early math skills are "significantly stronger predictors of later success in school than any other skills, including reading and attention skills".[9] Numeracy does not imply that all children can become mathematicians but it does require all children to achieve numeracy that enables them to function ably in occupations they pursue, avoid financial traps, and live within their means. Life for people who are innumerate has become increasingly hazardous; for one thing, the pervasiveness of scam operations has amply demonstrated how vulnerable they are. There are also those who prefer to maintain the myth that math proficiency is too difficult for most people so that they can advantage themselves. That education systems have, for decades. perpetuated the myth that math proficiency is unattainable for large numbers of children is symptomatic of the dysfunction that has long been present in education and still remains.

Logical-mathematical thinking begins in kindergarten

When children are introduced to foundational logical
concepts in preschool and practise and achieve them in
kindergarten, they are usually prepared for the arithmetic
operations (adding, subtracting) they meet in grade one. When they
learn to solve word and number problems in grade one, they gain
confidence in their ability to succeed in more challenging
numeracy tasks. Positive attitudes toward number and concepts
that begin in the kindergarten/primary years set the scene for math
proficiency throughout schooling and, with effective teaching,
children do well in math.

Kindergarten is prime time for building mental structures,
those neural connections in the brain that influence children's
ability to reason, remember, and learn. Structure-building is
facilitated by a play environment that fosters cognitive
development and by teachers who understand the cognitive-
developmental tasks of childhood as children learn to manipulate
number symbols and make a successful transition from
preoperational to concrete operational thought. The cognitive
transition relies also on parents who know what their child is
learning at school and learn how they can extend concept learning
at home.

Facilitating the cognitive transition from preoperational to concrete operational thought

The cognitive transition that occurs from about age four to
six or seven, as children move from dependence on sensory
perception to 'knowing' and understanding concepts, relies on
their ability to distance themselves from believing only what their
senses tell them. This cognitive transition is as dramatic as
children's rapid progress in language, physical and social
competence although conceptual changes are sometimes harder for

parents to detect. We see that the future working world has already arrived and requires cognitive skills that stretch the human intellectual capacity for reason and logical thought and creative, divergent thinking and invention. It is essential that children acquire the math skills they will require when they enter high school and postsecondary education and have added these skills to their repertoire. Logical thought and children's natural "creative orientation" should be fostered during and maintained beyond kindergarten/primary education which is a precious period of optimal cognitive growth. As mentioned in Chapter 1, during the preoperational period (about ages two to five or six) the "number of connections among neurons (synapses) is 50% greater than in the adult brain". During adolescence, the brain's synaptic connections are "pruned" and "neurons that have not been used extensively suddenly die off".[10] The kindergarten/primary years are therefore prime time for children to develop logical concepts and confidence in number. Brain development during these years influences their learning trajectory throughout their schooling.

Most children demonstrate concrete operational thought by age seven but the transformation makes several demands on them - and on whoever is teaching them. Simply telling children what they need to know and explaining concepts in words usually fails if children have not witnessed the transformation themselves or understood the relevant concept, usually through hands-on play. "Seeing is believing" is never more applicable than to the preoperational child. A developmental task for kindergarten children is to gradually understand that something is true despite what their eyes and ears tell them.

Hands-on play with concrete objects facilitates children's 'uncovering' of basic concepts. For example, a preschool child may say that a group of five oranges and a stack of five pennies means that there are more oranges than pennies because he is still focusing on the size of the oranges compared to the pennies. After many experiences like 'counting the pennies and counting the oranges' to verify the number in each grouping, he begins to understand that the concept of 'fiveness' does not change no matter what he is counting.

Play experience with concrete objects gradually liberates the child from dependence on the senses in order to 'know'. He 'discovers' that something can be true despite what his senses tell him. This enlightenment while forming concepts eventually allows children to 'know' by manipulating symbols that stand for number, instead of the actual objects, and they begin to trust what they know more than what they perceive. The confidence to depend on number symbols to perform arithmetic operations like adding and subtracting, in the absence of the props (i.e., play materials), is an important developmental milestone. In kindergarten, children also begin to understand concepts that differentiate things (e.g., same/different, equal/unequal, part/whole, animate/ inanimate). These cognitive transitions and others prepare children for arithmetic – sums and subtractions - using number symbols that begin to hold meaning for them.

Concept formation

Concepts are the "building blocks of knowledge" that enable children to organize and categorize information. [11] In early childhood, basic logical-mathematical concepts that include number, class (set) and order (seriation and sequence) provide a foundation for later mathematical competence. Concept of class, called *classification* (i.e. the ability to sort things into categories children define), involves the ability to connect the features and characteristics of objects according to their similarities; later, children transfer this concept to differentiating facts, themes and ideas. Concept of *seriation* refers to the ability to put things in order by following certain rules and using tools such as measured sets of objects (e.g. metric-sized rods like Cuisenaire rods) to put the objects into a series that conforms to certain rules. *Sequence* refers to the order in which events happen such as breakfast, lunch and dinner, or first, second, third. If children do not develop the basic logical-mathematical concepts before they have to perform arithmetic operations in grade one, they have to rely on drill, repetition and memory instead of their ability to understand using number symbols. Reliance on drill and memory may work for a while but without understanding an arithmetic operation, children will inevitably encounter a roadblock. Solving word problems and building on their understanding of basic calculations may present a challenge for them.

Concept formation enables children to construct their foundation for logical thinking. For example, when children reliably understand number concept, it is likely that they have achieved *"conservation"* of number - that is, the ability to recognize that the "amount" (e.g., number, volume) of objects remains the same despite changes in the configuration or physical features such as the size of what they are counting or measuring. *Conservation* demonstrates that children have achieved the cognitive maturity – in this case, distancing from the senses - that allows them to believe that something holds true in spite of how it appears based on what their senses tell them. Learning to trust and apply concepts is fundamental to logical thinking and reasoning.

As they are important building blocks for arithmetic operations, the three logical concepts discussed in this chapter - i.e., number, classification and seriation - are often referred to as "pre-math" or "math readiness" concepts. I use the term *"arithmetic"* to describe how we use operations with number symbols as *tools* of mathematics, as we add, subtract, and later, multiply and divide so as to calculate accurately when solving a math problem. *Mathematics* is, among other things, the science of knowing how, when, and where to apply concrete tools (symbols) and also formulas, theorems and principles to problem solving.

Children need to understand symbols and basic tools, what they mean and how to use them in the primary school years before they tackle "more complex explorations such as reasoning, investigating mathematical ideas, extending their understanding, reflecting, and making generalizations". [12]

Learning concepts and thinking logically develop early through planned and free play experiences with concrete objects. An old quotation by Sherman and Kay, 1932, describes the important role of the play environment: "Children develop only as the environment demands development". When children 'discover' something new as they play, they become motivated and curious to find out more. Whether or not they uncover concepts through play depends on the "things" and activities in the environments where they play. The concepts we want children to 'uncover' should be inherent in the activities. For example, when children play with parquetry, the small, flat, wooden pieces of various shapes and colours, when put together in various ways, form interesting shapes and endless patterns that children discover and rediscover as they move pieces around on the table.

Children's first-hand interactions and close observation of things and phenomena in the environment lead naturally to concept formation and "knowing" that something is true because they have witnessed the transformation themselves. For example, they learn that a heavy item does not need to be larger than a light item in order to sink in water when they compare objects that sink and those that float, like pennies to balloons. Playing with ramps and miniature cars leads them to make connections between speed, weight, the angle of the ramp, and distance. Discovering connections through active interaction with things is more meaningful and durable for the child at this early cognitive stage than memorizing a fact or a formula. This is 'discovery learning' as it was intended.

Concept of Number

Children's enthusiasm for sorting and ordering challenges, using numbers as tools to find answers (early problem solving), and learning about many aspects of everyday life (data gathering), are at a high point in kindergarten and grade one. Number concept begins in preschool by learning the sight and sound of number (sensory perception) by singing counting songs and rhymes. They learn the function and social significance of number (knowledge) by seeing numbers on homes, telephones and measuring devices; and they recognize how connected number is to life, which is an incentive for learning math. By labeling the number symbols, one-two-three – and attaching a number symbol correctly to a group of objects, either three-dimensional or two-dimensional (in print or on screen), they learn to use number symbols as tools.

Children make a small cognitive leap when they practise creating equal sets of objects (while they are also learning to classify), using one-to-one correspondence (e.g., give each bunny one hat), that may also involve seriating two equal sets of objects and counting both sets to ensure that they each have the same number of objects. Number concept emerges as children understand that number (e.g., 'sixness') does not vary in spite of changes in the size, shape or configuration of each group of six objects being counted, a stage described as *number constancy* (the invariance of number) that is usually achieved in kindergarten. Children have *conserved* number (*conservation*) when they reliably demonstrate this concept, usually by or early in grade one.

Children who have fully integrated the concept of number are equipped to perform operations such as simple adding and subtracting that are grade one tasks. Otherwise, the potential exists for children to misunderstand the operation they are asked to perform (e.g., adding), and they memorize sums, for example, 'two plus two is four", that does not confirm that they understand the operation. Children go through several steps in learning number concept, often in a predictable order, and usually in timeframes that depend on the child's play experience and individual coaching.

Steps in learning number concept

- recognizes the sight and sound of numbers – the child recites number in rhymes and songs
- learns the social significance and meaning of number – e.g. numbers that tell me how tall I am;
- labels the number symbols: 1, 2, 3, and so on;
- creates sets using one-to-one correspondence (e.g. one cookie for each child;
- recognizes equal sets; e.g. there are the same number of hats as there are bunnies;
- counts accurately and meaningfully (understands quantity) – i.e. consistently
counts all objects in a set without *double counting* or *skip counting*
- retains the constancy of number quantity in spite of differences or changes in the properties of the objects counted –that is, the quantity does not change in spite of the difference in size, shape or configuration of the objects. At this stage, the child understands that number exists independently of what she perceives.
- conserves number – child reliably demonstrates understanding of number constancy

Impact of number concept on other learning

Connecting aspects of daily living to numbers, calculation, and problem solving usually convinces children that numbers and calculation are tools that help them solve real-life problems. When their experience of number moves from the sensory and knowledge realms to the creation of relationships between number and things, the learning challenges increase. Number constancy that calls for a small cognitive leap, may fade in and out for a while until children have had sufficient experience comparing sets of objects and making equal sets. Computer software involving number activities provides practice that promotes understanding of concepts but only after children have had many play opportunities with three-dimensional objects. Children are ready for arithmetic operations when they conserve number which is a marker in the transition from preoperational thinking to concrete operational thinking. When these transitions do not occur, children need additional time and opportunities to play with concrete objects that move them from dependence on the senses to 'knowing' because they have understood the concept.

Classification - concept of class

The rule that children learn to follow in order to classify a group of objects is: **all objects in the total group of objects to be sorted must fit coherently (i.e. following the criteria established for each set) into one of the sets; that is, no objects in the total group may be left unclassified or misclassified.** The ultimate challenge of successful classification for kindergarten/primary children involves their ability to determine one or more criteria that may be applied to each coherent set of objects they create from a group of random objects. Before children achieve this stage in ability to classify, they go through incremental learning stages. They begin by sorting objects into sets when the criteria for each set (e.g., colour, shape or size) have been predetermined by the teacher who chooses the objects to be sorted; that is: sort this group of objects (i.e. presented in three distinct colours); then, sort a group of objects in three shapes and name each shape set – (such as, circles, squares, triangles). These are obvious visible criteria

that guide the child toward making three sets each of one
consistent colour, or one consistent shape – i.e., a set of circles,
squares, triangles. These activities familiarize children with the
classification task: that is, form sets where something is the same
for each object in the set and label the set.

The selection of play materials in the group to be sorted
should guide children initially to classify according to obvious
criteria they can see. As they become more skilled in classification,
the groups of objects to be sorted should become more diverse and
the criteria less obvious perceptually. For example, children enjoy
sorting sets according to their *function,* i.e., this set is things you
use in the kitchen; or, later, this set is things that are *animate or
inanimate* (knowledge criteria) that children have acquired from
experience and teaching rather than through the senses. The
gradual formation, redefinition, and reclassification of objects by
varying the criteria for the sets eventually leads to understanding of
sets within sets, e.g., sub-sets and hierarchies within sets such as
these are petunias, roses and marigold sub-sets (within the
'flowers' set).

Children usually become quite absorbed in classification
tasks that seem and are like puzzles to them when they have to sort
in increasingly challenging ways. If the materials they are given to
sort are challenging and interesting, children remain absorbed in
the task for long periods. I would keep a plastic shell of a pumpkin
filled with various small objects that I would change periodically
for my children (and grandchildren) to sort. It would keep them
busy for an afternoon on a rainy day; my job was to keep changing
the objects to be sorted and increasingly challenging in order to
maintain their interest. Thomas Homer-Dixon claims that
encouraging children to keep sorting (classifying), naming new
criteria for their sets and finding new ways to classify, builds
flexible, nuanced minds capable of "ingenuity" and invention. [13]

When learning the concept of classification, the linking relationships are as important as the discrete pieces of information that comprise the concept. For example, "these objects form a set because they are all used for cooking, even though they are all different in many other ways". Young children need direct experience with concrete objects in the environment that they can touch, match, combine, or separate. Gradually, they build the neural connections in the brain that later enable them to classify things according to abstract criteria. In the early stages, concepts are formed by constructing relationships among objects that resemble each other in one way (or two or three ways): for example, "these objects are the same because they all feel fuzzy"; therefore, they belong in the "fuzzy" set although they may be different in all other ways.

As they gain experience, children's attention moves from objective, concrete physical characteristics that differentiate the sets they form to less obvious criteria based on what they 'know' (knowledge) such as animal habitats (e.g., water, land, air) or the composition of objects – the wooden ones, plastic ones, rubber ones. From sorting according to knowledge-based, factual criteria, and subjective criteria such as things that are beautiful/ugly, happy/sad, safe/dangerous, children progress toward sorting random groups of objects in which they decide the criteria they will use to create each set These play activities are the essence of *discovery learning*. Rather than guessing or estimating or predicting, classification involves deliberate rational thinking in order to sort a group of random objects for which the similarities or distinctions become increasingly nuanced and abstract. Classification is a logical concept that, like number, can never be exhausted. Learning to classify in increasingly discrete way builds mental structures and cognitive flexibility, creativity, and original thinking; classifying is like a fitness exercise for the brain.

Children need sufficient time and play experience with
sorting tasks to achieve as much differentiation as they have time
for. Becoming skilled in the formation of classes and hierarchies of
classes and subsets promotes divergent thinking, the ability to find
and understand subtle differences, and, later, make discrete
distinctions among things or ideas. An ability to differentiate small
details contributes to thinking skills that lie at the heart of
creativity and invention. Classification tasks, done with purpose
and planning, provide practice for persistence and task orientation
(ability to focus on the task at hand). Consider the brisk mental
activity involved in defining the criteria for sets, undoing and
redefining sets, each time finding original criteria that are not
readily observable or known; and then using combinations of
physical, knowledge-based or abstract criteria to define their sets.

The ability to define, redefine and differentiate sets of
things according to increasingly abstract criteria is related to
science. Classification skills are essential to natural science (e.g.,
classes of trees, vegetables, animal life) and to understanding
physical science phenomena such as objects that attract versus
repel, and things that dissolve/don't dissolve. The teacher's task is
to ensure that sorting tasks become increasingly less obvious
through the senses and lead children to rely more on what they
know and understand. "As soon as a child is old enough to
understand sorting and organizing, it will enhance his cognitive
skills and his capacity for learning if we teach him to organize his
world." [14]

Children do not achieve a logical ability to classify on a set
timetable or at the same time. Some children understand how to
classify in a few play episodes; others take longer. Play materials
for classification activities should remain in the learning
environment for as long as it takes all children to master each stage
in learning the concept. Taking longer does not imply that these

children are not as bright; it means that they need more hands-on
experience with things and more perceptually-based (sensory)
sorting tasks before they tackle a knowledge-based or more
abstract classification task. When the goal is that all children
achieve the logical-mathematical learning outcomes, the need for
regular monitoring, assessment and recording of children's
progress as they develop each concept is non-negotiable. We have
known for decades that having performance standards for children
to achieve is ineffective unless teachers also possess the skills for
assessing, measuring, and recording their learning progress. [15]
For classification activities see [16] in the Notes for Chapter 8.

Concept of Seriation

**Seriation is the ordering of objects by size from a
common baseline always going in a straight line, in one
direction only.** The ability to order the objects in ascending or
descending order, by planning ahead, not using trial and error,
with the same gradation in size separating each item in the
series, is the learning outcome for concept of seriation. Toddlers
are usually introduced to this concept by playing with familiar
nesting toys, e.g., Russian dolls. In preschool and kindergarten,
specific-purpose play materials like Cuisenaire rods help children
move from exploratory trial and error play to arranging play
materials vertically or horizontally by correctly estimating the
consistent *gradation* in size from one object to the next in the
series and maintaining a common baseline. The set must be
complete in order for children to grasp the concept. The essential
problem to solve in seriation is 'what comes next in the series?'
and to correctly estimate the order of the items ahead of time,
keeping in mind the governing principles – i.e., one gradation in
size difference between each item in the series, common baseline
and straight line in one direction only.

As children engage with seriation activities, they explore the relationship between each of the items; they compare, match, join and divide, initially using trial and error. Eventually, they 'discover' that each two items in the series is different in size by exactly the same amount as the previous two items. This concept requires them to move away from a perceptual analysis of the task. Typically, they forget criteria like "all objects in the series must be on a common baseline" and "the series goes in one direction only" and they have to start over. Seriation requires children to mentally create relationships between the graduated objects, account for the governing principles and complete the series in one try with no errors along the way.

Why is seriation an important concept to understand?

Creating relationships by seriating a standardized set of objects involves keeping in mind the governing factors, such as equal gradations in size from one object to the next in the series, a common baseline for the series, and moving left to right in a straight line and in one direction only. Understanding simpler relationships such as big-bigger-biggest makes it is easier to understand the logic of number and to tackle ordinal relationships such as first, second, third. As with number and classification concepts, seriation requires children to focus on the less obvious aspects of the task. Seriating helps them integrate notions of pattern (e.g. intervals) and structure (e.g. part/whole) that are related to mathematics. The concept of seriation is embedded in mathematical and scientific problem solving – comparing and contrasting, measuring, and the importance of controlling several factors to achieve an accurate solution. Children also learn about probability as they estimate from unordered sets of items the order they want to achieve. For seriation activities refer to #17 in the Notes for Chapter 8.

Curriculum change in kindergarten

In the latter decades of the 20th century, significant

breakthroughs were made in our understanding of children's conceptual development. Among the most significant findings was that children's understanding of concepts is acquired through discovery and exploration during play with concrete objects, especially when the play materials ensure that the concepts are embedded within them for children to 'uncover' such as nesting dolls or cups, animal habitat puzzles or Cuisenaire rods. It took three or more decades to evolve an "exploratory, play-oriented, discovery learning" approach to kindergarten curriculum and learning. [18]

Math learning problems are encountered early

Children who move on to grade one arithmetic operations before they have grasped basic logical-mathematical concepts are often confused by adding and subtracting numbers. Instead of relying on concepts they understand, they resort to adding and subtracting based on what they can remember or count on their fingers; that is, they continue to depend on their senses. This approach works for the child until the arithmetic operations become more complex and variables are introduced such as adding and subtracting two-and-three-digit numbers and breaking whole numbers into fractional amounts. In math, where learning is cumulative (i.e., builds step upon step), they become confused, lose the thread of logical thinking, and decide that they can't do math. As Anna Stokke states: "When children do not learn one concept properly it is difficult for them to learn another concept on which it relies. This is why the malaise in math education starts early…when kids should be learning the basics so they can move on to the more difficult concepts". [19]

Science learning for kindergarten/primary children

Logical-mathematical concepts are also important for

learning about science and scientific thinking. Early science
concepts and skills include predicting, estimating, analyzing
information, tabulating, interpreting, forming conclusions and
reporting results. Another kindergarten mandate is to introduce
children to basic science fundamentals including those related to
the scientific method.

Natural science

Children are natural scientists and exploration,
experimentation and hypothesizing come naturally to them.
Among the many beautiful characteristics of young children is
their natural curiosity about the world, ability to wonder and
meander over the smallest details in nature and their drive to
explore natural phenomena and how things work. Science in
kindergarten involves "sciencing" which is an active process of
exploring, testing, finding patterns, observing changes, perhaps
recording changes, and asking questions. [20] "Sciencing"
employs the skills of inquiry, hypothesis, planning, deducing, and
finding answers, all skills that are used at a more sophisticated
level by scientists who apply the scientific method in their
research.

The key ingredient for sciencing is a well-provisioned
science centre and access to interesting natural space to explore
outdoors with tools for inspecting and dissecting things, resource
books, and collections of things to classify, use, take apart and
reassemble. Children's sciencing does not require pre-set activities
but rather the freedom to explore, discover and learn from
materials, resources and phenomena they uncover outdoors in
nature. The indoor science centre should be an exciting space with
naturally-occurring and diverse "things" to sort, sift, transform,
and inspect. For physical science exploration, basic equipment
would include a microscope, a counter or sink and a water source,

and storage containers. A resource table that includes pictures and
specimens borrowed from the local library or museum promotes
children's curiosity about the natural world and increases the
likelihood they will become dedicated custodians of our vulnerable
planet and environmentalists. Science goals should be addressed
outdoors, at least as much as indoors, and in all seasons of the year.

An indoor-outdoor approach to science in kindergarten
implies considerable change to the design and equipping of
outdoor space in school grounds. Schools should be able to access
natural space in the community, i.e. perhaps a park, a dedicated
nature preserve or conservation grounds where children discover
science phenomena and find outdoor specimens in all seasons.
Science exploration on field trips to nature conservation areas
should be part of kindergarten science especially for children in
urban centres. Many books about ensuring that children have
regular contact with nature, including Richard Louv (2005, 2008,
2016, 2020) who coined the term "nature-deficit disorder") [21]
and Scott D. Sampson [22] provide ideas for exploring, concepts to
address, and phenomena for parents to investigate outdoors with
children.

Kindergarten science programs should support children's
transition from dependence on physical-perceptual criteria toward
a logical understanding of science concepts in the primary school
years. Activities should test their commitment to "seeing is
believing" and enable them to make a transition to "knowing and
understanding" based on direct investigation indoors and outdoors.
This transition to concrete-operational thinking in science should
occur naturally while the child is learning the logical concepts but
this seldom occurs in kindergartens today. One reason is that
schools do not use the outdoor learning environment nearly
enough. Science activities indoors are too often 'one-off' activities
that make few meaningful or durable connections to science

phenomena. A class nature study project that is ongoing and proceeds gradually by incorporating observations, deriving conclusions and gaining knowledge related to a topic that is pursued in some depth leads children to a meaningful understanding of the related concepts and to make important connections over an extended timeframe. Primary school science learning is another area for curriculum reform.

Physical science

Space should be allocated in the science learning centre for physical science with materials that encourage children to experiment and test phenomena they can observe directly such as light sources, melting and freezing, and weights. It is important to choose physical science activities where concepts are directly observable by children such as discovering the relationships among speed, incline and distance rather than unobservable phenomena. It is important to remember children's dependence on "what I see I believe" even as they are making the transition to logical understanding. Until they demonstrate evidence of concrete operational thinking, avoid science activities that encourage magical thinking such as those that generate unobservable change in which the transformation cannot be seen, as in the case of the pull of magnets or electric current. Focus instead on observable changes such as floating and sinking, changes in water (melting, freezing, condensing), speed, weight and distance. No kindergarten program is complete without space and time to explore physical science phenomena, ask questions and pose hypotheses or 'what-ifs?' Conducting simple investigations to discover causes and effects often leads to exciting discoveries that children remember and may seed a lifelong interest in science.

Spatial concepts such as: above/below and directions such as right/left and forward/backward may be learned in the science

centre and during active play. When children climb, crawl through
tunnels, and build bridges, they learn about distance, space, depth,
height, and weight. Recognizing patterns, predicting what comes
next and finding out what fits together occurs in the construction
area. Primary school science should enable children to conduct
investigations that lead them to question, predict, observe, adjust,
and communicate findings. As children explore and test ideas, they
begin to see themselves as investigators and problem solvers.

Reaction to national and international mathematics test scores

International and national test scores and rankings in math
have shone a light on math curriculum, teaching methods, testing
regimes, and teacher training. The performance of Canada's 15-
year-old children on the OECD's 2013 Programme for
International Student Assessment (PISA) scores in mathematics
showed a decline of nine points from 2006 to 2013 when the
Canadian ranking fell to 13th place from the top ten. The recent
PISA test scores (2019) have shown improvement in Canada's
ranking for grade eleven math to seventh place after Japan, Korea,
Estonia, Netherlands, Switzerland, and Poland, a happier result,
but not one to crow about. The performance of children in the 2018
Ontario math test for grade six children was bleak. Less than fifty
percent of children in grade six met the grade-level provincial
standard for competence in math. [23] Educators, employers and
the general public clamoured again for change to math curriculum
but math problems persist.

From the turn of this century, many routine production jobs
have been replaced by "knowledge worker" jobs that require
sophisticated verbal, logical-mathematical and technological skills.
[24] During the past twenty years, warnings about the changing
ratio of skilled to unskilled jobs have hit home with parents,
especially those who experienced dramatic workforce change

firsthand and had to retrain and find new livelihoods. Technology dominates in many workplaces and increasingly performs the functions of former routine production workers. Corporations continue to demand workers with sophisticated skills to fill complex emerging roles and highly-skilled jobs. With the market for routine jobs declining, along with their remuneration, a decision by children to avoid mathematics and science places damaging limitations on lifelong career prospects and personal economic security.

Declining math proficiency among graduates has affected our nation's productivity and competitiveness for nearly three decades. Canada has experienced labour shortages for the STEM careers (Science, Technology, Engineering and Mathematics) since the last decade of the 20th century. John Manley in 2013, then CEO and president of the Canadian Council of Chief Executives, called the shrinking pool of skilled workers a "national emergency" that he blamed on "shortfalls in our education system". [25] The search for solutions to the "national emergency" turned attention to how math, in particular, (and science) are taught in schools.

Blaming 'discovery learning

After decades of complaints by corporations, think-tanks and parents who were unable to help their children with math homework, ministries of education launched the 'discovery learning' math curriculum early in this century across several provinces. They convinced themselves that conventional drills, memorizing tables, and following rules and formulas for solving problems were too pedantic, 'boring' and explained why children failed to understand math. Some educators feared that rote learning methods were undermining children's motivation to inquire, think logically, devise a rational solution to problems, and explain their answers. They were not entirely wrong about that. Education

ministries, however, established 'discovery learning' curriculum
claiming it was the 'right answer' to elementary school math
problems whereby children would "create math through
investigating and exploring". [26] The math problems that
appeared soon after were particularly acute in the junior division,
grades four to six and by grades seven and eight too many children
feared math and either dropped it as soon as they could or enrolled
in non-academic, applied math courses.

'Discovery learning' had been heralded for several decades
(after the 1970s) for its success in early childhood development
and learning that was amply confirmed by research. [27] Ministries
of education were convinced that discovery learning, which had
been so successful with young children, would solve the math
issues in junior and intermediate classrooms. Rote learning and
memorization of tables, rules and other tools used in elementary
school math were largely abandoned and replaced by inquiry,
estimation and probability. The discovery learning curriculum
emphasized "reasoning" one's way through math problems and
"breaking problems down into component parts" and "thinking
through through the steps to follow" in order to 'estimate' the
answer. [28] Direct teaching approaches for applying principles
and rules were sidelined, even forbidden. Teachers confessed they
had been required by school officials to stop using the 'old'
methods or trying out newer systems for learning math.

Teachers were advised to embrace the new curriculum,
after only scant professional development at various intervals, and
to boost the credibility of discovery learning to the public. The
approach soon produced large numbers of elementary school
graduates who struggled with math fundamentals and were unable
to understand high school math. Test scores declined and further
data showed that adolescents were increasingly avoiding math,
unable to do 'mental arithmetic', and had trouble with basic math

problems.

Lost in the adoption of discovery learning for the junior and intermediate divisions had been an awareness that while discovery learning during the preoperational stage of development is developmentally-appropriate, children in middle childhood who are concrete-operational are ready for and benefit from teacher instruction in math, often need coaching, and find learning tables and formulas to be readily accessible tools they can use for problem solving. Although the concrete operational child continues to benefit from some experiential (hands-on) learning in math (and science), when children reach the junior and intermediate divisions they are ready for a gradual introduction to formal learning and more didactic teaching methods.

Discovery-based learning strategies were widely blamed for declining test scores and the shortage of graduates with proficient STEM skills. The public was encouraged to blame failure of the math curriculum on discovery learning - but for all the wrong reasons. That ministries of education had failed to recognize children's readiness for some structure and direct teaching in math from grades four to eight was a failure that ranks right up there with the decision to stop teaching phonics in the 1980s and the adoption of the "whole language" approach to teaching reading. Not only that, discovery learning was never intended to be a exclusive approach to teaching math to children who had already achieved concrete operational thought.

Trouble with math usually becomes evident when a child is required to move beyond basic arithmetic operations in the primary grades and to understand and apply fractions and decimals from grade four on. This is usually the time when parents with the means to do so engage a tutor to help their child with math homework and review lost ground. Children who do not have that advantage simply fall behind, deepening the social and economic divide in education between privilege and penury.

A most disturbing element about the failure of math education is that when interventions are unsuccessful, parents, even teachers (and sometimes the children themselves) conclude that the child "can't do math". All too often, children drop math or science or both subjects at their first opportunity. This decision limits their choices and precludes or delays postsecondary learning that depends on or requires mathematical proficiency (i.e. numeracy). This waste of human potential has become a serious educational issue in Canada today as it negatively affects the development of individual potential, undermines the competence of our human resources, and reduces national productivity and influence. Furthermore, to attract young people to programs that require math proficiency, some postsecondary programs were forced to lower expectations of students' math readiness for undergraduate courses and sometimes their exit outcomes as well. This unfortunate adjustment has not increased Canada's competitiveness globally.

Middle childhood is a stage when children build knowledge that becomes an endless source of curiosity and interest. They love collecting weird objects, memorizing jokes, solving puzzles, and tackling new challenges. With the right teaching and coaching, added to understanding concepts and having learned how to apply reasoning and logic, children are likely to see math as a series of numeric puzzles to solve. The concrete-operational child is ready for learning that requires memory, following rules, logical reasoning, order, and repetition in order to understand subjects like math and science that have an internal orderliness, form and logic.

Instead of capitalizing on children's concrete operational 'readiness' for formal learning and instruction, ministries of education extended discovery learning without understanding where, when and with whom discovery learning is appropriate. Their decision might not have been as devastating if the application of some discovery learning methods had been treated as 'value-added' instead of abandoning formal learning methods and direct teaching that had worked. Not only that, but the absence of records showing that children had achieved logical-mathematical thinking meant that junior and intermediate division teachers could not assume that their incoming students understood the basic logical concepts that would prepare them for more complex arithmetic operations and problem solving.

A nation-wide debate about how math should be taught in schools continues. A cry for "back to basics" teaching methods is recurrent, but that is not the answer either. The Ontario government introduced another "new math curriculum" for implementation in the fall of 2020 but the timing was complicated by the pandemic. Teachers had neither received sufficient notice of the changes nor the training they needed. The outline for the new curriculum suggests that statements such as "adding number facts", "coding", "concepts about equal sharing to make fractions easier to understand starting in grade one" and "mandatory financial literacy" will be fleshed out over a four-year period for implementation of the new curriculum. [29] The danger is that another new math curriculum will be hastily installed before adequate consultation with teachers and parents and sufficient testing to ensure that it will improve math outcomes. Most important of all, teachers have to be well-trained and sufficiently prepared to teach the new math curriculum.

Improved teacher training for mathematics is an important first step

Skills-based math teaching for children in middle

childhood that is balanced with logical thinking, reasoning and inquiry learning to promote problem-solving and flexible thinking should guide reform for math education. The parents who prefer to go back to basic math are right in some sense. As Mighton states, "You need to combine discovery with guidance." [30] Teacher certification that includes standards for math, pre-service teacher training related to teaching math and ongoing, in-service professional development are essential prerequisites to making meaningful improvements to children's math performance.

Positive, energetic dispositions for teaching math that begin by knowing how to support and guide children's understanding of fundamental logical-mathematical concepts may be realized with changes to teacher recruitment and hiring practices and teacher training. Improved training for math teaching should enable all teachers to explain math concepts clearly and discern where children are experiencing difficulty. Teachers need to know how to match math-readiness activities to children's developmental levels and be able to coach them over hurdles in understanding concepts. They should be trained to observe and assess each child's comprehension of logical-mathematical concepts and to identify areas where children need more hands-on practice with concrete materials.

Assessments of children's learning progress should be entered into an individual education plan (KIEP) for each child that would identify where a child's learning may be stalled and note in the child's KIEP any gaps that need further attention. Recommendations should be made in the KIEP for the next steps to be taken in order to help the child move forward. Persistent gaps, after more practice and coaching, should be described and added to the KIEP for the next learning level which means that children might 'carry' some learning outcomes in math from one school year to the next during the primary division, K to grade three. This would ensure that children do not miss important conceptual steps in their math education - another reason why primary education should be treated as a "learning continuum" rather than broken up into discrete grades.

Over many decades, too many children leave a grade having only partially achieved the learning outcomes for that grade level, not only in math. As math learning is cumulative, i.e. builds on concepts already learned, problems with math compound each year unless children's gaps in learning are fully addressed in a timely way. If parents were aware of the math learning outcomes for each grade level, where their child's gaps in math learning may be, and the ongoing practice and coaching that is needed, they would be better prepared to help children with math homework and monitor their progress.

Children should become numerate and able to apply math fearlessly and competently in their everyday lives and for the working world of the future. Math education is long overdue for significant evidence-based reform. Children also need the emotional stamina and self-control to persist when they encounter obstacles in learning and an ability to fully engage with the task at hand. These learning-to-learn skills require ongoing practice and support from teachers and parents throughout all their elementary school years.

Parents are their children's first and most important teachers

Homes usually contain items that may be used by children to practise and learn logical-mathematical concepts. Parents have opportunities to challenge and question children in a playful way to attract their attention and maintain their interest in new learning. A trip to the supermarket, a visit to the park, a car trip to explore new places all offer opportunities to learn with children. By finding the

inherent learning in everyday tasks, parents can connect play,
learning, and the effective use of time for their children. The
distinction between play and work disappears when children count
with you as you put away, match objects, form sets during tidy- up,
and, especially, detect differences and likenesses among naturally-
occurring objects outdoors.

Parents are their children's first and most important
teachers. All they need are keen powers of observation, enthusiasm
for playful interaction, and eagerness to connect with their child
through learning. The right questions at the right time and the
opportunity to reflect with them on what they see and do helps
children understand the usefulness of all learning, including
mathematics and science, to so much of life.

9

THE CREATIVE MIND

"If we really want kids to develop as creative thinkers, we need to make the rest of school – in fact, the rest of life – more like kindergarten." Michael Resnick. [1]

<u>Young children are natural artists</u>

Young children are natural artists in much the same way they are natural scientists. They are curious investigators and sharp observers of their environment and they like to represent through various media – paint, crayons, role play, movement - what they understand about their world. Howard Gardner claimed that children have a *first draft* sense of what it means to draw a picture, tell a story or invent a song and this sense should be nurtured well beyond early childhood or it will fade away. [2] Children's imaginations and creative instincts flourish during early childhood but, unless they are encouraged and tended well into middle childhood and beyond, they are redirected by the constraints of curriculum and instruction-centred learning imposed by schooling.

In kindergarten, children are willing to express themselves and try many outlets for their imaginations, curiosity, and creative urges. When they begin formal education, sometimes as early as grade two, academic regimens compete with children's natural inclinations. In formal schooling, it's as if the left brain seeks to dominate the right brain's craving for self-expression and artistic outlets as the child learns to cope with standardized and testing and rigid performance expectations. Creative impulses do not conform easily to an unyielding structure imposed by the influences of formal learning.

Young children need help and encouragement to maintain, beyond the primary years, what Gardner referred to as their "creative orientation", those flashes of inspired associations we witness as they play and explore. [3] Otherwise, the academic and behavioural conventions of grade school, coupled with expectations that children perform well on standardized tests, all too soon overwhelm their creative instincts and readiness to abandon themselves to their unique insights and experimentation. A new challenge in primary education is to sustain children's natural instincts for creativity into the junior division while also ensuring that they meet developmental and educationally-sound learning outcomes.

To nurture creativity beyond early schooling children need time to pursue interests, explore, test and experiment without suffocating strings attached. When schools become data-driven places where standardized test scores are valued more than freedom for children to invent, use trial and error, and follow diverse learning pathways, any hope for extending their "creative orientation" is swamped by tasks, pressures to 'cover' curriculum and testing routines. Education systems have not yet connected declining scores in math and science to reduced time for creative pursuits such as music, movement activities and creative projects that exercise complementary skills, habits of mind, symbolic thinking, and problem solving. Kindergarten is prime time for nurturing children's innate ability to represent an idea they have in mind, express themselves in all developmental domains and use diverse media, a range of tools and divergent approaches to setting goals and achieving outcomes.

It is more than ironic that governments and education systems still assume that children can remain creative and inventive throughout their schooling when they are exposed to the same teaching strategies and expectations that were employed during the Industrial Era of the 20th century – conventions like sitting still in class, following rules and instructions intended to maintain order and uniformity, and staying within the lines, literally and figuratively. Stifling expectations like these seemed acceptable in an era when children were schooled for an industrial world of assembly lines, standard protocols, and rigid production targets. Manual labour then was controlled and supervised and did not require workers to exercise self-discipline, creativity, and an ability to think for themselves.

A 20th century vision for education no longer applies in an age when living successfully and workplace expectations call for flexibility, novel thinking, and much better than functional literacy, numeracy and creativity. If the future needs more people who can create, invent and innovate, that vision that cannot be realized by offering a workplace training course for adults and expecting transformed performance, long after traditional schooling has imprinted its standards of conformity, uniformity, convergent thought processes, and habits of mind. A creative mind develops early while the brain is developing rapidly and mental structures are being built. Education has to prioritize the goal to sustain children's originality, natural creativity and independent thinking from kindergarten and throughout their schooling. Reframed education should promote dispositions, values and learning outcomes that are essential to the development of human potential, mental and physical health and a creative mind.

Transforming schools to foster and sustain a creative orientation

The many contradictions in education today are stark; continuing to reduce resources and time spent to promote creative thinking is one more reason why parents should participate in education reform that is relevant to original thinking and invention. "Scarce are the innate problem-solvers and innovators…or eminent creators, people particularly good at life's tough calls…Creativity is essentially homeless". [4] In order for Canada to remain competitive and prosperous in a global world, educational transformation should begin now. The pandemic may have started this ball rolling and elicited a line of thinking, experimentation, apparent willingness to take some risks, and openness to change that were barely entertained until now.

Successful transformation depends very much on the language we use. *Transformation* implies a significant change of form and substance in order to move from one state to another. The term "*innovation*" is often used liberally, as if it can be a stand-in not only for the implementation of new ideas, products and systems, but also for originality and invention. Canada's former governor-general, Julie Payette, laid out clear definitions in a 2016 speech to the Public Policy Forum's Growth Summit in Ottawa on October 12, 2016. "Invention is not innovation. Innovation is an economic and social process, a means by which productivity is improved and better ways of organizing and operating are achieved as a society. It's about developing new ways of doing things and creating value – value that will stimulate growth. Innovation involves the work of bringing an idea, a new product to the market in order to create wealth, progress and stimulate growth".

Invention, on the other hand, is an outcome of original and creative thinking that arises from a fertile environment and climate that fosters ingenuity and a disposition and drive to create something of value. An *invention* is something devised, often protected by a patent and a product of someone's original thought

process. To be inventive contains elements of creative thinking,
purposefulness, and planning. *Originality* arises from the power of
imagination and creative thinking to produce an idea, an art form
or a process or product that has not been experienced or seen
before; it possesses a freshness and novelty that may inseminate
novel thoughts and creativity. To be original is to create something
new, either by design, in artistic form, or by using words or
mathematics to explain something that is new and does not imitate.

What is creativity?

Schirrmacher [5] said that *creativity* is perceiving things in
new ways, thinking unconventionally, forming unique
combinations and patterns, and representing an original idea or
insight that may be artistic, literate, mathematical, musical,
scientific, constructive, or theoretical in nature. People are creative
in diverse ways – literally, figuratively, perceptually, linguistically,
emotionally, logically, socially, and physically - and "being
creative" does not imply being creative in all developmental
domains. Wright [6] concluded that creative impulses are related to
thinking styles - to visualize, imagine, test, create analogies, and
think in metaphors; they are also present in rational thinking,
planning and predicting, analysis, synthesis, and evaluation or
judgement. A consensus seems to exist that creativity stems from
unconstrained thought that poses a wide range of questions,
examines input from many sources, hypothesizes connections
among several potential inputs, and pursues divergent styles,
perspectives and media to so as to produce creative solutions.

Creative thinking and disciplined execution are related.
Most people agree that creativity involves originality. A product of
some kind, something concrete or even a new process or an
abstract theory is usually the intended outcome of a creative
project. There is a close connection between creative thinking and

also being able to represent a creative idea or vision. The product of representation should always resemble the idea or vision that seeded the idea for a creative investigation or project. The creative outcome should reflect a measure of authenticity (i.e. be true to the original vision and plan). A moment of inspiration that is not linked to either a plan or a vision usually remains just that and is often unmoored and of little lasting consequence.

This perspective suggests that creativity is neither a "flash in the pan" idea nor one inspired insight or product that springs seemingly out of nowhere and is attached to nothing in particular. Creativity is more often the outcome of a disciplined approach, careful planning, and faithfulness to the plan. This is the difference between "messing about" in the search for inspiration versus learning to use the tools of creativity – e.g. words, artistic tools, mathematical formulas, seeing a convergence in research results – in inspired but relevant ways. Creativity is connected to the execution of an idea, and, in its purest form, involves disciplined thought, vision and inspiration. It is also related to learning to learn skills, e.g. self-control, ability to delay gratification, block out distractions, attend to the task at hand, and the mental discipline to formulate and follow a plan. It is the relationship between inspiration and perspiration that gives meaning and authenticity to a creative product.

The origins of creativity

There have been many attempts historically to understand the origins of creativity and how it can be cultivated in children. Paul Torrance linked creativity with the ability to produce something unique, useful, and original using both divergent (open-ended, wide-ranging) and convergent (deductive, general to specific) thinking to achieve an intended result. [7] He connected having a plan and the realization of a result that approximated the

plan to creative ability and he measured the creativity of the
outcome accordingly. For Torrance, the significant characteristics
associated with creativity included *fluency of thought, flexibility,
elaboration, originality*, and resistance to giving up before
achieving the goal. Mackinnon had a similar view; that creative
behaviour involves having original or unusual ideas that are related
to authentic situations or goals, and planning, thinking through,
and sustaining the ideas until a reasonable outcome is achieved. [8]
He saw creativity not as a flash of inspiration and but as deliberate,
purposeful activity associated with disciplined habits of mind, skill
and knowledge about how to use tools and media to achieve a
creative result. Today's discussions about nurturing creativity in
childhood and beyond suggest that, for creativity to be sustained,
children need freedom to envision their own product, to explore
materials and supplies, to experiment, take chances and risk failing
now and then, to be resilient and ready to start over, to
acknowledge their successes, and seek new challenges.

Some creativity experts claim that creative thinking skills
should be actively taught from kindergarten and throughout
schooling. [9] "Actively taught" in kindergarten means providing
environments that nurture children's self-expression and
encouraging them to explore, imagine and represent what they are
thinking, perceiving, and feeling. Educators used to believe that
"actively taught" meant direct teaching of specific skills and
asking children to make the same products, within the same
timeframe so as to achieve a result that resembled a prescribed
standard.

Today's mission for kindergarten/primary schooling is not
to "teach creativity" but to provide the environments, experiences
and an emotional climate for children to think and express their
thoughts, hone their perceptual (sensory) abilities, practise skills
for representing their ideas and plans (e.g. as in sociodramatic

play), and feel confident to judge their own efforts. This argument does not recommend abandoning limits and letting children do as they please, nor does it encourage 'messing about' with materials indiscriminately. It does make a case for nurturing ideas, protecting children's natural urges for self-expression, and guiding them to plan how they will represent their thoughts and ideas. This case encourages personal choice and independence, reinforces intention and purposefulness, and rewards children for independent thinking, individuality, and industry all within an emotionally empowering climate. We seldom find that creative geniuses in any field were raised or educated in an environment of constraint and strict conformity to someone else's standards. A teacher once said: "Art has the role in education of helping children become more themselves instead of more like everyone else". [10]

Much of what children learn in kindergarten happens without being directly taught. They have their own ways to engage in hands-on, active learning from which they absorb ideas, images, feelings, and motivations. They do the same when they are creating an artistic product, inventing a script for role play or performing movements to music. Parents often want their children to be creative but do not connect their need for quiet contemplation with the ability to amuse themselves and to satisfy their craving for experiences that they choose. Instead of allowing children to become bored now and then and to reflect, dabble and dream, sometimes parents decide it is best to fill and organize children's time. Similarly, teachers, when interviewed, claim they enjoy exuberance and creativity in children. Studies show, however, that they often "respond negatively to character traits associated with creativity – such as impulsiveness, independence and nonconformity". [11]

"Children who start out the smartest do not always end up the smartest." [12] People who are deemed to be creative are not

necessarily the ones with the highest grades in school. "A high
score on intelligence tests and an ability to regurgitate facts aren't
necessarily predictors of creativity".[13] In fact, the creative mind
is more likely to resist following the strictures of formal schooling
and to avoid learning skills or knowledge they consider to be
outside their interests and not worth their time. Creative children
are often those who test the teacher, confound their parents, and
resist limitations that constrain their freedom to act, pursue their
own thoughts, have their own ideas, and challenge convention.
"Highly creative kids tend to have spikier grades...In subjects that
interest them they excel and shine, but in areas that don't interest
them they tend to underperform". [14]

The executive functions, including self-regulation, self-
assessment, and impulse control, contribute to thinking creatively,
artistry, producing something novel, and originating an idea or
production. Creative thinking depends on a *divergent thinking* style
that considers various approaches to problem solving or
representing a thought. Divergent thinking needs flexible but
disciplined minds. Children often thrive when they have to
consider an array of ideas that are not necessarily linked to one
another in conventional ways. However, traditional education has,
for decades, educated children for *convergent thought* patterns that
emphasize control, linear thinking and staying on a prescribed
path. The popular old Golden Book, Tootle the Train, (1943) was
an example – "stay on the tracks no matter what". Curriculum has
usually implied conformity – to timeframes, content, standards and
results - as children were educated to fill specific societal needs
and roles.

Recall the discussion in chapter 8 on the logical concept of
classification that promotes flexible, creative thinking. When
looking for diverse ways to sort a random group of objects,
children should be encouraged to explore many pathways in their

quest to identify criteria that might define unusual groupings or
sets. The fact that they are also bound by rules to use all objects in
the random group of things to be sorted imposes some limitations
and disciplined thinking that are essential to creative thinking. A
viable creative project seldom begins without some boundaries that
are imposed such as the tools to be used, a word limit, or artistic or
creative conventions to observe. Flexible, divergent thinkers learn
to explore diverse pathways for producing their planned
masterpiece or invention within some limitations and still find
ways to express their own perspective on a subject or issue.

Education reform has to grapple with all that accompanies
significant change such as a new vision, a revised purpose and
mandate, changes to curriculum design, and more diverse
educational delivery approaches, including new venues for
learning. The greatest impact of education reform would be an in-
depth rethinking of how to evaluate learning. This might begin
with the observation and assessment of children's current learning
needs, a plan for the next steps in learning, the definition of criteria
and benchmarks to verify progress, and the evaluation of children's
demonstrated achievement of integrated learning as described in
learning outcomes; these steps are the subject of Chapter 10.

The role of exploration and curiosity

Young children are good observers and notice fine details
that capture their attention for surprising lengths of time before
they move on to something else. Their determination to expand
their boundaries and explore new environments overrides most
other impulses. Rather than looking inward for inspiration and
reflecting as an adult might do, they generally look outward in
search of sensory and physical stimuli for their developing brains.
Children like to collect raw data about the environment using eyes,
ears, taste, touch, and smell and then store this information for

future reference. Curious children are intent upon stocking their creative 'cupboard' with ideas and images they might use for later enterprises. The more diverse the activities and materials for the child to explore and experience, the richer the child's store of images and ideas for representations and projects. The takeaway here is that teachers and parents are challenged to provide a range of enriching experiences for children. Schools should be well resourced indoors and outdoors, and mandated to provide experiences that may influence and be remembered. Parents usually try to do whatever they can, often with very few resources, to expand their children's repertoire of images, events and ideas to stow away for future reference.

The role of kindergartens in sustaining children's natural creativity

Young children are called natural artists and young scientists with a "creative orientation" because they are curious, have active imaginations, and try to express them in diverse ways. In kindergarten, children represent what they see and experience using a number of media – language, song and music, movement, role play and drama, visual arts, and construction preferably using an array of naturally-occurring (and some fabricated) loose materials including wood pieces, logs and branches, rocks, stones, bricks and boards. Children between the ages of four and six are curious about nearly everything they encounter and unselfconscious about their representations of what they imagine and experience. Although they are happy when adults notice what they have achieved, they neither need nor expect an opinion or assessment of what they produce. They are generally content with their own evaluations. An affirming approach for parents and teachers to sustain children's creative impulses is by questioning them about their play, understanding the plan children have in their heads, showing interest in what they are attempting to achieve, and suggesting or providing resources they might use if their enterprise becomes bogged down. They should avoid passing judgement.

Canada's innovation agenda is intrinsically related to a new, timely and viable educational mission for the primary division (K to grade 3) to preserve and extend young children's natural creativity well into the school years and beyond. When an adult acknowledges that a creative activity has kept a child engaged for a considerable time, he is providing feedback that the child's time was well spent, the project was worthwhile in its own right and that using her skills and imagination to follow her plan and create something new is a valued enterprise. Allowing children to apply their own standards to a production is a fundamental part of the creative process that should be recognized and supported. Owen stated that creativity is a precious orientation that "is about offering time and space to understand and experience the processes involved – which need personal qualities of application, struggle and testing, alongside qualities of cooperation, collaboration and mutual criticism". [15]

Planting the seeds of creativity, originality, and invention

Planting the seeds of original thinking and invention to foster creativity means investing in what we say we want, instead of preaching one thing and doing something quite different. Nurturing creative thinking is not just about planning more art activities and bringing easels back to the classroom (although that is also important). It also means raising meaningful questions for children to tackle, arranging for them to explore a range of indoor and outdoor venues, introducing new materials and supplies, and planning thoughtful experiences. For example, teachers might read a story about a child who lives in a condominium and wishes he had a playground close to home. Then, they might visit a condominium, look for nearby places to play, think of ways around the problem as they see it, and propose a viable solution and alternative endings to the story. There is no doubt that this approach challenges teachers to be energetic, resourceful, and creative thinkers themselves.

Community spaces such as libraries, art galleries, museums, recreation centres, and public services such as water supply and food production make interesting venues for children to understand the many aspects of creative thinking that go into building a community and making it work for people who live there. Venues that offer local history, art and timely exhibits related to festivals and seasonal events are particularly interesting for children. Teachers usually identify the learning to be gained by visiting a venue to find opportunities for children to interact with staff or equipment and ways they can research background information for a project beforehand. Mayer proposed that contemporary art museums should become the "very hub of human creativity" which suggests that education should take smarter advantage of community resources like these. Such institutions are "crucial to a thriving society...Every child should be taught the basic skills they need to take full advantage of art museums". [16]

We talk about educational reform, yet we continue to tiptoe around its edges leaving a still-regimented system in place, with much the same classroom design, curriculum and emphasis on teaching to the test. Egan stated that to sustain children's creative thinking past age seven, schools should "encourage critical thinking rather than knowledge acquisition, problem-solving skills rather than familiarity with past problems, and openness to change rather than commitment to a set of ideas and institutions". [17] John Holt described the dichotomy between children's approach to learning and the schools in this way: "The child is curious. He wants to make sense out of things, find out how things work, gain competence and control over himself and his environment and do what he can see other people doing. He is open, perceptive, and experimental.... School is not a place that gives much time, or opportunity, or reward for this kind of thinking and learning". [18] This points toward another goal of schooling for the 21st century.

To achieve the desired result, change related to the use of time in schools, provision of opportunities for self-expression and creativity, curriculum that generates diversity more than conformity, and assessment and evaluation that recognizes independent, disciplined and creative thinking should be part of the transformation in education. "Thinking outside the box" should be more than a euphemism; it should drive reform, recast the purpose, design and management of education, and promote creative performance. Otherwise, children's efforts at creativity become so dominated by the structure, conventions, boundaries, and safety of imitation as to be unremarkable and certainly not a reflection of a "rich inner life" nor of their natural creativity.

Schools underestimate children's remarkable curiosity and eagerness to learn in their own ways. By imposing adult standards on what children should learn and measuring them accordingly, we rear anxious children and induce parents to be competitive on behalf of their children. It is wiser to have confidence that young children are natural learners who can usually learn for themselves and not solely because of the choices and efforts of others. Above all, kindergartens should protect children's natural tendencies toward creativity by eliciting their inclination for imagination and fantasy and their ability to think using symbols in ways that are meaningful to them.

Skills and tools that support creativity

Creativity cannot be taught, but immersion in the right environments provide opportunities to practise the skills and tools related to creative thinking, dispositions, and processes.

Awakening children's senses and their ability to process sensory
input accurately should be fine-tuned when children are young.
Perceptual (sensory) processing skills and acuity (accuracy) are
important support systems for developing creativity. Physical
environments that contain a wide range of creative materials and
tools – e.g. blocks, art supplies, props, musical instruments, and
display and workspace are a good place to start. Children like to
represent what they are thinking and planning using artistic tools
they choose, to express emotions through stories they tell, move
their bodies and perform actions to music, and invent scripts for
role play. Access to a wide range of materials found indoors and
outdoors, such as cardboard boxes, sand, and pebbles, fallen
leaves, and drawing instruments, spark curiosity, imagination, and
industry. Children need time to freely associate the diverse things
they find with the plans they conjure up. Outdoor natural spaces
are central to arousing creative instincts and aspirations. Feelings
and sensibilities are awakened, tastes are cultivated, and minds are
opened to possibilities, perspectives, hypotheses and questions, and
ideas and inventions. The longer a child experiences and engages
with natural environments, the more likely their minds will remain
open to novel thoughts and their creative juices will flow, blossom,
and persist.

Well-organized environments inspire a "creative orientation"

Space, time to think, question, do and appraise contribute to
novel thinking and ideas. Organization is as essential as a warm
climate of approval and the confidence to initiate an activity and
express oneself. Disorganized space encourages disorganized
thinking; ineffective or insufficient resources frustrate self-
expression. Space requirements for music and movement require
an area for active play outdoors and indoors – an empty classroom,
a gymnasium or hallway would do - just as science requires natural

areas to explore and find things to use in experiments and artistic
creations, like pods, seeds, acorns, leaves, and stones. Children
enjoy nooks and crannies among plants and shrubs that shelter
butterflies, wildflowers and birds that can inspire drawings,
projects and become places to hide and store treasures they find.

The organization of space for creative pursuits should send
messages that this is a place where children explore tools and
media, plan, realize a vision they have concocted, work together or
alone, find resources, and execute their plan. Ideally, this space
would allow room for fabric arts and sewing, needles, threads,
glue, fasteners, tape measures, various remnants of cloth, and a
cutting table for fabric and patterns. (In Scandinavia, I saw
children using small sewing machines; they would also observe
their teachers sewing placemats for the tables or making curtains
for a puppet theatre.) There should be a sheltered woodworking
space, preferably outdoors, with a bench and tools, aprons, a wood
supply bin, glue, nails and screws, clamps, measuring tapes,
pencils, and paper. Sharing space by periodically moving in and
out of the classroom things like sewing centres and replacing them
with woodworking materials, or putting aside some large
equipment to make space for a marching band should always be
possible. Classrooms that remain the same from September to June
do little to foster and sustain a creative orientation.

Sociodramatic play facilitates creative self-expression

Children's natural inclinations for self-expression through
pretend play and drama require many opportunities in kindergarten
for sociodramatic play (collaborative role play) as described in
Chapter 3. When their immature creative urges and free
associations through pretend, drama and role play are supported,
children's natural lack of self-consciousness is protected and more
likely to remain alive into the school years and beyond. When the

curriculum and schedule emphasize everyone doing much the same
thing at the same time, and when content takes precedence over
process, the program emphasizes how to "make every kid the
same, versus allowing their creative potentials to emerge". [19]
Sociodramatic play is an especially useful vehicle for protecting
and furthering a creative orientation. The classroom should have a
protected area for role play that promotes thinking on one's feet,
memory, imagining, and imitating. Sociodramatic role play is so
integral to divergent and creative thinking that adult development
programs often use role play in leadership training.

Aesthetic development in kindergarten

Gardner referred to aesthetic development as a *key
understanding* that allows people to discriminate between what is
beautiful and not beautiful and understand the difference between
artistic worth and kitsch.[20] Aesthetic development involves a
taste for quality and an appreciation of harmony in art and design
that develop in an environment that nurtures sensitivity to beautiful
things. The kindergarten that is stocked with creative works and
objects that are well cared for, displayed in an orderly space, with
children's artistic works as well as those of famous and local artists
and artisans cultivates aesthetic sensibilities in children that can
last a lifetime.

Young children crave exposure to nature and natural
phenomena, beautiful things to hold and look at, a changing
environment, unstructured experiences that ignite wonder,
admiration, and respect. As they explore and investigate, children
cultivate charming insights about the world as they see it. John
Mighton claims that maintaining children's sense of wonder and
curiosity is essential to achieving their full potential and creativity.
[21] Disney characters, television culture and artifacts representing
the latest cartoon symbols may not be ideal ways to support

wonder and curiosity. These might be downplayed in a
kindergarten that strives to cultivate an aesthetic sense in young
children, but, as children are attracted and attached to them,
eliminating them entirely might defeat the purpose. Decorating the
kindergarten classroom with children's works of art and
reproductions of famous works of art, both two- and three-
dimensional, usually compete successfully with pop culture
artifacts. Beautiful items collected from the natural world should
be displayed where children can examine and touch them. The
sound of music that supports contemplation and imagining can also
be a reflective accompaniment to creative play and projects.

Artistry and self-expression

A by-product of the standardized testing movement is that
children have become more anxious and fearful of failure, a state
of mind that may stem from feeling they should impress the
evaluator. This incompatible condition imposes undue stress on
children who want to learn; it inhibits playfulness and willingness
to risk immersing themselves in unconscious processes that elicit
unique and original connections between things and ideas. The
state of being playful, unafraid and motivated occurs when
children are set free in an environment that challenges them on
many levels – physical, social-emotional and cognitive – to make
progress, achieve intended results, and feel proud of their
productions. When kindergartens do not allow playfulness to
dominate the climate of the classroom, it is harder for children to
lose themselves in the moment, fully engage in an activity, allow
their imaginations to flow, use skills and symbols they understand
to execute their plans, and represent ideas that flow from their
imaginations.

Children's self-expression is limited when they are required
to follow someone else's plan and idea for a creative activity or

project. When they are asked to copy a prescribed pattern that makes their product look much like everyone else's, they are engaged in crafts, not creativity. Artistry is a process of knowing which media to use to create a particular effect or result and is also the creative capacity to imagine a product and a process that represents what the child has in mind rather than someone else's vision. For children to invent and create with art supplies, uninterrupted time and open-ended supplies – e.g. paints, papers, brushes - are crucial. A tape recorder, puppet theatre and a stage are relevant resources for drama and shows. For role play, costumes and a set as a backdrop may help children elaborate and extend their script.

Creativity with music

The ability to accurately hear and replicate melody, pitch, tone, and rhythm appears early in children who possess musical intelligence. Most children love singing, listening, and moving to music, playing an instrument, and responding by keeping time (clapping). Children who have had musical training also tend to be good students and perform well on most academic tasks. Howard Gardner found that musical intelligence is "a distinct way of knowing" that emerges earlier than most other special talents. [22] Knowing that music promotes playful interaction, academic proficiency, release from stress, and emotional wellbeing makes school-based musical training an important component of elementary school education.

Music facilitates language learning and should be part of every young child's experience at home and at school, indoors and outdoors, but it is not heard often enough in elementary schools. If it is present at all, one often hears children sing the tired old songs that their parents learned when they were young. The 'oldies' such as the ABC song, Inky, Dinky Spider have been beloved children

(and adults) for generations, but so have the compositions of
Gershwin and Porter whose music endures but no longer
dominates the adult music scene. If there is a musical gap left to be
filled by composers and musicians, it might be to compose vibrant
new songs for children from the time they begin to mouth words.
Music and singing should capture imaginations, introduce new
sounds and words, tell stories, poke fun and laughter, and elicit
fond memories. In Canada's classrooms, the introduction of songs
in languages that also reflect the ethnicities of the children should
be a regular feature of the music program.

The impact of music on health, creative interpretation, and skills
for self-expression

Music germinates ideas, makes connections, challenges
children to recognize and replicate patterns, and use sound symbols
to represent thoughts and actions. Developing a relationship with
music while young lasts a lifetime; when children grow up without
music, they are not only less likely to become sensitive to music as
adults but they seldom discover its stress-reducing impact on
mental health. Music has the capacity to transport children
emotionally from one environment to another, soften sadness,
resurrect memories, and lighten mood; it is a crucial resource for a
generalized sense of wellbeing and thinking good thoughts. Music
mediates stress, pain, loneliness, and despair, and enhances
pleasure. It helps children sleep, energizes them after a rest, and
engages them in activity outdoors and indoors. Their response to
music is similar to how they respond to a beloved pet: their
expressions and moods change, their attention is engaged and they
respond emotionally.

Music affects creativity by motivating self-expression and
adding beauty, depth, and variation to life. Stories told to music

improve children's ability to connect musical sounds to characters in a story and reinforce links between the senses, words, and sound symbols. Indoors and outdoors, space should be converted for movement activities to music such as marching, dancing and gliding like a skater, along with storage for musical instruments, recording and playback devices.

Music supports learning in all domains – physical, cognitive, social, emotional – and it motivates creative impulses and invention. Parents are wise to ask teachers how music outcomes are addressed in the kindergarten/primary years. Listening, singing and moving to music exercises the brain, strengthens connections among brain cells and influences perceptual development (senses), mind development (memory, symbolic thinking), and physical development (stimulation of the nervous system, coordination and motor skills). Music triggers self-expression as children pretend they are a famous dancer or assume the role of a conductor. Music creates an association between hands and painting or drawing at the easel as they listen to a story told through music. Symbolic thinking is enhanced by the addition of music to imitating the actions of an animal or a character in a story.

Building a creative mind with unit blocks

Play with blocks is particularly rich in creative potential as well as learning in all domains. Many teachers never had opportunities to play with unit blocks, and teacher training seldom addresses their significance with respect to children's overall development. Unit blocks were invented in Boston by Caroline Pratt in 1914; prior to that date, other blocks had already been deemed important play materials in the kindergartens of Friedrich Froebel (his Gifts and Occupations) and Patty Smith Hill's blocks of the late 19th and early 20th centuries that fastened together with pegs, holds and grooves. When unit blocks are unavailable in kindergartens, many reasons are given, including 'blocks are messy' and 'difficult to tidy up'. The most common reason cited is lack of space. A reason might also be that teachers do not know all the skills, concepts, and habits of mind that children learn by playing with these dynamic and creative learning materials.

There is an interesting story about Frank Lloyd Wright, the famous 20th century American architect, whose mother Anne invested in two or three sets of plain, abstract wooden blocks for her young preschooler. In later years, Wright attributed his architectural genius to regular play with the blocks and credited his mother for his illustrious, creative career over six decades. This story does not imply that children who play regularly with unit blocks will become famous architects but play with unit blocks can nurture spatial intelligence on a scale that may lead to creative genius. These abstract, unadorned, plain wooden blocks, usually made of well-sanded birch or maple, are the ultimate 'responders' to children's actions on them and facilitate learning of concepts related to shape, metric measurements, balance, pattern and design, perceptual skills, numeracy, and attending skills. As they also attract small groups of children who like to collaborate in planning and building, they contribute to social development and the executive functions. Children rely on their creative insights and abilities to fashion these abstract pieces of wood into a structure that represents what they have in mind.

As with most materials for creative play, the more children play with unit blocks (or any plain, unadorned blocks that are large enough to build an impressive structure), the more skilled they become in using abstract materials as symbols to represent something else. Their shape, metric sizes and smooth surfaces are easily manipulated by children's small hands and are especially effective in allowing their unit block creations to become anything they imagine them to be. As they have no embellishments that suggest or restrict what children might do with them, building with them is left up to children's imaginations to create a structure that resembles the plan they hold in their mind's eye. The popular, articulated blocks such as Lego, Unifix, Lincoln Logs, and other construction sets, although entertaining and instructive, often guide children toward a specific type of structure. They are not a creative substitute for abstract unit blocks in their plain shapes and sizes. Building a fire station with Lego or other articulated blocks calls for different skills than those needed to build the same structure using unit blocks that require children to use their imaginations to supply the colours, contours, and decoration that the articulated sets provide for them. Unit blocks neither prescribe the design of structures nor how children should use them.

Unit blocks should be accessible to children every day and the furniture for storing them should be open shelves that children can access and tidy up easily after using them. Rules for their use should be made clear to children – i.e., no throwing, hitting, or crashing of a structure, always tidy up after building and keep them within the boundaries of the block area. Locating the unit block play area close to the creative arts or role play centre allows children to use them for a project or role play episode they have in mind. The unit block area should be bounded on three sides and carpeted (thin, dense carpeting) to dampen noise, enable children to sit and kneel comfortably, and provide a solid, flat base for the block structures. Programs that make good use of unit blocks often post photographs of children's structures in the classroom for children to enjoy long after they have been replaced. The difference in composition and creative learning potential from the art materials and supplies, musical instruments and role play props makes unit blocks an essential addition to any program that claims to foster and sustain children's creative orientation.

When properly employed in kindergarten and grade one, unit blocks are well worth the cost and space needed for children to play with them effectively and store them properly. Ideally, parents should request and even fundraise to help schools invest in at least two sets of unit blocks for each kindergarten/primary classroom because they are one of the best investments for promoting imagination, creative thinking, planning and representation that schools (and, perhaps, parents) can make.

Science, creativity, and invention

Children are "natural scientists" and like to engage in the skills of *sciencing* from an early age. When they are encouraged to explore things physically and with their senses, and to look for patterns in what they observe, make connections and ask 'what if' questions and experiment, they are developing creative thinking for scientific inquiry and investigation. Preparing children for science and reaching conclusions implies that teachers should encourage them to freely associate patterns with potential causes, investigate puzzling phenomena that cannot be understood through the senses alone, formulate questions that lead them to explore further, and use the results of investigations to ask more questions. The investigation skills learned in childhood are early versions of inquiry and analytic skills needed for scientific research.

Thinking outside the box

Learning to think outside the box includes *divergent thinking* that can break through old boundaries, topple outdated conventions, and overcome structural, systemic impediments. Thinking outside the box does not begin in high school or postsecondary education; it emerges as children experience environments that nurture and sustain imagination, symbolic thinking and the creative impulses that are active early in life. If

272

and when this nation truly begins to value creative thinking and
reinvents education to liberate children's learning potential and
capacity to originate, invent and innovate, schools may be
motivated to discontinue practices that were designed to promote
assembly-line conformity and conventional protocols for the
Industrial Age.

In the past century, it seemed appropriate for children to sit
still for long periods, absorb standard, uniform 'content', and
arrive at the same right answers, about the same time, using
established teaching and learning methods. Expectations and
practices like these are not conducive to learning outcomes,
aspirations and talent development that call for thinking outside the
box. Schools, governments, and corporations today cannot expect
children to learn skills and achieve the goals of creative thinking
and inventiveness by doing very little that is different from past
practice. The new mandate for education should be a curriculum,
learning environments, venues and practices that respect and
protect creativity, foster independent thinking, and encourage an
inquiry and *sciencing* mindset.

Resourceful teachers who are also skilled observers and
assessors and are able to intervene effectively when children have
a question, encounter an obstacle or need additional resources,
enable children to reach creative goals. Teachers and parents seed
thinking outside the box when they 'accompany' children in their
project efforts. Creative minds are developed when children are
encouraged to use technology for investigating and reporting
instead of resorting to screens to amuse themselves. When children
are looking for ideas for their projects, technologies may expand
children's thinking and learning horizons by answering some
questions and making useful suggestions. Teachers and parents are
also instrumental when they interact with children to help them
feel confident that they are becoming creative thinkers and

inventors as well as effective learners.

Some essential elements of education reform involve "thinking outside the box" and taking advantage of new and better venues for helping children retain their creative orientation such as learning outdoors, in natural environments, and taking advantage of community resources to introduce children to the creative enterprises that are 'out there' in the world beyond the school. The use of playgrounds has declined as parents became overly preoccupied with their children's safety at the expense of their physical development, reasonable risk-taking, and the opportunity to discover and appreciate nature's artistry and abundant resources for creative activity. It is another contradiction that urban developers are still permitted to remove trees and other natural vegetation from new residential developments and parks and even replace them with artificial surfaces and climbing structures.

When we understand how creativity originates and how to cultivate it, we find many practices in communities, schools and homes that undermine children's creative orientation. Reducing art and music programs in schools makes it less likely that children will choose to explore artistic media. When the unit blocks are stored in a cupboard that is open only for special reasons, they seldom become sufficiently acquainted with these abstract materials to exploit their creative potential. Teachers who allow children in the role play area only when their seatwork is finished deprive children of an especially rich creative medium. Children need many opportunities to tackle creative challenges and execute their plans.

Instead of encouraging children to conform and deal effectively with and within current systems and structures, we need to educate them to create the systems and structures. [23] School jurisdictions typically abandon creative thinking outcomes and activities when "back to the basics" movements arise or education budgets are cut back, or when schools value standardized test results more than wonder, imagination and invention. The notion of 'job readiness' and preparation for the world of work tend to shove aside personal ideals for living well, self-improvement, enrichment, and character development. Investment in arts education and sustaining children's natural creativity declines or disappears when schools choose to value competition, fitting in, and measure children according to how well they achieve the same learning as everyone else. Systemic change in primary education that would foster creative potential appears and is quite different from past values and practices.

In the third decade of this century, business professionals, politicians and government leaders still raise concerns about the decline in creativity and low levels of innovation in Canada relative to other countries. They question the education system's emphasis on facts, content and data and knowledge acquisition that has a short lifespan especially in times of rapid change. The complaints of teachers who are disenchanted with the limitations under which they work, the scarcity of teaching resources, and the time they spend on administrative tasks are turning into a resounding movement that parents should support. Updated and expanded pre-service training for teachers that addresses new modes of education delivery, diverse venues for learning, and individualized teaching that releases children's potential in all domains are urgent priorities for primary schooling to launch children on a learning trajectory toward higher performance levels, creativity and invention. The voting public would be wise to support the cost of education that promotes creative minds, disciplined thinking and learning outcomes that are suited to a vibrant, alive, democratic society. "We need to understand that classroom education is merely one phase of a continuous process of learning, discovery and engagement that can occur anywhere and anytime. We need a learning system that fuels, rather than squelches, our collective creativity." [24]

10

RELEASING CHILDREN'S POTENTIAL

"Still, in times of perplexing, unprecedented, and dangerous threats, we can learn much from childhood imagination – that wonderful capacity to generate endless "How abouts". For our species to succeed and prosper through this century, as it has during earlier eras of peril, we'll need to activate our ability to imagine possibilities. Sometimes it's a mistake to fasten too quickly on constraints; it just makes these constraints appear inescapable and robs us of any chance for genuine change."
Thomas Homer-Dixon, 2020 [1]

Public education is a follower; it weaves new ideas or trends into an old framework instead of imagining a future that is framed by changes in the environment, in peoples' needs and aspirations and new ways to ensure that a nation moves forward and benefits all its citizens. The education sector nearly always resists taking that one big leap that can improve lives, enhance personal and collective security and advance national interests. At this time, that one big leap means rejecting a centuries'-old approach to testing, grading and evaluation in schools in order to adopt an approach that fits the new context – one based on expectations related to the skills, knowledge, understanding, and character that children should achieve to be prepared for change that has already occurred and what likely lies ahead.

Education is at a crucial turning point; this institution should not return to the 'old normal'. The pandemic opened a window on where the new path might take us, foundations that need to be remade and the resources and investments that will be required. The unknowns have to be considered and choices made after broad consultation, including with parents, and listening to input on what the values, priorities and outcomes of a re-imagined education system should be. To prepare for robust change that will take Canada and its people into the new era that is well underway, we must be ready to leave the old era behind. There is no point doing the same thing over and over and expecting different results.

This juncture is telling us that most children are adaptable, accepting, and willing to try something new. Those who are daunted by change they have already confronted will need to see and understand a clearly laid plan, a path forward for them and assurance of support. All signs suggest that we need an education system that facilitates improved human performance which depends on children's achievement of their individual potential. In addition to higher levels of competence in learning and know-how, this means greater capacity to empathize and share, to be thoughtful and creative and to invent and innovate so that our nation will continue to influence others, thrive economically, and protect values that matter. Canadian education systems have been standing still, apparently unable to tackle serious issues that confront us now and have for decades. We feel troubled by the insufficiencies and indecencies we see, such as racism, violence, and inequity, but we do not act effectively. Furthermore, Paul Bennett states that "Our public schools, initially established as the vanguard of universal, accessible, free education, have lost their

way and become largely unresponsive to the public they still claim
to serve". [2]

The pandemic exposed the deficiencies in our education
systems and forced public schools to alter delivery strategies and
teaching methods. Education acquired an unanticipated mandate to
make meaningful change but still remains under severe constraints
and without the essential resources, investment and aforethought
that would ensure excellence and relevance to current realities. Our
hope for a better future and an education system that addresses 21st
century conditions may reside in educating children to rise even
further to challenges, eschew the expectations and entitlements of
recent generations, and see themselves as thinkers, inventors and
animators for a healthier, more secure future - a society with a
generous heart, talents, and the creativity to make life better for all.

To set new goals and expectations, the education
establishment has to set aside its attachment to conformity and
uniformity within schools, delivery systems and evaluation
methods that are no longer viable. Whereas industrialized society
of the 20th century adopted a standardized delivery system,
content-driven curriculum, and evaluation approaches that used
standings and rankings to direct children to destinations that would
serve industrial requirements, today's priorities and needs are
different. For the foreseeable future, we need an education system
that adopts a new vision and achieves a better future instead of
clinging to the much greater risks inherent in maintaining the status
quo. Some recent pockets of ingenuity in the sciences and
technology have demonstrated that when human potential is
supported and fully exploited, some immediate, formerly
intractable problems can be solved. Education needs to embrace
pockets of ingenuity and reframe education so that it can finally
capitalize on individual potential and improved performance
overall. [3]

Business, government, and education have been challenged for well over two decades to be creative and innovative in order to compete globally and survive economically. One example is found in the corporate offices that have reinvented their environments to provide a measure of privacy for workers, many of whom have to date spent their careers in open concept environments in which working in teams and sharing open space have been the norm. Progressive organizations today find that working alone can be at least as essential to invention and novel thinking as groupthink and collaboration. [4] The psychology of the workplace is playing catch-up with those organizations that have already changed their expectations of worker performance, now encourage independent work and reward individual enterprise and innovation.

The pressure to recast the ways we live, learn and work is already upon us and we should not look away. That means acting in areas that have a direct impact on our lives and over which we are entitled to exert influence – in this case, education. This is not the only institution that requires a major re-think. Parents should feel sufficiently empowered by their knowledge about schooling and the education system to challenge its authority and control. They should seize the levers that are available to them, an approach they have not yet energetically pursued. Parents need to express their insights on changes they see as important based on their own experience of the system and understanding of what their children should be experiencing and learning in school.

The paradigm shift - from instruction-based to learning-centred

To take the 'big leap', elementary education has to shift from an 'instruction-based' to a 'learning-centred' paradigm. The *instruction-based paradigm* focuses on the *'inputs'* to learning: some inputs are time-based, by dividing schooling into terms, school years and grade levels. [4] Curriculum inputs are centralized, teachers direct the learning, and learners are grouped into cohorts (classes) who mostly move through school together. Evaluation determines the content to be measured through tests, examinations and assignments that are averaged to produce a score that is linked to a grade range and descriptors that usually resemble: A = superior performance, B = good, C= average, D= low average and F=failure. Learning achieved has been judged according to how well the learner complies with expectations, demonstrates knowledge that relates to the inputs and applies it to contexts that are specified by curriculum guidelines. Education in the instruction-based paradigm reflects the norms of a bygone era and inputs and processes that are much the same for all learners. In that context, learning is discipline-centred (subject-based), focuses on mastery of units of knowledge, and the content and skills to be learned are often separated from their applications. [5]

The image of the child as a "blank slate" whose mind was to be "written upon" endured for centuries. Similarly, children today still learn in cohorts and receive the standard 'inputs', but they account individually for the prescribed learning they achieve. Applications of skills and content are anticipated in advance and the evaluation and grading of students are usually predicated on marking schemes and grading guidelines. Competitiveness is encouraged and 'rankings' are treated as important for earning rewards of some kind. Standing in a class or grade is too often assumed by children to be a measure of their relative worth, especially by those who are deemed to be 'successful' students, and also by those who feel like failures from their first encounter with low grades. Robin Barrow [6] described what happens in the context of instruction-based education: Schools classify people....as good students and bad students. That is a problem, because 'good student' tends to translate into 'poised for success', while 'bad student' means that you're doomed to a second-class

life". For more than a century, children and their parents have
quietly acquiesced to the degree of control that education systems
have had and continue to have over their psyches, lives, and
futures.

Evaluation in the *instruction-based paradigm*

For a century to the present, knowledge has been passed
(usually in lectures or formal lessons) by professors or teachers to
older students and children who soaked it up, studied texts and
notes for examinations and earned grades between A' s and D's or
F's. Students are sometimes referred to as 'A-students', 'D-
students', another indication that they are being evaluated instead
of the learning they achieve. The norm-referenced grading system
ABCD,F compares learners against each other in the same cohort
or classroom.

Standardized tests in the *instruction-based paradigm*

Testing is usually the way teachers have ascertained how
much content children retain and understand. As one way to test
children, schools and teachers have increasingly adopted multiple-
choice tests to simplify the processing of tests and examinations
and reduce the labour-intensive work of marking and assigning
grades. Multiple-choice tests designed by teachers and schools are
often unscientifically designed (not standardized) and often test
content, facts and memory. Over the years, they gained a
reputation among students as unfair and biased toward specific
interpretations of content and knowledge when other
interpretations or application were also plausible. Multiple-choice
test scores do not measure individual potential; they usually
represent learning achieved by following a specific learning
pathway and limited to how the knowledge, concepts or skills
being tested were taught.

Standardized tests are designed scientifically, norm-referenced and pre-tested on cohorts of students; they are used by educational institutions to evaluate the preparedness of students for a specific education or training program and to rank students according to their academic proficiency. They are also used to measure intelligence (IQ tests) and aptitudes, despite accusations that the standardized questions often contain cultural bias. In the past couple of decades, standardized tests have been used to rank public schools in terms of how well their students have mastered skills, acquired knowledge, and apply what they have learned. In Ontario, the Equity and Accountability Office (EQAO) administers standardized tests in grades six and nine, and as early as grade three which makes them pertinent to the kindergarten/primary division. The downsides of standardized testing are several; they encourage teachers to "teach to the test" in grades 3, 6 and 9 to ensure their school and class receive competitive scores. The tests may not always be an accurate measure of a school's 'quality' unless they also factor in its demographics, socioeconomic status and resources. Standardized testing takes valuable time away from teachers' other roles and the teaching support they would otherwise provide to each child individually.

Why the *instruction-based paradigm* no longer fits

In the instruction-based paradigm, the teacher delivers content that is pre-determined by curriculum; scoring and grading relates to how quickly and effectively students have conformed to standards set by either the teacher or the curriculum. Assumptions are made that most students are "average" and may therefore be taught using much the same teaching methods for all, as in 'teaching to the middle'. A bell-curve may sometimes be used to ensure that most grades in a class end up in the average range that is attributed to the large middle-pack of students, a practice that is somehow deemed to be a test of the integrity of the evaluation

process. The idea for decades has also been that any 'subject
expert' could be certified to teach, with a minimum of training and
practice teaching and some commitments to ongoing professional
development. Accountability by teachers and schools to parents
and children for their child's learning performance and the
outcomes they achieve has been close to non-existent.

Teachers compose grading guidelines with examples of
anticipated levels of performance on a test or assignment related to
the inputs they provided. For courses, a final grade of 60% is
intended to represent the extent to which the student achieved the
results anticipated and is treated as evidence of how much they
were required to learn was correctly absorbed and applied. A 60%
result signifies success on slightly better than half the course
requirements but still enough to be granted a pass or credit for the
course that deems the student to be ready for the next level of
learning. Children usually do not know ahead of time what will be
tested on an examination or test so preparation often involves a
guessing game. Grades and evaluation at the end of a semester or
school year are 'summative' which usually means that the learner
cannot try for a second time in the same semester or term to
achieve the expectation that was applied. Applications of the
instruction-based approach to evaluation and grading persist in
most schools, colleges, and universities.

Today's economies cannot function adequately with large
numbers of apparently-qualified graduates who demonstrate
average achievement. Sixty percent (or even 75%) does not meet
the higher performance standards required for the largest share of
employment in the Information Age, nor to sustain the progress
and level of security to which our society has become accustomed.
The prevalence of the twin curses of grade inflation (perpetrated by
the schools) and rampant cheating (by students, many of whom
'figured out the system') have endured over many decades and at

all levels in the system. Many counterproductive practices of the
instruction-based paradigm remain embedded in the system and
appear to be intractable, and the old grading systems remain one of
them. There have been, however, significant attempts to move
toward a 'learning-centred paradigm' that should be encouraged so
education systems can focus on what matters and most children
may thrive.

The *learning-centred* paradigm

This paradigm emphasizes the achievement of integrated
learning that may be described as learning outcomes which allow
learners to follow a range of acceptable pathways toward the
demonstration of clearly-defined outcomes on their own timetable.
Individual education plans, (known in this book as KIEPs for
primary school) may be attached to the learners' demonstrations of
learning outcomes that represent integrated learning that is
verifiable over time, more than once and in several contexts.
Learning outcomes allow children to learn in several venues, not
only in a classroom setting. The teacher's role is to plan, facilitate,
instruct and coach children in the learning to be acquired and to
observe, assess, and evaluate children's individual demonstrations
of the learning outcomes.

Learning outcomes describe culminating demonstrations of
integrated learning that are neither lists of discrete skills nor broad
statements of knowledge and comprehension. Statements of
learning outcomes describe complex role performances that rely on
embedded knowledge, skills and concepts that may be applied in
several contexts. They are usually determined by an educational
jurisdiction – a nation, province or large education authority - to
represent meaningful, significant, demonstrable 'performances'
that should be achieved by all learners in order to move to the next
learning level – for example, from the primary to the junior

division - or to be eligible for a credential such as a high school diploma or an elementary school leaving certificate. The determination of learning outcomes to be adopted by a nation or province or other large jurisdiction would be made following input received from an organized consultation process that should include representation by parents, business, large corporate and non-profit organizations, governments, educators and others. The use of learning outcomes as standards would reflect the education mandate derived from the consultations. They should suit the time and context for which they are established that today demands more complex performances by learners, flexible, independent and creative thinking, skilled applications and innovation, and the emotional stamina, rigour and self-discipline needed to achieve higher standards.

Statements of learning outcomes describe complex role performances that integrate knowledge, skills, concepts, and understanding; they represent essential, transferable learning to be demonstrated and verified, more than once, and in more than one context. [7] The learning outcome statements for children in the primary division should be relevant to developmental norms and tasks and the learning they should acquire to build a strong foundation for the next stage in learning. Progress in the demonstration of learning outcomes should lead children on a pathway toward ongoing growth and success in learning and be relevant to expectations of self-reliance and full participation in society. The rate at which children progress would depend on their demonstrated learning and readiness for new learning challenges that are described by the statements of learning outcomes for the next stage. Low expectations produce low levels of performance; expectations that are too high foster frustration, alienation and eventually, despair. We know where alienation and despair lead and the overwhelming cost to society of youth who see no way forward and whose potential contribution to society is wasted.

Where might reform lead?

The early years of schooling build the foundation for learning which is why teachers in the early years should be well-trained and supported, highly professional and skilled, and remunerated accordingly. They should have access to state-of-the-art environments and resources for their teaching roles and be authorized to command special resources for children, including those with delays or disabilities, and expect a timely response. This professional expectation may lead to further differentiation in the certification of teachers, a graduated pay scale that also provides a defined career path for teachers and calls for a viable performance appraisal system. As cost-effectiveness is usually a make-or-break condition for significant change to occur, the upgrading of early childhood education training standards and programs, and changes to job descriptions, responsibilities and role differentiation in the primary division should be addressed.

Teaching methods and learning outcomes in the *learning-centred paradigm*

One impact of the learning-centred approach would be to broaden the environments for learning with the classroom as the central hub for learning and to make better use of community resources and the natural outdoor environment for projects, discovery learning, and practice. Learning might be acquired and demonstrated in a classroom environment, authentic outdoor setting, a gallery or conservation area, or a gymnasium or another space that allows for movement and social interaction. Learning outcomes are embedded in performances that are transferable to a wide range of experiences and circumstances; this allows for several ways and contexts in which the culminating performances may be demonstrated and a number of pathways that children may take to achieve the integrated learning.

Learning outcomes support interdisciplinary learning that might include a number of teaching methods - play-based activities, direct instruction and demonstrations, practice sessions, project learning, times for exploration and experimentation, group times for planning, reflection, discussion and conversation about discoveries, visits and outings, and research and learning by reading. The timely and relevant application of 'interdisciplinary learning' could encourage more teachers to be creative and lead to greater breadth and diversity of the learning experiences provided for children.

Implementation of the learning-centred approach might alter the role and responsibilities of teachers and the terms and conditions of teaching contracts to account for reconfigured professional roles. For example, teachers might be 'contracted' to teach a cohort of children for their four or five years in the primary division to allow the teacher to follow the progress of the children she has known since kindergarten. Teaching contracts might also assign primary division teachers to work in teams with a cohort of primary school children in ungraded classrooms where they learn at their own pace in multi-age settings. This approach might imply revised teacher classification categories that correspond to the specific roles and responsibilities of teachers and account for training, experience and merit based on performance appraisal that would replace the seniority principles that seldom favour the interests of children and learning.

Ongoing assessment that is improvement-oriented (formative evaluation) characterizes this paradigm that measures the demonstrated achievement of integrated learning instead of grades that represent 'approximations' toward specified

performance expectations. Assessment of children's performance
would be supported by anecdotes, samples of children's work and
other demonstrations of their ability to integrate knowledge, skills
and understanding described by the learning outcomes.
Observation and assessments would be integrated with the teaching
and learning activities; the demonstrations of performance should
be transparent and described in teachers' observation notes. The
statements of learning outcomes would likely evolve over time as
the system is evaluated and the people affected by it adjust to
revised strategies and expectations.

Projects as a learning strategy and opportunity to demonstrate culminating performances

The learning-centred paradigm makes frequent use of
projects that allow not only for interdisciplinary learning but also
for observation and assessment of integrated learning
performances. Projects provide occasions for children to explain,
plan, and collaborate, share and entertain ideas, observe and
acquire new perspectives, be creative, and practise learning-to-
learn skills, meeting goals and solving problems. The evaluation of
a child's achievement of a learning outcome is not based on a final
examination or averaged scores in a series of tests or assignments.
It is based on verification that the performance demonstrates that
the child has integrated learning that factors in knowledge, skills
and understanding.

For example, a multi-age class of primary school children
are building an elaborate town on a large table with blocks,
miniature replicas of town buildings and fixtures, and a skyway
road with bridges, using miniature track and matchbox cars. A
grade one child has been building a road with the track to enable
his matchbox cars to navigate a turn close to the bottom of a bridge
ramp without rolling off the track. He has to understand the

relationship between speed and the angle of the ramp and factor in
the distance the cars have to travel in a straight line from the
bottom of the ramp before it can navigate the turn successfully.
This performance integrates skills related to: angles, weight of the
car, speed, measurement, distance, perception, perspective-taking,
eye-hand coordination, testing and experimentation, and a number
of learning-to-learn skills and executive functions. When projects
happen regularly, for a short or a longer timeframe, they offer
occasions for children to demonstrate integrated learning that
reflect the reliability of a child's learning achievement.

Brief history of an attempt to shift to a *learning-centred* paradigm
in education

A little dose of reality related to the challenges inherent in a
successful paradigm shift offers insights into how to proceed, what
might happen, and the importance of persevering to achieve an
improved, relevant evaluation system.

Goals and objectives for the instruction-based paradigm
have been modified from time to time to respond to demands for
change that emerged from societal and economic crises. The first
half of the 20th century, still in the Industrial Age, mobilized
education for predictability, conformity and classifying students
for an industrialized economy. In the mid-1960s, community
colleges were inaugurated to train students to fill growing numbers
of vocational jobs. Universities expanded in the 1970s to
accommodate more students in business, engineering, sciences and
social sciences as society became more complex and differentiated
and many leadership positions opened up. The 'massification' of
postsecondary education that ensued made colleges and
universities the preferred destinations for high school graduates
and adults who required retraining for new employment sectors.
Routine production jobs were increasingly limited to industrial and

in-person service jobs that were already under economic and
financial pressure.

As vocational programs grew rapidly, by the 1980s college
training programs were urged by their program advisory groups to
target job-specific performances to ensure that graduates would be
'job-ready'. The identification of 'competencies' related to
vocations were derived from in-depth analyses of the tasks and
discrete skills embedded in specific roles and jobs which framed
curriculum and diploma requirements for college training
programs. [8] The competency-based education system (CBE)
persisted in colleges until the early 1990s when employer and
business representatives for programs again recommended that
student performance, especially in generic skills should be
upgraded. One response from the Ontario Council of Regents
established a task force to write generic skills competencies for
programs; they were designed to improve communication,
interpersonal and leadership skills, mathematics (numeracy),
analytic skills, and computer literacy at levels relevant to a wide
range of vocational roles. [9] By 1993, as needs for improved
performance evolved rapidly, the Ontario Ministry of Training
Colleges and Universities (MTCU) responded to further calls from
employer advisory groups who wanted more efficient training that
would ensure integrated learning for more complex levels of
performance including leadership roles. The College Standards and
Accreditation Council (CSAC) was established in 1993 with a
mandate to recommend program standards for college programs.
[10] The timing coincided with the appearance of a new approach
to curriculum and the evaluation of learning referred to as
Outcomes-Based Education (OBE). [11]

The concepts of *"personal mastery"* and *"systems thinking"*
described by Peter Senge (1990) [12] that were also gaining
popularity in the early 90s resonated with the needs of business for

better systems for distribution and management to support the
explosion in technology and global trade. The massive economic
shift that was occurring intersected with demands for a
competitive, highly skilled workforce that would generate
invention and capacity to innovate. The technology sector was in a
rush to compete internationally to meet the demand for more
sophisticated devices. The introduction of outcomes-based
education (OBE) into Ontario colleges in 1994 with its
descriptions of learning outcomes expressed as *complex role
performances* appeared to address the demand for graduates with
the integrated skills and understanding needed to perform complex
roles and function at higher levels of complexity and reliability.

Colleges appeared ready at the time to embrace a
"paradigm shift" from an instruction-based approach to specific
skills-based training toward the establishment of program 'learning
outcomes' and learning-centred principles for curriculum as well
as innovative program delivery and teaching methods. Descriptive
statements of *learning outcomes* that reflected complex role
performances quickly became the new framework for college
program curriculum design. At the time, many anticipated that
learning outcomes would fundamentally change the nature and
direction of college education. However, to implement learning
outcomes as intended meant that colleges needed to take the "big
leap" and change the evaluation and grading system from
instruction-*based grading and rankings* to the *learning-centred*
approach in order to complete a paradigm shift. Verifying the
demonstration of complex role performances meant that former
dependence on students' mastery of content and discrete skills as
appropriate measures of achievement would have to be jettisoned.
New ways of assessing complex role performances and integrated
learning for academic credit and certification had not yet been
tried, tested and confirmed by programs. Instead, several colleges

began to experiment with benchmarks and rubrics that described
approximations toward the achievement of a learning outcome that
could be 'graded' in traditional, instruction-based ways.

Instead of developing a compatible evaluation system for
the performance of learning outcomes, 'strands' of OBE were
merged into the traditional *instruction-based* system for evaluating
and assigning grades. The demonstration of learning outcomes
amounted to evaluating and assigning grades or credit for
achieving the skills-based benchmarks or incremental steps toward
the learning outcomes instead of verifying the achievement of the
integrated learning and complex role performances as described in
the learning outcome statements. The paradigm shift was derailed
by failure to take the "big leap" that called for adopting a
compatible *learning-centred* approach to evaluation, a shift that
might have become transformative for education as a whole. The
choice to merge an old grading system with the use of learning
outcomes to define curriculum was never acknowledged to be a
'make or break' choice. In this case, the tepid partial shift in
paradigm meant that not much changed and the achievement of
higher levels of performance of integrated learning remains
unfinished business for the colleges.

Education systems in general continue to avoid
accountability for the quality and effectiveness of programs they
offer. They retain control of testing, evaluation, grading, rankings,
and certification requirements. They maintain their dominion over
delivering content and focusing on specific skills instead of
ensuring that children and students learn to think, integrate and
apply. "Teaching to the middle" and subjective interpretations
endure related to whether and who would be capable of higher-
level performances. The adoption of learning outcomes as an
instrument for new ways to design curriculum, without also
making the shift to compatible teaching methods and a related

evaluation of learning achievement has no legitimate claim to educational transformation. It is just another example of trying to weave a new approach into an old framework with indifferent results.

Adopting a *learning-centred* paradigm for kindergarten/primary education

In the *learning-centred paradigm,* the learning process is actively controlled by the learner whose demonstration of a learning outcome reveals whether the performance meets the standard described. The following section describes how the intentions and principles of outcomes-based education (OBE) appear to fit and might be particularly appropriate for evaluating learning in the kindergarten/primary division.

The philosophy, principles and applications of OBE, along with a shift to the learning-centred paradigm would emphasize *verification* that learning has occurred before the child moves to the next stage in learning. This intention, if faithfully applied, could offer children their best opportunity for success at the next level. Children would advance at their own pace instead of being pushed forward by a time-driven curriculum to the next grade. The removal of grade levels in the primary division would let children learn at their own pace, an important consideration given the unevenness of development and cognitive maturity in the early years to about age eight. OBE allows children to advance at their own pace instead of being pushed forward by a time-driven curriculum to the next grade level before they are ready.

The learning-centred paradigm allows children to follow

diverse learning pathways and the context in which a child demonstrates an outcome may differ from that of other children. For example, a kindergarten or grade one child might demonstrate understanding of a concept or an outcome that had eluded him in the classroom, on a visit to a zoo, a conservation area, or in a gymnasium. An ungraded primary division – would make no firm distinction as to grade level – that is, whether a child is in grade one, two or three. It would allow children time to form a solid foundation for the junior division on their own timetable within the five-year timeframe, depending on whether kindergarten is one or two years. When children are ready to move on to more difficult learning challenges, they are relieved of the pressure to overcome gaps in the learning prerequisites while simultaneously trying to learn new skills and concepts – for example, learning to add and subtract while still trying to understand number constancy. Children who are slower to achieve the learning foundation for the junior division would be identified sooner and appropriately coached along the way throughout the primary division. The first four or five years would be dedicated to building a strong foundation for all later learning.

New venues and delivery systems for learning-centred education

Communities and their various resources might become practice and demonstration venues for learning-centred education, including experiential learning that is interdisciplinary, as children develop social cognition and perceptions, literacy and communication, and creative thinking in the context of selective experiences. Group times in schools would continue in large or small groups for direct teaching or interactive times devoted to social-emotional skills and character building. Essential knowledge and specific skills could still be tested in quizzes. "Culminating assignments' - verbal, written, numeric, or graphic - might be assigned to a child or to small groups and class projects.

What do learning outcomes look like for the kindergarten/primary division?

Learning outcomes require the child to demonstrate a level of performance that represents 'culminating demonstrations of integrated learning'. For kindergarten/primary, these 'culminating demonstrations' might look like: _clearly explains_ the _meaning_ of a story that the child has _read_ by _using facts_ from the story _as evidence_ to _support the meaning_ the child has _understood_ - an outcome that might be considered developmentally appropriate for about a grade three level. An outcome for seven-year-olds (about grade one) might be: _demonstrates the ability to correctly choose_ either _to add or subtract numbers_ in order to _find the answer_ to a word problem. Culminating demonstrations of performance would combine skills, knowledge, understanding, and relevant dispositions (such as persistence) that are considered to be developmentally appropriate and would build on the learning outcomes already achieved.

Assessment would not focus on outcomes that are related to age or grade level as much as it would factor in the learning outcomes that have already been achieved and readiness for more complex integrated learning. This approach would also benefit children who learn rapidly and like to be challenged. For children who consistently perform beyond a normative developmental level, the learning outcomes in their KIEP would be adjusted and enhanced to maintain their interest and provide opportunities to enrich their learning horizontally. Training should ensure that the teaching repertoire of primary division teachers would enable them to adjust the ways and contexts in which children demonstrate the learning outcomes and select and access resources that enrich children's learning.

Children's progress from the point at which the learning

begins toward the achievement of learning outcomes would be noted through ongoing observation of the child's participation and success with a range of activities and tasks. The teacher in the learning-centred paradigm observes each child, with notebook and checklist in hand, to see how she approaches an activity, figures out the inherent concept or skill, and either completes the task, tries again, or moves on to another activity. In the process, the child might ask the teacher for help; the teacher might make a suggestion or ask a question to determine how much she understands. The child either finishes the activity successfully, or tries over again, or moves on with the approval of the teacher who might suggest she try the same activity tomorrow. Teachers' notes provide evidence related to each child's participation and levels of success with a range of specified activities.

Learning-centred kindergarten/primary classrooms

All children, including those with disabilities, should have an individual education plan that represents how far they have progressed in their learning and the steps to be taken next. Adaptations for children with disabilities would comprise a significant part of their IEP; for other children, adaptations to the KIEPs might include various pathways children have taken to demonstrate the learning outcomes that usually reflect the ways they learn best. This approach implies that from JK to a grade three level, children's learning would not be graded. Their progress to a specific point, how they tackle the learning outcomes, and the outcomes they have achieved would be noted and recorded in the KIEP, as well as the recommended next steps in learning. The progress of children who excel and learn quickly and the enriched learning they tackle would also be noted.

The knowledge, skills and understanding of the concepts embedded in learning outcomes would be presented in a developmentally sound sequence. Success with a series of learning outcomes would ensure a sound foundation upon which a child would move forward to the next level. At the end of the five years, most children should be ready for more formal learning at a grade four level, having progressed at their own pace, with an individual plan and teacher attention to each child's progress and learning needs at each stage. The learning-centred approach is especially pertinent to subjects like reading, writing, math and science where much of the learning is incremental and cumulative.

Children who continue to require extra time and teaching support, or who have not achieved the learning outcomes for the primary division might need specialized classes or resource teachers and an individualized curriculum and IEP in the junior division. Knowing that they are making progress at their own speed and in their own way, enables children to focus on learning and feel pride in their successes. They also learn where and how they learn best. A learning-centred approach to primary education is child-centred and emphasizes the strengths they can build on. By the end of five years of primary schooling, children experience school not as a test of their relative worth, nor proof that they are unable to learn the way school is set up to instruct them, but a place where they can be successful and be themselves.

Types of evaluation

Two different approaches to evaluation represent the two different paradigms and determine the next steps in learning.

Summative evaluation is used regularly in the *instruction-based paradigm* to evaluate students at the end of a term of instruction. It passes judgement on a child's achievement using a grade to indicate the extent to which she is deemed to have succeeded and her ranking relative to the other children in the cohort. The grade assigned is intended to indicate the quality of the child's performance overall, usually based on a mix of scores and grades received for tests, assignments and examinations. Summative evaluation in schools assigns grades according to: A=excellent, B=good, C=average, D=poor, F=failure and sometimes Incomplete. Various statements may be employed in summative evaluation reports such as "needs more work", "has not achieved his potential", "excels beyond required performance", but the evaluation delivers a verdict that usually has specified consequences. The grades earned are meant to represent a level of quality or proficiency that may destine a child for higher learning, or for other destinations, all of which have related consequences.

Formative evaluation involves ongoing assessment and is relevant to the *learning-centred paradigm*. In primary education, this approach is used to identify whether and how a child is learning effectively and where they may be experiencing difficulty. Formative evaluation does not assign a final verdict, pass judgement or rank the child; it does provide feedback and guidance on how the child should improve his performance and makes recommendations related to the next steps in learning that would be documented in the KIEP. Formative evaluation allows for learning progress over time and provides feedback to parents and professionals who might be a resource teacher, health care professional, principal, or head teacher. In this context, parents know where their child is on a learning trajectory, the pathways (i.e. activities and learning experiences) toward achieving the learning outcomes, and what the next steps should be.

Formative assessment in the learning-centred approach records areas where a child may need more support, or a specified learning pathway, or perhaps coaching to overcome a hurdle. At certain junctures, a child may need to be redirected toward alternative outcomes to stretch her abilities, enhance her learning or to experience success, bearing in mind that challenging children and having expectations of performance is always important in learning. Evaluation in the learning-centred approach is 'improvement-oriented' to enable children to be and feel successful and motivated as they set new goals, gain confidence, and ultimately perform at higher levels. Formative evaluation recognizes the importance of individual differences, the influence of disabilities and seeks to discover the child's potential and aptitude for certain skills, knowledge, and styles of learning whether academic, hands-on, creative, or experiential. Formative evaluation is compatible with learning outcomes as demonstrations of integrated learning at all levels.

The identification and education of children with disabilities

One of the most damaging inequities in our education systems is the late identification of children with developmental delays and disabilities who needed early, immediate intervention in order to prevent or forestall further negative impacts on children's perceptions of themselves as learners. Timely preventive strategies that provide resources and extra support for the child have a significant impact on their ability to overcome some deficits or delays before they become permanent disabilities. The introduction of the learning-centred paradigm for primary education, in company with individualized programs and teachers who are trained to plan and implement KIEPs, would improve the early identification of learning deficits and delays, both present and potential, while the child's brain is at its most 'plastic'. The absence of timely identification of disabilities, that is usually attributed to cost factors, is impossible to defend given the much heavier cost society must bear for conditions that go untreated, not to mention the waste of individual human potential.

Individual education plans for all children would draw

greater attention to children's developmental progress. It would
enable teachers who have been trained to observe and recognize
delays to seek testing, the intervention of resource teachers, and
preventive or rehabilitative treatments that need to begin as soon as
the deficits are detected. In many jurisdictions, the testing of
children is delayed until they are in the junior division and, too
often, treatments are available for only a fraction of the children
who need intensive support from the time they are first identified.
So, not only does the identification process often occur too late to
correct or prevent the problem, many children never receive the
interventions they are entitled to receive. An individualized,
learning-centred approach to primary education has the potential to
reduce the inequities of the system as it is currently practised.

Individual education plan summaries (KIEPs) instead of report
cards

Within the instructional paradigm, parents typically receive
report cards at the end of each school term and at mid-term which
also provide reference points for parent-teacher interviews. Report
cards require teacher comments for nearly every entry; for
kindergarten/primary children these reports are usually narrative
descriptions of the child's progress instead of grades. Parent-
teacher mid-term interviews usually occur once per semester. In
the learning-centred paradigm, kindergarten/primary assessments
would include teachers' reflections from observation notes,
anecdotal evidence, and the learning outcomes the child has
achieved. Reports would include specific recommendations for
enabling the child to make further progress at the next stage.

Evaluation in the primary division should be framed in the
context of children who are beginning their learning journey and
need to prepare for what lies ahead. Questions for a consultation
process on education reform might include, "what foundational

learning should primary level children demonstrate in order to be
successful learners later on"? Specific learning-to-learn skills
would be one reasonable answer. Additional questions and answers
have already been identified throughout this book.

Evaluate learning achievement instead of children

The adoption of the learning-centred paradigm would
consider the learning outcomes that should become *standards* for
assessing achievement and readiness for further learning. Grading
approximations toward the achievement of learning outcomes that
measures how close the child comes to meeting the standard are
inconsistent with the learning-centred paradigm. Learning
outcomes should provide clear descriptions of the performances to
be demonstrated that, in the primary years, would include asking
children to explain what they have learned or ensuring that they
apply the learning correctly in more than one context.

If evaluation in kindergarten/primary schooling were to
shift from the instruction-based paradigm to the learning-centred
paradigm, the breakthrough change would contribute to unleashing
human potential, capitalize on a diversity of aptitudes for learning
and guide children toward fruitful learning pathways. Achieving
one's potential does not mean that more children would become
astronauts; it does mean that more children would have the
opportunity and support to achieve optimally, to find a niche in
which they are able to participate fully, to become self-reliant and
resilient, and believe that they are able to make a positive
contribution to something larger than themselves. Hands-on
demonstrations, and asking children often to 'explain', would
nurture and identify abilities such as understanding, choosing and
deciding, and forming judgements.

Primary teacher training with a learning-centred focus

In a learning-centred context, kindergarten/primary teachers allow children to learn at their own pace and often independently. The teacher's role becomes that of instructor, facilitator, coach, keeper of records, assessor of progress and achievement of learning outcomes, and designer and manager of the learning environment. The assumption is that teachers in this model need to understand the nature of learning, how to employ play activities and experiences effectively as vehicles for learning, and how to observe, record, assess, and report accurately on children's progress. Teachers require a broad repertoire of instructional and coaching skills, and the ability to link play activities and projects to children's developmental levels, interests, and preferred ways to learn. They possess group management skills for instruction, discussion and practice sessions and provide settings for the assessment of skills, knowledge, conceptual understanding and integrated learning. Teachers are also team members, parent advisors, leaders of extracurricular activities, and spokespersons and representatives for schools and education. Teaching is a demanding profession that deserves greater recognition and reward for the complex role performances that are required to be a successful educator in this century.

In this context, teacher training becomes a mission to turn an aspiring teacher into a professional with the disposition to work closely and positively with children and parents, the drive to continue their own learning, the energy to find and follow through on bright ideas, and the enthusiasm to motivate learning by others. Training programs for kindergarten/primary teachers should emphasize knowledge of child development, the nature of early learning, observation, record-keeping and assessment skills and how to construct and implement KIEPs and report to parents. Teachers should be knowledgeable in education theory, psychology and philosophy, primary school pedagogy, and acquire

skills related to observation, data collection and research skills.
Finally, but not least, primary division teachers should be trained
to plan and teach physical education programs that also integrate
interdisciplinary learning.

Teacher performance appraisal in the learning-centred paradigm

Formative evaluation is advised for teacher performance
appraisal, during teacher training and throughout the probationary
period and one's professional life. A professional development
plan is a useful device for performance appraisal that records areas
which require updating or improvement.

Experienced teachers usually anticipate specific questions
from parents at their mid-term meeting; their answers require
preparation, tact, and an ability to offer positive guidance to
parents. Parent-teacher meetings can be stressful for teachers who
have not prepared summaries based on their interactions with the
child, specific skills and examples that substantiate verbal or
written comments. Parents should be able to assume that
assessment reports are authentic representations of their child's
learning status because they are supported by evidence. The
accuracy of notes and assessments depend on regular observations
and selection of anecdotal and physical evidence to support
teachers' recommendations. These learning outcomes should be
practised throughout teacher training and demonstrated in order to
qualify for interim teaching appointments. Regular appraisals of
the performance of probationary teachers should identify strengths
and weak areas that need more practice and help from mentors. A
development plan for each probationary teacher should accompany
the appraisal that is conducted by a principal, a master teacher or
another trusted educator. The idea is to support and encourage the

probationary teacher by providing authentic, constructive feedback based on evidence and notes of classroom visits.

Appraisal of teacher performance should become a regular event for teachers that is recognized by professional certification standards governed by the "college of teachers" (where they exist), which are the regulatory bodies for teachers. Appraisals for certified teachers (usually after two years of probationary teaching) should be conducted at intervals of every four or five years, and the appraisal system should include an annual report presented by the teacher to the principal or other designated official. Teacher unions should support updated certification standards established by ministries of education or a college of teachers, including at times when they should be reframed to meet new government legislation, curriculum guidelines and standards. Contract agreements for teachers should include: the right to professional development days; merit increases; special support when new curriculums or teaching approaches are introduced; and the potential for sabbatical leaves, based on professional aspirations and merit, once every seven years or so. The profession should demand a clearly-articulated career-path for teachers. Teaching contracts should reflect the demanding, crucially important work teachers do, as well as the high standards of performance and professionalism expected.

The impact of the pandemic on children's education

In a world that cries out for people who are capable of complex role performances which rely on critical and creative thinking, original ideas, and ability to find and apply real-life solutions to complex problems, a 60% average proficiency in the foundational cognitive and creative learning domains is not a sustainable educational outcome. Accountability for educating and improving the performance of Canada's future human resources

belongs to the education sector. Children should not be held
accountable for their failure to learn and achieve in a system that is
no longer working for them. Instruction-based grading and
evaluation has emphasized children's 'ability' as if it were
something that children could control without astute, well-
informed teaching and educational interventions, accurate and
relevant assessment, effective delivery systems, and sufficient and
timely services for children who live with disabilities. Teacher
training and authentic performance appraisal, fair and realistic
certification requirements, the availability of essential resources,
and the management of education and the schools are all
accountable for the learning outcomes achieved by children.

Deficiencies in any of these obligations and
accountabilities of the education system lie at the doorstep of the
education establishment and governments to ensure effective,
relevant, efficiently-monitored, and well-funded education services
that meet the needs of the society they serve. Appraisal of teacher
performance should factor in the quality of learning environments,
the resources available to teachers and children, the venues and
delivery of education services, the currency and soundness of
curriculum, and the performance of management and the education
system. Teachers cannot achieve improved performance in the
absence of high-quality, relevant teacher training, up-to-date
resources for teaching, and regular, supportive performance
appraisal that is tied to professional development plans. Parents
should have a formally-recognized role in school evaluation and
teacher performance appraisal; they should press hard for authentic
accountability by the system and for sufficient, improvement-
oriented government funding for all aspects of education.

Evaluating children is different from evaluating the
learning they achieve. Education has been walking a fine line
between both for much too long. Schooling is not about labeling

children, controlling their ultimate educational destination and determining their future career potential. It is about facilitating and assessing the learning children achieve; to do otherwise is to treat children as commodities who can be measured for their worth to society. It is children's right to be served by an accountable education system and to be supported so they are able to achieve their potential. It is a parental responsibility to help their children become fully engaged in learning and to provide, within their means to do so, a range of experiences that enhance their learning and contribute to a "rich inner life". To do this well, parents need a voice, recognition and respect by the education system, and help when they need it to support their child's learning. Parents have a right to an equitable and just education system they can depend on through difficult times such as their daunting experience throughout 2020-21.

Ironically, the pandemic uncovered some inconvenient truths about education that could, if they continue, block, impair or derail essential change. It revealed that schools and teachers have little confidence in their own ability to devise alternative ways to assess learning using technologies, projects, and culminating assignments. Although the need for teacher preparation and know-how were reasonable explanations for the considerable time it took schools and teachers to partially adjust curriculum and learn to use technology sufficiently to eventually deliver curriculum online, it also exposed the system's limited repertoire of teaching strategies, delivery methods and emergency preparedness. More startling was the lack of awareness of what constitutes *"essential learning"* at each grade level so that teachers could advise parents about where their focus should be as so many of them struggled to school their children at home. This stressful juncture for education also uncovered a stumbling block to reform that has for centuries allowed education to maintain its authority and control over a large

share of how our society functions: *it continued to hide or deny the
deficiencies in the education system.* Evaluation and grading
systems have for decades served as a gatehouse for individual
progress, opportunities for some and not for others, and children's
eventual destinations. School closures due to the pandemic
exposed the tyranny of grades and rankings and the raw control
schools have over families and children's destinies and still do.

Closing thoughts

Re-imagined public schools might become not only venues
for classrooms and learning resources, indoors and outdoors, but
also multipurpose venues for creative projects, after-school
programs in the arts, music, sports, recreation, as well as before-
and after-school child care. A teacher might even assume
responsibility for a cohort of children whom she would teach and
guide throughout the kindergarten/primary division that is a unique
period when children's minds are being shaped. This idea has been
floated before but the obstacles were regarded by education as too
challenging and numerous to surmount. A serious pan-Canadian
consultation process should consider all the issues that arose
during the pandemic and new strategies for teaching and
evaluation, some of which are already in the process of being
invented or refurbished.

A paradigm shift should favour new ways to assess
progress and learning achievement that are rooted in knowing,
understanding, and thinking proficiency that frame nimble minds,
thoughtful reflection and the promotion of competent performance
in pursuits that reflect children's optimum learning potential. A
key vision for education is to respect individual diversity, release
talent and energize individuals, and also pay its dues to a nation

and a planet whose future depends on big ideas to solve big
problems in most areas of human endeavour.

More effective nurturing of individual minds and
development in all domains and throughout childhood would
contribute to building a society that works better for all. Big, bold
ideas gain traction in limber minds - those conceptual and creative
minds that learn from the past, find the relevant threads to guide
the improvement of teaching and learning, and, with that in place,
the overall performance of all our institutions which depend on a
sound, relevant education system. Greater investment by
governments in educating our future human resources, instead of
propping up fading Industrial Age institutions, services and
resources, are essential for Canada and Canadians to 'own' the 21st
century.

Meaningful educational change seldom occurs voluntarily
and without external pressure. Adopting ideas from here and there,
without enough evidence of their effect or relevance, does not
replace comprehensive education reform that fits the context where
it will be implemented. So much has been published in Canada
about Finland's system of education that offers a global example of
excellence, but the Finns are the first to say we should envisage an
education system that would work within our own culture,
heritage, and vision of the future, instead of imitating their ideas
and force-fitting them into our context. We have seen how fruitless
and disruptive ill-considered change can be, and how easily it can
derail an otherwise sound prospect for relevant education reform.

Our education system is at the nexus of what Daniel
Kahneman characterized as a context in which it is necessary to
"think slow" rather than "think fast". [13] To "think fast" at our
current juncture would be to plaster over the cracks that have been
exposed in education, and borrow technologies for only as long as

we need them to keep our existing delivery systems, curriculums, grading systems, and environments intact. To "think slow" would be to enlist parents, teachers and thinkers from many disciplines - philosophers, scientists, researchers, business leaders - in an in-depth, nation-wide consultation process to re-imagine a creative and relevant approach to educating our children for today and tomorrow, starting with the kindergarten/primary years.

Meaningful reform could transform goals into learning outcomes, 'instructors' into designers, planners, coaches, facilitators, and evaluators of learning achievement. Child-centred education would enable children to become proficient actors, agents and inventors rather than receptacles for content and imitators of what has gone before. A genuine desire for reform would turn parents into resource persons, agents of change, and empowered partners. It is my hope that parents will choose to accept this mission.

Notes

Chapter 1 The Nature of Learning

1.   Piaget. Jean 1969a. The Science of Education and the Psychology of the Child. New York, NY: Viking. Jean Piaget was a Swiss-born genetic epistemologist (1896-1980) whose seminal research at the University of Geneva on children's cognitive development and how children come to *know* and understand has influenced early childhood education since his works were interpreted from the original French and published in North America from the 1970s on. His research and books on cognition and the development of thought in children from birth to adolescence led to the cognitive-developmental theory of the nature of children's learning and the four main stages of cognitive development: sensorimotor, preoperational, concrete operations and formal operations. "*Assimilation, accommodation* and *equilibration*" are Piagetian terms that describe the psychological process of learning. Piaget. J. & Inhelder. 1969b. The Psychology of the Child. New York, NY:, Howard. 1991. The Unschooled Mind: How Children Think and How Schools Should Teach. New York, NY: Basic Books, and Gardner, H. 1989.To Open Minds. New York, NY: Basic Books.

2.   "brain-based assessments". Doidge, Norman. 2007. The Brain That Changes Itself: Stories of Personal Triumph from the Frontiers of Brain Science. New York, NY: Penguin. pp. 37-42.

3.   "use it or lose it". This phrase refers to the significant "pruning back" of the synaptic connections in the brain that occurs in adolescence to those connections that were formed during early childhood but not used. This supports the belief that early education should expose children to many diverse learning experiences. "It is probably best to strengthen weakened areas while all the extra cortical real estate is available." N. Doidge. Ibid. p. 42.

5.   Neo-Piagetians replicated much of Piaget's research and promoted his findings in North America from the 1970s on. They were instrumental in the formation of the cognitive-developmental tradition that evolved Constructivist theory in early childhood education. The central message of Constructivism is that children build their own mental structures ("schema") in the brain through their hands-on manipulation of concrete objects in the environment. Prominent neo-Piagetians include: Rheta DeVries, David Elkind, Lawrence Kohlberg, Constance Kamii, and many others.

6. "Instruction-based practice" refers to teaching and learning that is based on traditional schooling that employs conventional teaching methods such as direct teaching, rote learning, drill and practice as well as grading systems and rankings of students.

7. Piaget believed that children's play is instrumental in their cognitive development as young children learn through their active interaction with concrete objects in the environment.

8. Diamond, Adele. (2007). Ways to achieve the goals of education: insights from neuroscience, psychology and teaching. Bulletin of Tibetology. pp.35-70.

9. "malleability of the natural child". French philosopher Jean-Jacques Rousseau used this phrase that lent support to Maria Montessori's description of early childhood as a "sensitive period" for learning that is primarily bound by the senses and depends on children's physical and sensory interaction with their environment.

10. Lawrence Kohlberg's (1972) description of the cognitive-developmental model of early education that became a pillar of the Constructivist theoretical school in education. His seminal paper is entitled "Development as the Aim of Education. Harvard Educational Review. December, 1972. Vol. 42 (4). pp.449-496.

11. "Formation of mental structures" (structure building) references Jean Piaget's finding that children construct "schema" or neural connections in the brain as they interact with their environments and manipulate concrete objects in their play that leads to thought even before they use language to express their thought.

12. "Developmental tasks" refers to child development theory which proposes that certain abilities to act, behave, learn and understand may be considered 'normal' within an age range and a developmental stage although they are not achieved by all children within the same timeframe. The term is found throughout the literature of the neo-Piagetians who refer to the developmental tasks of children at various ages and stages such as: a developmental task for the five-year-old may be to learn to skip in a cross-lateral fashion and, usually at age six and seven, to learn to read. There is wide variation among these developmental norms especially in terms of the time when these tasks are achieved by children as they depend on experience as well as maturation. It may be beneficial to think of developmental tasks as a sequence of anticipated abilities that may occur within a broad timeframe.

13. Cognitive-perceptual or physical-perceptual skills describe the perceptual tasks of development that are manifested by the brain's ability to **process** the perceptions that are received from the senses (cognitive-perceptual skills) and the physical reception of the sensory signal – seeing, hearing,

touching, tasting, smelling – that depends on the physical **acuity** (accuracy) of the sensory receptors that pick up the signal (physical-perceptual skills). Both are important in learning to read.

14. Gardner, Howard. 1989. Frames of Mind: The theory of multiple intelligences. New York: Basic Books. (pp. xiii-xxxix). Also: Intelligence Reframed. Multiple intelligences for the 21st century. New York: Basic Books; 2004. (Multiple intelligences after twenty years).

15. Project learning. Lilian G. Katz & Sylvia C. Chard. (1989). Engaging Children's Minds: The Project Approach. Norwood, NY: Ablex. Lilian Katz advocated projects for children during the early childhood years as an informal, play-based, interdisciplinary learning approach for children to practise and acquire many developmental and learning skills while working together on a project that is interesting and meaningful to them.

16. Bloom, Benjamin. 1956. Taxonomy of Learning Domains. This taxonomy was devised to promote higher levels of thinking in education rather than just learning facts and acquiring knowledge through rote learning. The taxonomy from the lowest level to the highest proposes a hierarchical sequence in the levels of thinking: knowledge, comprehension, application, analysis, synthesis, evaluation or judgement.

17. The "pioneering research" refers to one famous example, i.e. the Perry Research Project conducted in the 1960s in Ypsilanti, MI by David Weikart, later founder of the HighScope Foundation. Further studies on the long-term value of preschool education were conducted by James Heckman of the University of Chicago and winner of the Nobel prize in the economics of human development who confirmed the economic benefits of investing in early childhood education to reduce deficits and strengthen the economy. His studies and others confirmed the lasting benefits of early childhood education for underprivileged children on their later school success, as well as benefits that continue to be felt and seen later in life.

18. "Discovery learning" is a term used in many contexts. In early childhood education "discovery-oriented" learning describes the preoperational learning process whereby young children learn through hands-on exploration of the environment. It is also attributed to young children's uncovering of logical concepts related to early math and science learning. In the primary and junior divisions, the term has been used to describe methods whereby school children are required to figure out concepts for themselves instead of being instructed using direct teaching methods. John Mighton (2020: 136) finds that discovery learning is useful in middle childhood to describe the process of solving complex problems that probably have more than one right answer. Some educators use the term interchangeably with "inquiry-based learning".

19. "balanced approach" Mighton, John. 2020. All Things Being Equal: Why math is the key to a better world. Toronto, ON: Alfred A. Knopf Canada. A

"balanced approach" in this context refers to math teaching for elementary school that is advocated by John Mighton (founder of the JUMP series of books and successful Canadian playwright) and also Anne Stokke of the University of British Columbia. Both suggest that math teaching today should pursue a balanced combination of direct instruction and discovery learning that would help make learning mathematics accessible to more children.

Chapter 2 Learning to Learn

1. Shenk, David. 2009. The Genius in All of Us: Why everything you've been told about genetics, talent, and IQ is wrong. New York, NY: Doubleday. p. 113.
2. "Executive functions" are the management functions of the prefrontal cortex of the brain that influence how we manage our emotions, reactions and behaviours in order to achieve goals. They include ability to persist, exercise self control, and resist distractions, all of which should be introduced and practised in kindergarten.
3. Galinsky, Ellen. 2010. Mind in the Making: The seven essential life skills every child needs. New York: HarperStudio.
4. Ibid.
5. Diamond, Adele. 2011. *Interventions shown to aid executive function development in children 4 to 12 years old.* Science. Vol. 333 (6045). pp. 959-964.
6. Tough, Paul. 2012. How Children Succeed. Grit, curiosity, and the hidden power of character. New York: Houghton Mifflin Harcourt. pp. 92-95.
7. "nature-nurture debate". This refers to a 20th century debate in psychology about whether one's genetic inheritance or the conditioning role of the environment has the greatest impact on human development. The behavioural scientists insisted that the environment and conditioning were most influential, while the child development researchers of the time believed that genetic inheritance, nurturing and maturation were most significant. Today, most psychologists believe that both nature and nurture (heredity and environment) play a significant role.
8. The child development "maturationist" movement of the 1950s (led by Arnold Gesell) promoted the concept predictable ages and stages of development
9. Meaney, M. 2001. *Nature, nurture and the disunity of knowledge.* Annals of the New York Academy of Sciences. 935: 50-61
10. Cain, Susan. 2012. Quiet: The power of introverts in a world that can't stop talking. New York, NY: Crown
11. Ibid.

12. Little, Brian. 2014. Me, Myself and Us: the science of personality and the art of wellbeing. New York: HarperCollins.
13. Gardner, Howard. 2004. *New introduction: Multiple Intelligences after twenty years.* In Frames of Mind: : the theory of multiple intelligences. pp. xiii – xxxix. New York: Basic Books.
14. Tough, Paul. 2012. How Children Succeed. Grit, curiosity, and the hidden power of character. New York: Houghton, Mifflin, Harcourt.
15. Ibid.
16. Dweck, Carol. 2006. Mindset: the new psychology of success. New York: Penguin Random House.
17. Galinsky, Ellen. 2010. Mind in the Making: the seven essential life skills every child needs. New York: HarperCollins. pp. 4-6.
18. Diamond, Adele. 2011. *Interventions shown to aid executive function in development in children 4 to 12 years old.* Science. Vol.333 (6045): pp. 959-964.
19. Whitebread, David. 2010. Play, metacognition and self-regulation. In P. Broadhead, J. Howard, and E, Wood. *Play and learning in the early years. From research to practice.* London, UK: Sage. p.163.

Chapter 3 Teaching the Way Children Learn

1. Sternberg, Robert. 1987. The Triarchic Mind: A new theory of human intelligence. New York: Harcourt Brace Jovanovich.

2. Friedrich Froebel opened the first kindergarten in Germany in 1857 that provided a framework for kindergarten education.

3. Lev Vygotsky, a Russian researcher on children and play emphasized the importance of social interaction on cognitive development and the role of language in facilitating thought. Although he was a contemporary of Piaget, he was not initially associated with Constructivist theory but was later acknowledged to be a cognitive developmental scientist and a member of the Constructivist School.

4. Montessori and Piaget were contemporaries (1920s to mid-century) whose work influenced Constructivist theory that is widely practised in early childhood education, "developmentally-appropriate practice" (DAP) and cognitive-developmental theory.

5. "Scaffolding" is a teaching practice in which the adult offers coaching support to the child during the learning process and provides concrete objects (play materials) that enable a child to perceive/see a concept he is trying to understand. "Scaffolding" emerged from the concept of a "zone of proximal development" (ZPD) which is perceived as a gap between what the child already

knows and what he needs to understand to achieve prescribed learning. Scaffolding may take the form of asking questions at the right time to help a child delve deeper into the obstacle he has encountered in order to uncover a problem in his thinking. Jerome Bruner was an early promoter of scaffolding as a way of helping children learn.

6. Moyles, J.(2010). Foreword. In P. Broadhead, J. Howard,& E. Wood. Play and Learning in the Early Years. London, UK: Sage. (p xii).

7. Shipley, Dale. 2012. Empowering Children: play-based curriculum for lifelong learning. Fifth edition. Toronto, ON: Nelson Education. p. 35.
8. Ibid.
9. Rubin, K., Fein, G., Vandenberg, B. 1983. *Play*. In, P.H. Mussen (series eds.) & F.M, Hetherington. Handbook of Child Psychology: Socialization, personality, and social development. Fourth edition. pp. 693-774. New York: Wiley.
10. Gardner, Howard. 1982. Art, Mind and Brain. New York: Basic Books. Children are born with a natural "creative orientation". The science related to creativity proposes that schools should strive to extend this creative orientation beyond early childhood or it will diminish because of the influence of prescriptive teaching methods that compete with children's natural creative tendencies.
11. 'non-literal play'. Bettelheim, Bruno. 1987. *The importance of play*. The Atlantic. 262 (3). pp.35-46.
12. "volitional fortitude". It is similar to willpower that is linked to motivation. Tough, Paul. 2012. How Children Succeed: Grit, curiosity, and the hidden power of character. New York: Houghton Mifflin Harcourt. p.92.
13. Galinsky, Ellen. 2010. Mind in the Making: The seven essential life skills every child needs. New York: HarperCollins.
14. Whitebread, David. 2010. Play, metacognition and self-regulation. In P. Broadhead, J. Howard and E. Wood. *Play and Learning in the Early Years*. London, UK: Sage. pp. 161-176.
15. Lilian G. Katz. 1994. The Project Approach. Champagne, IL: ERIC Clearinghouse on Elementary Early Childhood Education.

Chapter 4   Governance and the People in the School

1. Bennett, Paul. 2018. *Canada's bureaucratic school system needs a top-to-bottom overhaul*. The Globe and Mail. Toronto, ON: October 2, 2018.
2. School boards frequently lock horns with local governments because school boards have exclusive jurisdiction over matters affecting schools even though their decisions may run counter to municipal policies and

the interests of citizens. The relationship between provincial
governments and school boards has grown looser over time and the
supervision by governments of board behaviour and policies has lagged
and sometimes causes significant administrative disruption.

3. In 2018, Nova Scotia dissolved seven English-language school boards
leaving only the Acadian board in place, and established a 15-member
Provincial Advisory Council of Education representing all regions of
the province including one member representing African Nova Scotia
and one for First Nations communities. Their Minister of Education
claimed that the governance changes are necessary to strengthen the
system and will result in "better outcomes for the province's 118,000
public school students". Article by Caroline Alphonso. *Nova Scotia
school boards collapsed into one council.* The Globe and Mail.
Toronto: March 30, 2018.

4. School closures. Boards identify schools where the child population has
declined; some classrooms are closed down and others become mixed-
grade classrooms. As school enrolments decline further, lists of
potential school closures are announced to the community a few
months (sometimes years) prior to each school's closure. School boards
are required to conduct meetings of parents and the public to receive
feedback on the closures and input on the plans for a new school. This
process is sometimes referred to as an *'accommodation review
consultation'* (ARC). Boards are not obliged to respect the
recommendations of the ARC and seldom, if ever, do so. Neither do
they consult meaningfully with municipal governments about the real
impact of school closures on neighbourhoods and families.

5. Louv, Richard. 2008. Last Child in the Woods: Saving our children
from nature-deficit disorder. Chapel Hill, NJ: Algonquin Books. This
book raised alarm about children's lack of spontaneous access to the
natural world on children's outlook on life and the environment as well
as on their mental and physical health. He insists that that children need
spontaneous, physical contact with nature on a daily basis - to run
around outdoors, feel the impact of nature in all seasons, and develop a
relationship with the natural world that would encourage them to care
about the environment and buttress their mental health.

6. Decades ago, large tracts of land were set aside for schools and their
playgrounds where children played before and after school. The large
new schools on the fringes (edges) of communities usually occupy
compressed outdoor space that may be dominated by car parks close to
the school. New enterprises are redesigning and equipping outdoor
spaces for elementary schools in some municipalities that allow for
group learning and promote natural spaces for play, exploration and
physical fitness.

7. Garden areas in school grounds provide a curriculum thread for
gardening projects throughout the school year as children plan their

gardens in the winter, prepare a garden plot in the spring and plant
seeds, and tend and harvest their garden in the warmer months and
when school resumes in September. Gardens ensure that children have
regular contact with nature all year and more reasons to be outdoors.
They also offer a rich interdisciplinary context for learning many new
skills, to investigate and observe natural science phenomena and to use
their math and literacy skills as they plan the garden. These gardens
often become a welcome community resource for families.

8. College of Teachers. This is an Ontario regulatory body for
    professional teachers located in Toronto that administers the interim
    certification and professional certification processes. They are
    accountable for the professional conduct of teachers and are the
    authority that reviews and sanctions unprofessional conduct. The
    college establishes the "scope of practice" for teachers and also
    provides resources and professional development courses. Ontario is
    currently the only province to have a regulatory college for teachers.

9. The College of Early Childhood Educators (in Ontario), performs
    similar duties to those of the College of Teachers and works to enhance
    the professional status and credibility of early childhood education
    specialists.

Chapter 5 Social and Emotional Readiness for Learning

1. Haass, Richard. (2018). A World in Disarray: American foreign
    policy and the crisis of the old order. New York: Penguin.

2. Goleman, Daniel. 1995. Emotional Intelligence: New York, NY:
    Bantam.

3. Fulghum, Robert.1986. Everything I Need to Know I Learned in
    Kindergarten: Uncommon thoughts on common things. New York:
    Ivy Books. This is an old chestnut with a light touch that contains
    several memorable truths. Often quoted.

4. Uebergang, Joshua. 2010. A Complete Review of Social
    Intelligence by Daniel Goleman. http://ezinearticles.com.

5. Goleman, Daniel. 2008. Social Intelligence: The revolutionary new
    science of human relationships. New York: Bantam.

6. Smilansky, S. & Shefataya, L. 1990. Facilitating Play: a medium
    for promoting cognitive, socio-emotional and academic
    development in young children. Gaithersburg, MD: Psychosocial
    & Educational Publications.

7. Eliot, Lise. 1999. What's Going On In There? How the brain and
    mind develop in the first five years of life. *Sex differences in
    intelligence. pp. 430-436.* New York, Bantam.

8. Kuper, S. and Jacobs, E. 2018. *Why are boys falling behind at
    school? In developed countries girls outperform in the classroom.*

How to close the gap? Financial Times. Saddle River, NJ:
December 14, 2018.

9. Canadian Council on Learning. 2011. What is the future of
    learning in Canada? Ottawa, ON: October 11.
    www.changelearning.ca

10. Kuper, S. and Jacobs, E, 2018. *Why are boys falling behind at
    school? In developed countries girls outperform in the classroom.
    How to close the gap?* Financial Times. Saddle River, NJ:
    December 14, 2018.

11. Eliot, Lise. 1999. What's Going On In There? How the brain and
    mind develop in the first five years of life. New York: Bantam
    Books.

12. James, William. 1877 paper entitled *"Habit"* quoted in David
    Brooks. 2015. The Road to Character. New York: Random House.

13. Bettelheim, Bruno. 1987. A Good Enough Parent. New York:
    Random House.

14. Ibid.

15. Fullan, Michael. 2002. *The Change.* Educational Leadership. May,
    2002. pp. 16-20.

16. Borba, Michele. 2002. Building Moral Intelligence: The seven
    essential virtues that teach kids to do the right thing. San Francisco,
    CA: Jossey-Bass.

17. Tough, Paul. 2012. How Children Succeed: Grit, curiosity, and the
    hidden power of character. New York: Houghton Mifflin Harcourt.
    pp. 83-86.

18. Duckworth, Angela. 2016. Grit: the power of passion and
    perseverance. First Canadian Edition. Toronto, ON: HarperCollins.

19. Kronman, Anthony T. 2015, quoted in David Brooks. The Road to
    Character. New York, NY: Random House. p. 57.

Chapter 6   Physical Literacy

1. Louv, Richard. 2008. Last Child in the Woods: Saving our children
    from nature-deficit disorder. Chapel Hill, NJ: Algonquin Books.

2. Active healthy kids Canada. 2014. "Is Canada in the Running?"
    Among 14 nations tested, children received only Cs, Ds and
    Incomplete, as well as an F in overall physical activity, participation in
    organized sport, active play, (too much) sedentary behaviour, and (too
    little) government investment in school-based physical programming.
    In 2018, Canadian children earned a D+ for physical activity in a
    public report that blamed Canada's dismal showing on: "too much
    screen time" and the fact that children do not walk to school as they

should. ParticipACTION Report Card on Physical Activity for Children and Youth, June 2018.

3. *"Where's Waldo"* and other Richard Scarry books for children that provide practice in depth perception and ability to detect figure from ground - that is, the ability to pick out tiny details on a busy page of drawings.

4. *Peter and the Wolf* is a symphonic fairy tale for children that is set to music produced by various orchestral instruments each of which is identified with a specific character in the story. The story set to music by Serge Prokoviev was published in 1936 and since recorded by several orchestras and narrated by classical actors. It has provided valuable practice for auditory discrimination, recognizing the sounds of orchestral instruments and active listening by children over more than eight decades.

5. Hutchinson, Alex. 2019. *Culture of fear is holding children's fitness back;* article published by The Globe and Mail, Toronto, ON. September 24, 2019.

6. *Is Canada in the Running? How Canada stacks up against over 14 other countries on physical activity for Children and Youth.* The Report Card on Physical Activity for Children and Youth. 2014.

7. Ibid.

8. Statistics Canada. Health Fact Sheets. *Physical activity and screen time among Canadian children and youth: 2016 and 2017.* Ottawa, ON: Statistics Canada. April 17, 2019.

9. Bozikovic, Alex. *The new playground.* The Globe and Mail. Toronto: November 6, 2014.

10. Louv, Richard. 2008. Last Child In The Woods: Saving our children from nature-deficit disorder. Chapel Hill, NC: Algonquin Books.

11. Shipley, Dale. 1988. A Study of the Ecoles Maternelles in France. Unpublished report on the ecoles maternelles after a three-week study conducted on-site at a school in Arles, France and authorized by the French Embassy in Canada.

12. Life Expectancy. 2016. Statcan Health Fact Sheets. 2019. By 2031, it is predicted that high rates of childhood obesity and chronic diseases formerly attributed to adults will shorten the lifespans of children. www150.statcan.gc.ca.

Chapter 7 Language and Literacy

1. O'Sullivan, Julia. 2020. *There is a reading crisis in Canada: the pandemic will only make it worse.* The Globe and Mail. Toronto, ON: September 11, 2020.

2. Giroux, Henry. *Illiteracy and the authoritarian nightmare: an American view.* The Hamilton Spectator. May, 2016.

3. Council of Ministers of Education. (CMEC). 2019. Measuring Up. Canadian Results of the OECD 2018 PISA Study for 2018. *Canadian high school students among the top performers in reading according to new international rankings.* The article above references the view of Douglas Willms, former Research Chair in Literacy and Human Development at the University of New Brunswick.

4. The Organization for Economic Cooperation and Development (OECD) programme for International Student Assessment (PISA) conducts a survey every three years that measures the performance of 15-year-old students in reading, science and math. In 2018, about 600,000 students in 79 countries completed the PISA test in literacy with Canada achieving seventh place. Eighty-six percent of Canadian students who took the test performed at or above the benchmark (Level 2 with a base score limit of 407) with students from all 10 provinces/territories scoring an average of 520. Higher national scores were achieved by Singapore at 549 followed by China, Japan, Korea, Estonia and the Netherlands. The score of 407 is considered the baseline level of reading proficiency, a level that has been deemed insufficient for competent performance in the vast number of jobs in our new economy that remain unfilled in Canada. Caroline Alphonso, Education Reporter. The Globe and Mail. Dec. 3, 2019. Toronto, ON .

5. Reynolds, G. and Sulpizio, Simone. *How exercise could help you learn language.* New York Times News Service. New York. August 30, 2017.

6. Piaget and the Constructivists believed that thought comes before language and therefore it is important to provide sensory experiences through interactive play that promotes brain activity that leads to thought. The child will find the language he needs to say what he is thinking.

7. Pinker, Stephen. 2007. The Stuff of Thought: Language as a window into human nature. New York: Viking. p. 149.

8. Vygotsky, Lev. 1978. Mind in Society: Development of Higher Psychological Processes. Cambridge, MA: Harvard University Press.

9. Chomsky, Noam. (1978). Language and Mind. (extended edition). New York: Harcourt Brace.

10. Bruner, Jerome. 1983. Child's Talk: Learning to Use Language. New York: W.W. Norton.
11. Eliot, Lise. 2000. What's Going On In There? New York: Bantam. p. 353.
12. Pinker, Stephen. 2007. The Stuff of Thought: Language as a window into human nature. New York: Viking.
13. Perceptual skills such as cognitive-perceptual processing and physical perceptual acuity are different skills but they usually act together. Children may experience difficulties in one or the other perceptual skills or in both which is sometimes called sensory-processing disorder (SPD). Cognitive-perceptual processing refers to the child's ability to process the information that is received through the senses. Susan Wise Bauer, 2018, Re-Thinking School: How to take charge of your child's education. New York, NY: W.W. Norton cited a 2009 study in the Journal of Abnormal Child Psychology which suggested that up to 16.5 percent of elementary school children could be diagnosed as suffering from SPD which can impede children's learning in school as learning demands increase.
14. 'Whole language' approach to teaching children to read. This approach has been widely discredited but it was prevalent in Canadian schools in the 1980s and 1990s when teachers were obliged to adopt this approach and discouraged from teaching phonetics. This is another example of ministries of education taking an unproven idea and putting it into practice before it has been well researched and tested.
15. Fulghum, Robert. 1986. Everything I Need to Know I Learned in Kindergarten. New York, Ivy Books. A popular book, often quoted.
16. Doidge, Norman. 2007. The Brain That Changes Itself: Stories of Personal Triumph from the Frontiers of Brain Science. New York: Penguin. pp. 295-298.
17. Ibid. pp. 139-186.
18. Pinker, Stephen. 2014. The Sense of Style: The thinking person's guide to writing in the 21st century. New York, NY: Viking.
19. Dinehart, Laura. 2015. *Handwriting in early childhood education: current research and future implications.* Journal of Early Childhood Literacy 15(1). pp. 97-118.
20. Gray, Peter. 2012. *Unsolicited evaluation is the enemy of creativity.* www.Psychologytoday.com/us/blog/freedomtolearn October 16, 2012.
21. Piaget, Jean. 1955. The Language and Thought of the Child. New York: Meridian.

22. Beauchamp, G. and Kennewell, S. 2008. *The influence of ICT on the interactivity of teaching, education and information technologies.* Education and Information Technologies 13(4): 305-315.
23. Katz, Lilian G. 1994. The Project Approach. ERIC Clearinghouse on Elementary and Early Childhood Education. Urbana, IL.
24. Doidge, Norman. 2007. The Brain That Changes Itself: Stories of personal triumph from the frontiers of brain science. New York: Penguin. pp. 307-3010.
25. Ibid. p. 311.
26. Chumak-Horbatsch, Roma. 2012. Linguistically Appropriate Practice: A guide for working with young immigrant children. Toronto, ON: University of Toronto Press.
27. Ibid.p. 55-58.
28. Ibid. p.55.
29. Aamodt, Sandra and Wang, Sam. 2011. Welcome to Your Child's Brain: How the mind grows from conception to college. New York: Bloomsbury.

CHAPTER 8   Numeracy and Logical-Mathematical Thought

1. Mighton, John. (2020). *The right formula: why math is the key to a more equitable society.* Toronto, ON: The Globe and Mail. January 19, 2020.
2. Mighton, John. 2020. All Things Being Equal: Why math is the key to a better world. Toronto, ON: Alfred A. Knopf.
3. Human Resources Development Canada (HRDC). 2001. A report published by HRDC as part of the Vision 2000 series.
4. Brooks, David. 2013. *Thinking for the future.* New York: The New York Times International Edition. December 14, 2013.
5. Dweck, Carol. *The secret to raising smart kids.* Scientific American Mind. 18(6): December 2007. pp.36-43.
6. Doidge, Norman. 2007. The Brain That Changes Itself: Stories of personal triumph from the frontiers of brain science. New York: Penguin.
7. Shenk, David. 2010. The Genius in All of Us: Why everything you've been told about genetics, talent, and IQ is wrong. New York: Doubleday. p. 30.
8. Dweck, Carol. *The secret to raising smart kids.* Scientific American Mind. 18(6): December 2007: pp. 36-43.
9. Mighton, John. 2020. All Things Being Equal: Why math is the key to a better world. Toronto, ON: Alfred A. Knopf. pp. 30-31.
10. Doidge, Norman. 2007. The Brain That Changes Itself: Stories of personal triumph from the frontiers of brain science. New York: Penguin.

11. Charlesworth, Rosalind. 2011. Understanding Child Development. 8th edition. Belmont, CA: Wadsworth – Cengage Learning.
12. The Kindergarten Curriculum.2016. Ministry of Education, Toronto, ON: p. 85.
13. Homer-Dixon, Tbomas. 2000. The Ingenuity Gap. Toronto, ON: Alfred A. Knopf.
14. Levitin, Daniel. 2014. The Organized Mind: Thinking straight in the age of information overload. Toronto, ON: Penguin Canada. p. 336.
15. Marshall, Ray and Tucker, Marc.1992. Thinking for a Living: Education and the wealth of nations. New York: Basic Books.
16. Classification activities. The easiest sorting challenges rely on the senses (what children see and touch), and then on what they know. In kindergarten, children sort according to sensory-based criteria followed by knowledge-based criteria (things they know) and similarities they determine for themselves such as vehicles with wheels/without wheels. Later, they differentiate within sets - for example, furniture: then bedroom furniture, living room furniture; later, they decide how differentiated to make their own definition of sets, i.e. according to one, two or maybe three criteria that define each set: e.g. things for measuring that are used in cooking versus things that measure distance and things for measuring weight. The objects they select initially often cross over the boundaries cited by the criteria they choose which means they have to start over and re-establish their criteria. At a later stage, children learn to sort random collections of objects into sets, and then sets within sets; for example, children sort their Hallowe'en treats first into broad sets first, such as wrapped versus unwrapped items, and then break down each broad set into sub-sets such as hard versus soft, or sweet versus sour, or chocolate versus licorice, and so on.
17. Seriation activities to play with your child. For these, you may choose to obtain seriated sets of objects, preferably Cuisenaire rods. Ask your child to put the rods in order of size and remind them of the "rules" to follow: common baseline and one direction only in a straight line. Observe what the child does. Let him use trial and error initially and get used to playing with the rods which are fun to hold and stack. Later, place the rods on the table with some gaps or mistakes in the order and ask the child to fill the gaps and put them all in order. Observe whether they follow the rules. Later, after they have figured out how to seriate the rods correctly before they actually touch them, find another set of seriated objects and ask them to make two seriated sets by matching the sets of rods using one-to-one correspondence. (This is "double seriation") After playing with the seriated sets for a length of time, they will plan and correctly estimate ahead of time the order in which each item in each set should be placed in order to create two seriated sets.

18. The Kindergarten Curriculum. 2016. Toronto: Ontario Ministry of Education. The Ontario Ministry of Education launched pilot projects for a draft full-day, play-based curriculum for kindergarten in 2010 that was revised and then legislated in 2016. The kindergarten curriculum advises teachers to "weave together the mathematical processes and related expectations from five mathematics categories as well as relevant expectations from other areas of learning (e.g. science and technology, language, the arts)". This helps to explain why children do not develop math skills, tools and understanding in a linear or compartmentalized fashion. The curriculum frequently addresses logical-mathematical concepts under headings like pre-math or math readiness. These are the five categories noted in the 2016 curriculum:

- Number sense and numeration (quantity relationships; counting; operational sense)
- Measurement (attributes, units and measurement sense; measurement relationships)
- Geometry and spatial sense (geometric properties; geometric relationships; location and movement)
- Patterning (patterns and relationships)
- Data management and probability (collection and organization of data; data relationships; probability).

19. Stokke, Anna. 2015. What to Do about Canada's Declining Math Scores? C.D. Howe Institute. May, 2015.
20. Zeimer, M. 1987. *Science and the early childhood curriculum: One thing leads to another.* Young Children. 43 (8): 44-51.
21. Louv, Richard. 2008. Last Child in the Woods: Saving our children from 'nature-deficit disorder'. New York: Algonquin.
22. Sampson, Scott D. 2018. How to Raise a Wild Child: The art and science of falling in love with nature. New York: Houghton Mifflin.
23. Education Quality and Accountability Ontario. EQAO. Test for Grade 6 math. 2018. www.eqao.com
24. The ratio of "knowledge worker" (high performance jobs) to routine production work (labour and in-service jobs) has been quoted in several books and articles since the Vision 2000 series of reports issued by the Canadian Government. Peter Drucker, 1959 in *The Landmarks of Tomorrow* was among the first to use the term "knowledge worker" jobs to describe the shift away from manufacturing/industrial and construction jobs in the late decades of the Industrial Age to jobs for 'knowledge workers' referenced later by Robert Reich (US Secretary of Labour) and others. Still later (1990), workers in high-performance jobs were referred to as 'systems analysts' by Peter Senge, author of The Fifth Discipline.

25. Manley, John. 2013. Report from the Chief Executive Officer and President of the Canadian Council of Chief Executives. This excerpt from the Report was contained in an article by Caroline Alphonso for The Globe and Mail, on December 3, 2013.
26. Ontario Ministry of Education. The Kindergarten Curriculum. 2016.
27. 'Discovery learning' that features exploration and discovery through play has been the subject of numerous research studies since the 1970s. The pedagogy was endorsed by the National Association for the Education of Young Children, (NAEYC) Washington, DC in the 1980s. Hundreds of books and articles that describe discovery learning were published and/or recommended by the NAEYC under the heading 'developmentally-appropriate practice' (DAP) for young children.
28. The Kindergarten Curriculum. 2016, Ministry of Education.
29. Ministry of Education. 2020. The new math curriculum for Grades 1-8. Toronto, ON: September 2, 2020. www.ontario.ca
30. Mighton, John. 2014. "Math scores: the sum of our fears". The Globe and Mail. Toronto, ON: January 11, 2014.

Chapter 9   The Creative Mind

1. Resnick, Michael. 2018. Quoted in, Katie Reilly. 2018. *When schools get creative.* The Science of Creativity. TIME special edition. p..85.
2. Gardner, Howard. 1982. Art, Mind and Brain. New York: Basic Books.
3. Ibid.
4. Mayer, Marc. 2020. *Society has turned its back on our creative generalists".* The Globe and Mail. Toronto, ON: January 11, 2020.
5. Schirrmacher, R. 1988. Art and Creative Development in Children. Albany, NY: Delmar.
6. Wright, Susan. 2010. Understanding Creativity in Early Childhood. London, UK: Sage.
7. Torrance, Paul. 1966. *Torrance Tests of Creative Thinking.* Norms Technical Manual research edition. Princeton, NJ: Personnel Press.
8. MacKinnon, D.W. 1971. *Nature and Nurture of Creative Talent.* In, R. Ripple. Ed. Educational Psychology. Readings in learning and human abilities. New York: Harper & Row.
9. Reilly, Katie. 2018. *When Schools Get Creative.* TIME: The Science of Creativity. 2018. p.85.
10. Clemens, S. 1991. *Art in the classroom: making every day special.* Young Children. 46(2): 4-11.Washington, DC: National Association for the Education of Young Children (NAEYC).
11. Mayer, Marc.2020. *Society has turned its back on our creative generalists.* The Globe and Mail. Toronto, January 11. 2020.

12. Dweck, Carol. 2006. Mindset: the New Psychology of Success. New York: Random House.
13. Begley, Sarah. 2018. *How parents can excite and inspire.* The Science of Creativity. TIME special edition. p. 90.
14. Grant, Adam. 2018. *How parents can excite and inspire. 2010.* The Science of Creativity. TIME Special. p.92.
15. Owen, N. 2010. *Creative Development.* In, I. Palaiologou. The Early Years Foundation Stage. London, UK pp.192-193.
16. Mayer. Marc. 2020. *Society has turned its back on our creative generalists.* The Globe and Mail. Toronto, ON: January, 11, 2020.
17. Egan, Kieran. 1999. *Children's Minds Talking Rabbits and Clockwork Oranges.* Essays on Education. New York: Teachers' College Press. P. 78.
18. Holt, John. 1972. How Children Learn. New York: A Merloyd Lawrence Perseus Books Group.
19. Puccio, Gerard. 2018. Quoted in Katie Reilly. *When Schools Get Creative.* The Science of Creativity. TIME special edition. P. 84.
20. Gardner, Howard. 1999. Art, Mind and Brain. New York: Basic Books
21. Mighton, John. 2020. All Things Being Equal: Why Math is the Key to a Better World. Toronto, ON: Alfred A. Knopf.
22. Gardner, Howard. 1983. Frames of Mind. New York: Basic Books. p.99.
23. Sternberg, Robert. 2018. In Katie Reilly. *When Schools Get Creative.* The Science of Creativity. TIME Special edition. p. 87.
24. Florida, Richard. 2010. The Great Reset: New ways of living and working drive post-crash prosperity. New York. Random House.

Chapter 10   Releasing Children's Potential

1. Homer-Dixon, Thomas. 2020. Commanding Hope: The power we have to renew a world in peril. Toronto: Penguin Random House Canada. pp. 27-28.
2. Bennett, Paul. 2020. The State of the System: A reality check on Canada's schools. Montreal, QC: McGill-Queen's University Press. p.3.
3. Homer-Dixon, Thomas. 2000. The Ingenuity Gap. Toronto, ON: Alfred A. Knopf.
4. Cain, Susan. 2012. Quiet: The power of introverts in a world that can't stop talking. New York: Crown.
5. Barr, R. and Tagg, J. 1995. *From teaching to learning: a new paradigm for undergraduate education.* Change. November-December. This article clarified the philosophical and theoretical differences between two competing educational paradigms over about three decades after the influence of behaviourist traditions in education faded in the 1980s.
6. Barrow, Robin. 2015. The Philosophy of Schooling. New York: Routledge.

7. *Learning outcomes* are statements which describe the demonstration of "culminating performances" of integrated learning (skills, knowledge, understanding); learning outcomes are the standards for evaluating the achievement of learning within Outcomes-Based Education (OBE). William Spady is credited with elaborating on the meaning and practice of learning outcomes and the language/terminology related to OBE that is important to an accurate understanding of the applications of the approach.

8. DACUM is an acronym for "<u>D</u>evelop <u>a</u> <u>C</u>urricul<u>um</u>" that provided the framework for developing job descriptions, identifying training needs, and prioritizing staff development initiatives. This method was used to identify the 'competencies' for *competency-based education* (CBE) in community colleges during the 1980s and early 1990s.

9. In Ontario, the Generic Skills Task Force (1990-1991) was established by the Council of Regents to develop the competencies for clarifying the generic skills in colleges that became official in 1991. Now referred to as "essential employability skills", the generic skills at that time identified literacy, numeracy, analytic skills, computer literacy, and interpersonal skills as essential components of college vocational programs.

10. College Standards and Accreditation Council (CSAC) from 1993-1994 established "learning outcomes" as the focus of curriculum design for college programs and replaced the DACUM competencies. Learning outcomes broadened the focus of vocational programs toward the demonstration of "culminating, complex role performances" that represent the integration of learning related to both the generic and the vocational skills as the mission for college learning and training. Toronto: Ministry of Training, Colleges and Universities (MTCU).

11. Spady, William and Marshall, Kit. 1991. *Beyond traditional outcomes-based education.* Educational Leadership. v 49 n2. October, 1991. pp. 67-72.

12. Senge, Peter. 1990. The Fifth Discipline: The art and practice of the learning organization. New York: Doubleday.

13. Kahneman, Daniel. 2013. Thinking Fast and Slow. New York: Farrar, Strauss & Giroux.

EMPOWERING PARENTS

INDEX

A

	112, 116-117, 153, 184, 234, 240, 246, 257-259, 262, 288-289, 296, 299-305
Assimilation	23-24
Attachment	127, 279
Attending skills	12, 54-55, 63-64, 214, 270
Attitudes	12, 17, 53, 60, 71, 129, 139, 142, 150-153, 180, 183, 222-223
Auditory discrimination	172-173
perception	167-168, 172
-motor integration	172-174

B

Back to basics	94, 245
Background/foreground	93-94, 170, 261
Balance	177-180, 187, 199, 214, 270
Balanced approach	47, 199
Barr, R. and Tagg, J.	281, 327
Barrow, Robin	281, 328
Basic fundamental movements	156, 163, 174
Bauer, Susan Wise	17, 197, 322
Beauchamp G, and Kennewell, S.	211, 323
Begley, Sarah	257, 327
Behavioural science	195
Best practice	44-46
Bettelheim, Bruno	81, 147, 148, 210, 316, 319
Blocks, unit blocks	90, 269-274
Body awareness	156, 159-160, 175, 179
Brain	5, 14, 18, 21-22, 26, 45-46, 52, 67, 72-73, 88, 134, 141, 160, 194-196, 202, 206, 209, 213-215, 221-224, 232, 249-251, 258, 269, 300, 311-316
Brain-based assessment	21
left-brain/right-brain	249-250
Brooks, David	146, 220, 319, 323
Bruner, Jerome	196, 322
Budgets	42, 100, 219, 275
Building	20, 43, 53, 73, 77, 81, 84,

S

T

U

V

Manufactured by Amazon.ca
Bolton, ON